Beyond the Bible Codes

A Flaming Shot in the Dark

by

Mark Vedder

Codes and patterns belong to no one. As such, you may copy any and all information in this book as you see fit. However, if you copy verbatim what I have written or use my illustrations, please credit your source so that (1) interested parties have a means to contact each other to further these studies, and (2) you do not embarrass yourself. Verification can be a long drawn-out process, and is best left as open as possible.

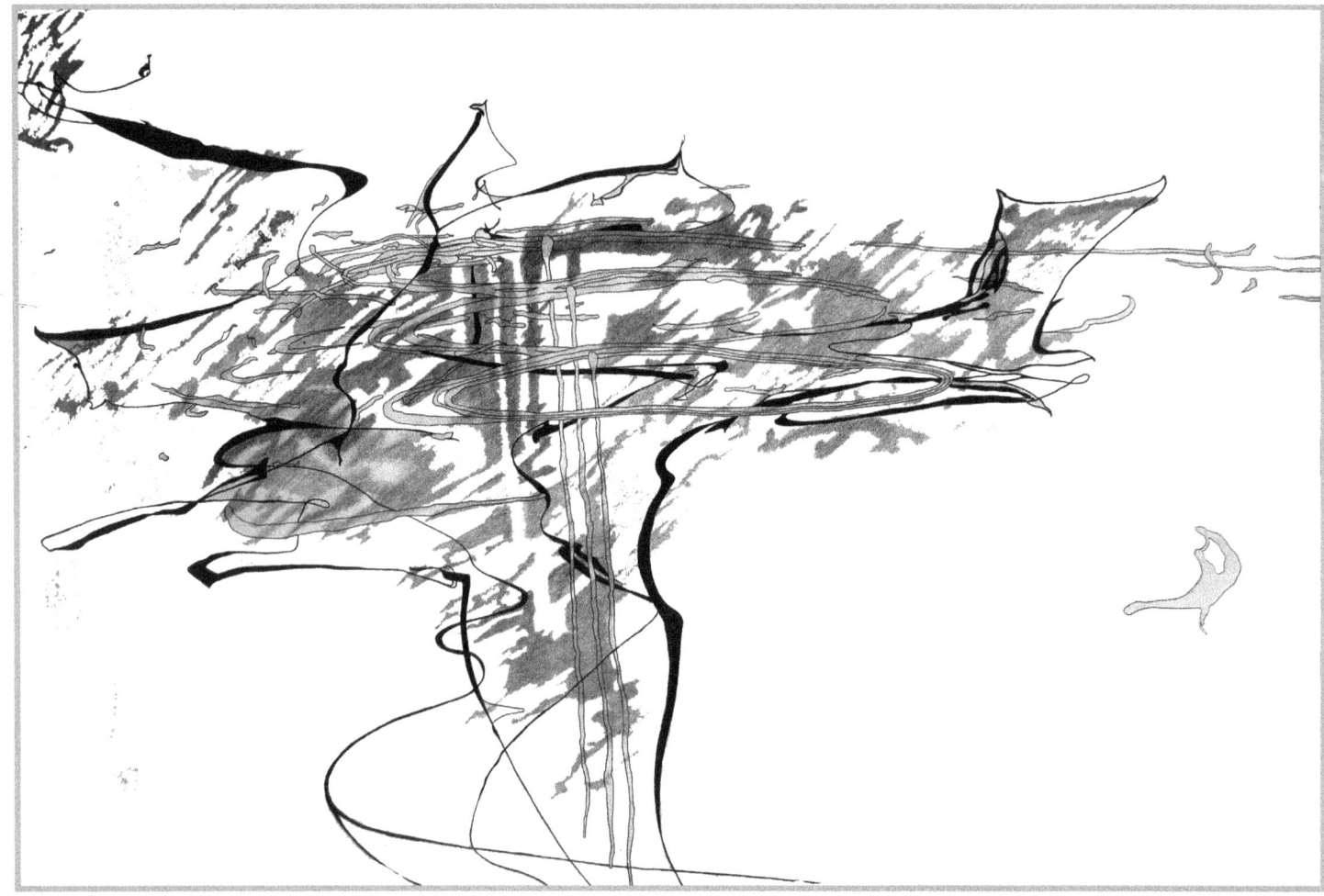

Publishing Rights Reserved © 2017 by Mark Vedder. This publication may not be reproduced for publishing without written permission of the Editor or Publisher. Quotes and extracts are permitted with credit of this publication as source.

Library of Congress Control Number: 2017909432
Vedder, Mark 1965–
        Beyond the Bible Codes/A Flaming Shot in the Dark/Mark Vedder
           p. cm
        Includes Introduction, Appendices
ISBN 978-1-941776-30-8

New England Bible Sales
262 Quaker Road
Sidney, Maine 04330
jptbooks@gmail.com
NewEnglandBibleSales.com
(207) 512-2636

2017
ISBN 978-1-941776-30-8
Publishing rights reserved
by
Mark Vedder
sufferingduckman@gmail.com

Table of Contents

Note to My Readers……………………………………………………………..…….1

Introduction……………………………………………………………………..…….2

The Elephant in the Room……………………………………………..…….…..…….4

   I The Problem, the Approach, and Its Inevitable Conclusion…..…………..……...7

  II Approaching the Solution………………………………………………..……...15

 III Tripping Over the Solution………………………………...……………..……..23

 IV Exploring the Unthinkable……………………………………………..……...30

  V Integration………………………………………………………………..…….36

 VI Regrouping: The Common, the Unique, and the Field………………..…..…...52

VII Opening Up the Game…………………………………………..……..……...59

VIII Almost to the Starting Line……………………………………..……….……...74

Appendix I 37 and 73………………………………………………..……….…...75

Appendix II The Meanings of the First 50 Numbers……………………..………...89

Appendix III Gematria Systems for Hebrew and Greek Letters……………..……...116

Appendix IV 153……………………………………………………………..……...120

Appendix V The Geometric Structure of the Hebrew and Greek Alphabets…………..128

Appendix VI A Simple Way to Understand the Meanings of Letters………………...133

Note to My Readers

This book and its discoveries was written in the sequence you find. In other words, the discoveries in chapter two were made when chapter two was written, and the discoveries in chapter three were not found until chapter two was finished and chapter three began to be written. So to read this is to take the exact same journey as did i in both discovery and writing.

However, now that the work is ready to be presented, certain clarifications are inserted that were not part of the original sequence of thought; most of these have been relegated to the Appendixes. The original journey is preserved as much as possible. The illustrations are done by myself, in some cases simply doodles drawn when the mind became overloaded. They are generally inserted where and when they were drawn.

Some of the processes of thought that run into dead ends are of virtually no use to you whatsoever; these are found mainly in Chapters 1 & 2; they are exceedingly detailed and do not resolve into proper patterns, yet are included as a record of the process taken to find the real patterns. I wrote as i thought and i thought as i wrote; it is somewhat akin to a diary in this manner.

As such **start with chapter 3 on page 23 for the actual discoveries** unless you are interested in the long train of thought that leads to there with all of its dead ends.

The appendixes are other studies which have been added to round out and provide a framework for the journey. Some are there for exploration, others are just cool by themselves.

A prime motivator for doing this work is the frustration i have had with all other books on Biblical numerics: they universally lack closure. One can point out that the number 7 occurs 1000 times in a chapter, but that demonstrates nothing if we do not know why it should occur 1000 times or what the point is other than a lot more than would be expected of 7's.

And a teeny side note: i do not capitalize the personal pronoun ("I"). It is one indulgence i allow myself in writing. The fact that English is the only language that does so is one influence; the other being that i find it a tad arrogant. But with texting coming into its own these days, this idiosyncrasy may be part of a larger palette than appears at first blush.

Also, **ignore any (or all) mathematics** except those that you are truly interested in. There are simply too many figures. I have included the entire journey leading to the discoveries, so unless you have oodles of hours at your disposal and love figures, they can be rather distracting. Read at whatever pace suits you, and enjoy yourself.

And lastly, the big question for many is "**Does this prove divine inspiration of the Bible?**" Really, i would rather that was *not* a question, but this is how many of us tend to think; we prefer blind proof over diligent investigation. So my answer? It is entirely up to you. I make no claims one way or the other. Yes, i have my own opinion and i trust that you have yours: this book is written to share discoveries; its influence or lack thereof is wide open.

Introduction

There is a line often repeated in detective stories when something is found which thereto had eluded all investigation, usually in response to the question, "How did you find that?", the famous line being, "Because I was looking for it." Ask yourself as you read these words: "What am I looking for?"

Edgar Allan Poe points out in *Eureka* that the two opposite methods of investigation, *in*duction and *de*duction, aptly compare to *creeping* and *crawling* in contradistinction to *intuition*. Yet the matter is never quite that simple; intuition by itself is, well... nutty. The fringes of every discipline are crammed with intuitive opinions that would have us 'at last' realize the 'newly discovered truth' that we are the products of alien DNA and it's best to avoid initiating a romantic relationship with a kinkajou while Mercury is in retrograde. These roughly useless opinions *do*, however help us to realize that intuition without discipline or research often fails to deliver when the subject is to be taken any further, or even seriously.

Tragically, the world of Numerics is notorious in this manner; those who engage in actual research do not have the time or aptitude to communicate, and for the most part, those eager to communicate wouldn't know a concept if it stopped biting them on the butt and baked them a chocolate truffle cake. Among the thousands of books published on the subject there *are* a few that are of some use. After thirty years of research, i know of three.

Recognizing then the fact that it is a contradiction of the unwritten Laws of Life to both research well and publish successfully, this particular work, an investigation into the underlying numeric codes of the Bible is being written (right now) before the actual fact of discovery has occurred. In other words, dear reader, i am sitting here writing this Introduction with absolutely no idea of how it will pan out. Once the investigation is fruitful and fully unfolded, the work will likely be clarified so that it makes sense and is hopefully somewhat useful. And of course it must be, as a marketing concession, made pretty; hence the pictures. The advantage of this approach is that if the research does not merit mention, you need never see these words. If you are reading them, chances are good that i will have succeeded, hopefully in a manner consistent with the original intention. Come along, we'll have fun.

So why does our Introduction initially introduce *intuition*? Because whether <u>inducing</u> larger patterns from a few isolated (though intriguing) examples, or <u>deducing</u> how numerics 'should' work from the logic inherent in those examples, the investigator inexorably finds himself adrift: "*Now what?*" being the common familiar ground to which one constantly returns. Intuition, however, is both limited by and impelled toward what one believes is possible, provided that one is willing to do the research to demonstrate said possibility.

Thus i *intuit* that the Bible is letter-perfect, numerically perfect, and of a logical order that is beyond the power of investigation. This immediately tells us that any attempt to *comprehend* the matter is out of the question, and if my currently estranged reader is ever to read these words, the methodology must seek instead to *apprehend* the matter. For if *every* aspect of *every* word, letter, number, and passage as well as every aspect of the collections of passages is 100% significant, then no matter where one looks, one finds. And therein lies the rub: if only two or three—or say a dozen—methods of organizing are used in the text, it would be simply a matter of isolating and identifying them. But if *all* methods that are possible to be used are being used, then we see no figure-and-ground by which our minds have learned to isolate and identify things. One cannot say 'Here is a pattern!' because there is no 'here' where a pattern isn't. It's like putting a chocolate truffle cake lover in a home made of chocolate truffle cake; he doesn't know where to turn.

Thus we can *intuit* that the best way to apprehend what is going on is to start with the most comprehensive (biggest) organization of the most detailed (smallest) elements of the subject matter. Such things like how many letters are in the entire Bible. And endeavor to discover from what they are, where they are, and how many are there, exactly *why* they are what they are and where they are in those particular orders. Fortunately for investigations of this nature, there are oodles of books out there written by very diligent men who have spent their lives doing nothing but counting these letters and arranging them in various kinds of lists, as well as arguing with other diligent men of the same cloth over whether another 'letter list' lists the letters better than the latter list (that was hard to resist).

And lastly i *intuit* that having believed that this investigation is possible, worthwhile, and itself waiting to already have been accomplished, the job is as good as finished. *Fait accompli*, with naught but the research and transcription yet to be done. . . and the *discovery*, of course, which process it is now high time to commence.

Wait! What about the Elephant in the Room?

Let's be straight to the point on this one. Most people who pick up this book will have made up their minds as to its veracity before ever cracking the cover. And virtually everyone will be searching for the exact point that i'm trying to prove. Which is too bad. Because i not only have nothing to prove, i do not believe that anything (whatsoever) *can* be proven. Even if we humans were built to utilize proofs, which we are not, history has clearly demonstrated that a person will believe what he wishes to believe despite any kind of overwhelming evidence to the contrary.

As a sidebar, i would gently suggest to any of my readers who have inadvertently swallowed the misnomer 'mathematical proof' that they pick up any book by the mathematician Ludwig Wittgenstein and leaf through it. The only thing mathematics can demonstrate is limited consistency within a presupposed system of primarily tacit assumptions. In simple terms, a 'mathematical proof' can only 'prove' that you were able to come up with the answer you wanted in the first place.

Evidence and *motivation* are inextricably linked by definition, the more so as we attempt to separate them. This is because the very act of isolating our personal motivation for answers from the 'scientific' evidence we use to get them relies on the presupposition that we are able to distinguish between the two; the which distinction cannot be defined until we actually have the answers we are motivated to find, because there is no way to predict in which direction an 'answer' will lie without preconceptions. It's like telling a tree where to put out branches. Or herding cats. The point is that pretending that motivation is not part of research leads, at its best, to circular thinking, and at its worst, pure deception.

Once upon a time, there was a doctor of 'philosophy of geology' who had spent his life's work building a theoretical model of the origin, history, and structure of a particular mountain range. Highly respected and published, he was hiking over the subject of his studies when he came upon a most peculiar boulder. Round and round the rock he went, staring in disbelief. After a thorough examination, the conclusion was undeniable: there was absolutely no way that this boulder could be there if his theory was correct. His life's work was effectively disproven.

Fortuitously, the boulder was located on a ledge, with a drop of nearly 900 feet. After a foray into the woods to find a sturdy branch and some back-breaking work, he was able to dislodge the boulder, which made its way down the cliff with not a little fanfare.

Exhausted by now, our good doctor took a well-deserved rest on the now-conforming ledge. "Well that's that," he stated with a satisfied sigh, "My theory is vindicated."

Does this actually happen? oh yes; every day and in every discipline. As to the journey taken in this particular book, there are those who will applaud it all with gusto. There are those who will pooh-pooh it out of hand. There are those who wish the Old Testament to have amazing patterns, but are dead set against there being even a hint of a pattern in the New. There are those who will demand consistent, predictable formulas, and those who will consult their 'spirit guide' to discover how to meditate properly on the discoveries.

While i love to share journeys like this with people, there is little to gain by caring about the presuppositions they bring along: it is so much useless baggage. Let us take, for example, two people who are discussing the date of when the world will end. I have no problem whatsoever with folks investigating the End of the World; an enormous amount of research is required, and in that process one is bound to learn *something* useful. The silliness comes in when they we wish to *prove* it.

ا حب البط : *The world will end on April 1st, 2041.*
我也如□ : *I must beg to differ. Tradition shows that the consummation of this cycle will coincide with the next harmonic convergence of the planets on September 8th, 2040.*
Duck: Well those dates seem pretty close. What makes each of you so sure?
ا حب البط : *He is wrong! He has no knowledge of the Only True Way, and his mother licks flypaper!*
我也如□ : *These traditions are from records that are in some cases thousands of years old. It is indisputable.*
Duck: Let me ask a few questions: first, are you both absolutely certain of your dates?
ا حب البط : *It is the truth. Let all who deny it be consumed by eternal darkness.*
我也如□ : *Oh yes. All previous predictions have come to pass just as anticipated.*
Duck: Since you are both so absolutely sure, here is my next question: Is there anything you can do about these dates to affect them, or to have them affect you?
ا حب البط : *The day has been chosen. None can alter it one jot to the left or the right. We are to have our hearts and lives prepared and wait for the day. He who disbelieves is a son of what proceeds from the end of a camel.*
我也如□ : *All cycles are part of the larger pattern of the cosmos. Nothing can alter its course. But the unintelligent and uneducated ignore the riches of tradition and knowledge, stumbling blindly in the darkness of their own ignorance.*
Duck: Um... okay, so we're having an argument about something that no one can do a thing about?

أ حب البط : *It is fixed.*

我也如□ : *We are but ants traveling along the Vine of Time.*

Duck: I suggest a course of action that will <u>definitively</u>, once and for all, prove these dates that we feel so strongly about.

أ حب البط : *It is already proven! What more could you add to the Holy Message?*

我也如□ : *Yes, pray tell; if you have the gift of discernment to demonstrate the truth, do tell us all.*

Duck: It is the <u>one</u> way to show who is right and who is wrong with no contradiction from the disbelievers or the ignorant.

أ حب البط : *Well?*

我也如□ : *Yes, please to tell.*

Duck: We wait and see.

Unfortunately, that particular suggestion is a tad too simple for many and an unnecessary amount of conflict ensues where we could be sharing ideas and—sanity forbid—learning from each other. Or at least enjoying each other's ideas.

So take this journey as you will. It includes the Hebrew scriptures as well as the Greek scriptures; i did not roll either language off the cliff. My own personal ideas may seep in through the cracks here and there, but they do not dictate the parameters of the journey.

Let's let the elephant back into his own realm to wander where he wishes.

"Bye."

I The Problem, the Approach, and Its Inevitable Conclusion

When i was attending Cornell University, my major (architecture) required that i take calculus. So i did. The first few days i was fascinated by some of the underlying ideas, and i frequently asked the professor to explain the proof or how precisely it worked. After about three days of this, he said, "Look, we don't have the time to explain how everything works. Just memorize the formulas until you can solve the problems."

If you are anything like me, that does not work. I did not have the *time* in my studies to memorize all the formulas . . .but if i knew how they worked, i would not need the formulas. Besides, i like to understand what it is that i am doing.

As it turned out, the midterm had a rather difficult final problem. Two blank sheets were provided for the writing down the process of working it out. I stared at it for a bit, and discovered that with geometry and some understanding of the nature of the dimensions of numbers, the answer was plain, and i wrote it down. No work sheets necessary.

When the tests were handed back, my answer was marked wrong. . . and i had been *so* sure that it was correct. As the professor reviewed the test, to my surprise i found that i had the right answer after all. I raised my hand and asked him why it was marked wrong. "You didn't show your work, so you must have copied" (no one else had gotten it right). I pointed out that i was sitting in the front row and that he was one of a crew of teachers sitting at a desk right in front of me. "Sorry, I can't give you credit for that, you'll have to take it up with the dean."

So i find myself sitting in the Mathematics Dean's office requesting credit for a problem that i had gotten correct. "*How* did you solve it?" So i showed him how. Then i had to sit there for a full fifteen minutes while he filled up a page and a half with calculations. He finally looks up and says, "Yes, it is possible to do it that way, but there is no possible way you could have known it, so I'm not giving you credit."

A lively discussion ensued, the upshot of which was his intellect being compared to that of the phylum Porifera (sponges) and me absenting myself from further attendance to the class. You can imagine how this helped my grade point average.

You see, we are all in this together. We *know* things on a deep level that is often impossible to communicate. And when we try, there is so often a system in place that wants us to do it *their* way. This journey is not going to be like that. I am a firm believer in thorough, deep research, but i am an equally firm believer in having fun, opening new doors, and believing the impossible. So let's have some fun. Anything that gets too complicated, just skip; this is not a university course; we wish to open up motivation and understanding, not bury them.

Let us start with the available facts. The number of letters in the Greek New Testament is still under discovery, so that fact will be taken into consideration when/if we get there. The Hebrew Old Testament, however, is as precise as one allows one's self to believe, and as such is an ideal place to begin this journey. The Pentateuch (first five books) is historically the single most studied collection of writings on the planet by a significant margin. We will ignore for the moment the proportional level of understanding garnered by this attention. But first let us address the disturbing fact that researchers have already been looking for these patterns through the entirety of this long history.

Moses does the background calculations for the first letter.

Yet consider that calculators have only been available for the last 70 years, and computers for the last 40. And neither are conducive to calculations that must distinguish between multiple *qualities* of the data being quantified; for this we require complex spreadsheets which in turn require programmers, which in turn require consistent paychecks, which in turn requires a legitimate and lasting pool of interest, which is seldom applied to pure discovery. So the actual advantages to our understanding of ancient manuscripts that belie standard analytical methodology at every turn are not perhaps as extreme as one might imagine. And we can eliminate an enormous segment of the competitive crowd because of bias alone; if one is searching to prove a particular point of view, one will always short-search. Likewise we can eliminate the skeptics and debunkers as it can be somewhat difficult to find something when you are absolutely convinced that it's not there—whether you are looking directly at it or not. Furthermore, the fanatics are out because they will accept just about anything, the less researched the better. Who does this leave? Just us, i guess; whoever 'us' is. If the gloves fit, step in the ring.

So let's have a look at the data for the first five books of Moses. Note that we are using the traditional Masoretic count; the Westminster Leningrad Codex and others have been compared, and for some reason the Masoretes seem to have had an 'in' to what works the best.

Chart 1: Number of Letters and Sum of Gematria in Each Book of the Pentateuch			
Book	Letters	Initial Observations of Patterns	Gematria (See Page 116)
Genesis	**78,064** ($2^4 \cdot 7 \cdot 17 \cdot 41$)	$(153) \times (.2222+2^1+2^2+2^3+2^4+2^5+2^6+2^7+2^8)$	**5,106,274** ($2 \cdot 97 \cdot 26,321$)
Exodus	**63,529** ($17 \cdot 37 \cdot 101$)	$5^1 + 6^2 + 7^3 + 8^4 + 9^5$ ...and a palindrome in base 5: 4013104	**4,639,025** ($5^2 \cdot 97 \cdot 1,913$)
Leviticus	**44,790** ($2 \cdot 3 \cdot 5 \cdot 1,493$)	$1(6^1) + 2(6^2) + 3(6^3) + 4(6^4) + 5(6^5)$ ...and a sequence in base 6: 543210	**3,137,240** ($2^3 \cdot 5 \cdot 107 \cdot 733$)
Numbers	**63,530** ($2 \cdot 5 \cdot 6,353$)	$4^0 + 5^1 + 6^2 + 7^3 + 8^4 + 9^5$ ...also $\quad 10(2^{10} + 73^2)$ See below for 63,53**2**	**4,350,277** (prime) *16,659,549 other books* ($2 \cdot 4^2 \cdot 73 \cdot 25,357$)
Deuteronomy	**54,892** ($2^2 \cdot 13,723$)	$3^3(.3333^3+1^3+2^3+3^3+4^3+5^3+6^3+7^3+8^3+9^3)$ Note that .3333... cubed is .037037037...	**3,777,010** ($2^2 \cdot 3^2 \cdot 5 \cdot 103 \cdot 193$)
Pentateuch Total	**304,805** 5 x **60,961** (prime)	$1^7-2^7+3^7-4^7+5^7$ $\qquad$ [63,801] $+1^2+2^2+3^2+4^2+5^2+6^2+7^2+8^2+9^2$ $\quad$ [+ 285] -5^5 $\qquad\qquad\qquad\qquad\qquad\quad$ [−3,125] $\qquad\qquad\qquad\qquad\qquad\qquad\qquad$ 60,961	**21,009,826** (sum 28, product 12^3) $21,000,000 + 2(17^3)$, or $2(17^3) + 3(7)(100^3)$

The total number of letters for Exodus is somewhat remarkable: $5^1 + 6^2 + 7^3 + 8^4 + 9^5$ can hardly be an accident. The fact that Exodus and Numbers are only one letter apart is most remarkable. Leviticus is equally promising with $1(6^1) + 2(6^2) + 3(6^3) + 4(6^4) + 5(6^5)$. Note also that Genesis uses powers of two and includes the decimal .22222 while Deuteronomy uses cubes and includes the decimal .33333. Right now we are avoiding statements like "*5^7 is 78,125; 61 means law, and the law is not introduced in Genesis, so 78,125 − 61 = 78,064, the number of Genesis' letters.*" Genesis' 153 multiplier is a highly significant pattern number. and may warrant its own chapter if we get that far. It could also be expressed as

$$4 \times (7^1 + 7^2 + 7^3 + 7^4 + 7^5) - (3^0 + 3^1 + 3^2 + 3^3 + 3^4 + 3^5)$$

When the two reversed "Nun" letters from 10:35-36 are included in Numbers, it can be expressed as

$$4 \times (\quad 1^4+2^4+3^4+4^4+5^4+6^4+7^4+8^4+9^4 \\ + (9^3-8^3+7^3-6^3+5^3) + (5^3-4^3+3^3-2^3+1^3) \quad) \text{ ...to make } \mathbf{63{,}532}$$

Deuteronomy can also be expressed as the series

$$(3^3(1^3)+3^3-3) + (3^3(2^3)+3^3-3) + (3^3(3^3)+3^3-3) + (3^3(4^3)+3^3-3) + (3^3(5^3)+3^3-3) \\ + (3^3(6^3)+3^3-3) + (3^3(7^3)+3^3-3) + (3^3(8^3)+3^3-3) + (3^3(9^3)+3^3-3)$$

and (in keeping with the **4x**'s in the previous examples) can also be expressed as

$$4 \times (\quad [8(9^3) + 8(8^3) + 8(7^3) + 8(6^3) + 8(5^3)] \\ - [8(5^3) + 8(4^3) + 8(3^3) + 8(2^3) + 8(1^3)] \\ + 3^5 - 3^4 - 3^3 - 3^2 - 3^1 \quad)$$

The Pentateuch Total puzzled me for a bit; i intuited that it would be a series using the 7th power… but also felt that 5 to the 5th should play a part. It turns out that all that was missing was the squares, as shown in the chart above. We might ask, *How significant are these series statistically?* Well, beware of statistics. I could tell you that the total number of 5-symmetrical examples like these from 1 to 5.2 billion is one in 2,415,614 (yes, i did make a list of them; it's 27 pages long) and i would be correct.

However, this would ignore the fact that a larger proportion of these fall into the *range* of the number of letters in the books (44,790 to 96,091). So the chances of a number being 5-symmetrical (like $1^2+2^2+3^2+4^2+5^2$) are actually 1 in 513, not one in two-and-a-half million; this is what i mean by beware of statistics. So 3 out of 5 of the books have a number of letters that could only happen 1 in 513 times. That seems somewhat significant. The other two use a multiplier (153 and 27 respectively, two very significant numbers) which drastically cuts down the statistical significance, but is still notable. So you decide.

And folks get quite creative with patterns. For example, it has been noticed that the two inverted Nun letters found surrounding Numbers 10:35-36, somewhat like parentheses, when included in the total of Numbers adds up to **63,504**, which equals the *digits* of Deuteronomy added to Numbers, as shown in the chart below. Correspondingly, adding the digits of *Genesis* to **63,504** equals the number of letters in Exodus, as shown:

Chart 2: Deriving the Values of Exodus and Numbers by Summing Digits					
	Genesis	**Exodus**	**Leviticus**	**Numbers**	**Deuteronomy**
	78,064	63,529	44,790	63,53<u>2</u>	54,892
63,504 = (3 · 3 · 7 · 7 · 12 · 12)	↓ →	= 63,504 +7 +8 +0 +6 +4		= 63,504 +5 +4 +8 +9 +2	↓ ←

Of course, the pattern stops there. Leviticus is sitting lonely with no participation and there is little else that one might hope to derive from extending this any further. The 3's, 7's, and 12's at the far left are explained by the fact that the 22-letter alphabet is divided into 3 mother letters, 7 double letters, and 12 elemental letters. But why double each one? The fact is, patterns like this are quite clever, but not *that* difficult to find. Let's find one.

The summed digits of each of the five books add up to **25, 25, 24, 19,** and **28** respectively, and as it is fairly simple to come up with a number near Exodus or Numbers (such as **29 · 30 · 73 = 63,510**) and add the appropriate digit sum (Numbers has **19**) which gives us the number of letters in Exodus (**63,529**). Then we need only explain the three factors of **63,510**: 73 is one of the two prime factors of Genesis 1:1, the book we arrived at (Exodus) is about the first building of God's house, and Psalms 36:8 says *"They will be abundantly satisfied with the fatness of your house; and you will make them drink of the river of your pleasures."* which has the gematria value of **30 x 73**. As to **29**, Ecclesiastes 7:10 has some advice about how to consider Exodus: *"Say not, How is it that the former days were better than these? for you do not inquire wisely concerning this,"* and has the gematria value of **2929**.

Thus three very significant factors, **29 · 30 · 73** plus the digits of Numbers with the added 2 Nun letters, **6+3+5+3+2** equals the number of letters in Exodus, **63,529**. Significant? Perhaps. Difficult? No, I did that while I was typing here; it took under five minutes.

This is like my friend who can 'prove' that a magnet is an unfolded hypercube by drawing his version of a hypercube and putting magnetic lines around it. To be fair, it's a very intriguing picture, but until he draws a useful conclusion, it is merely an *idea*.

The problem here is not that there are no amazing features; the problem is that they lead nowhere. Each discovery is unique and the buck stops there. Knowing that the letter total of the book of Numbers is equal to the 28th hexagonal prism if one adds in the two inverted 'nun' marker-letters from the passage in 10:35-36 (which are not letters proper so to speak; they also appear 7 times in the 107th Psalm.), or knowing that a 34-sided shape with lines drawn through all the vertices will have the same number of letters in Genesis as new vertices outside the shape, while fascinating, does not help us understand Deuteronomy's or Genesis' totals one whit. In short, after a sizable chunk of perfectly good time spent investigating, we feel *teased*. Someone is parsing out amazing features just enough to keep us interested, yet just sparingly enough to keep us stumped. At this point, when motivation to continue is being put through the wringer, it is good to remember that the spiritual world has a sense of humor, apparently at our expense.

But i realize that my gentle reader has not exactly been privy to the last baker's dozen of hours spent on this wonderful endeavor of chasing one's tail in a circle. Here are the basics. Genesis 1:1 and John 1:1 are two obvious keys, the one "In the beginning" being of old creation, the second "In the beginning" being of new creation. The first has the gematria total of **37 x 73**, the second of **39 x 93**. With a modicum of research, or a good pot of coffee, a calculator, and most of the firewood already stacked for winter, one can find enough incredible number games being played by these passages to almost justify the fact that it's only an hour until morning and no sleep has been had. In the course of attempting to justify the time spent, we come to grips with a few basics:

- Prime numbers are indicators of the *character* of each passage. 37 and 73, being the first set found in scripture, are rather special. Every time a new concept is introduced, a prime number is lurking around somewhere. See Appendix I.
- 39 and 93 (3 x both 13 and 31, again reversed numbers) appear every time something larger than this creation is the subject.
- Other prime markers begin to take on their own characters. For example, 61 is the key to Psalm 119, and appears every time the concept of 'law' is under scrutiny.
- The meanings of numbers are inextricably related to the content of the passages in which they appear.
- God's ways are strange.

That last point is probably the most salient. Like it or not, all the research in the world does not squeeze the secret out of the numbers. Yet all the research in the world is somewhat required to appreciate the parameters. So being good victims of the spiritual world's sense of humor, we do our homework.

Warning: The next several sections contribute virtually nothing to the discovery of the Pentateuch patterns. These will be in blue type to let you know what to skip. They are here because they are the process gone through while building up to the discoveries, and there is an outside chance that someday someone may read them.

The first bout with the calculator is to take every sum of letters of each book, as well as its reverse, and add it to every other number, as well as itself. We come up with the chart that follows. In this chart, G, E, L, N, & D stand for Genesis, Exodus, Leviticus, Numbers, and Deuteronomy respectively. And the little 'r' after each letter means the same value reversed. The order of the chart is in ascending amounts.

Chart 3: Summation of the Letters of Each Book of the Torah and its Reverse, Inclusive										
	Nr	Lr	Dr	L	Gr	D	E	N	G	Er
Nr 3,536	7,072									
Lr 9,744	13,280	19,488								
Dr 29,845	33,381	39,589	59,690							
L 44,790	48,326	58,070	74,635	89,580						
Gr 46,087	49,623	55,831	75,932	90,877	92,174					
D 54,892	58,428	64,636	84,737	99,682	100,979	109,784				
E 63,529	67,065	73,273	93,374	108,319	109,616	118,421	127,038			
N 63,530	67,066	75,274	93,375	108,320	109,617	118,422	127,059	127,060		
G 78,064	81,600	87,808	107,909	122,854	124,151	132,956	141,595	141,594	156,128	
Er 92,536	96,072	102,280	122,328	137,326	138,623	147,428	156,065	156,066	170,600	185,072

So what does this thorough attempt at discovery tell us? Absolutely nothing. I've now run through every imaginable permutation of the numbers and while there are piles of interesting data, none of it relates in any way whatsoever to any other figures. Once again, it's like someone is playing with the data even as it's being calculated. Do we give up? Of course not; we're still gathering information. And we have yet to calculate each relationship *subtracted* instead of added. So yes, here is our next chart:

Chart 4: Subtraction of the Letters of Each Book of the Torah and its Reverse										
	Nr	Lr	Dr	L	Gr	D	E	N	G	Er
Nr 3,536	0									
Lr 9,744	6,208	0								
Dr 29,845	26,309	20,101	0							
L 44,790	41,254	35,046	14,945	0						
Gr 46,087	42,551	36,343	16,242	1,297	0					
D 54,892	51,356	45,148	25,047	10,102	8,805	0				
E 63,529	59,993	53,785	33,694	18,739	17,442	8,637	0			
N 63,530	59,994	53,786	33,685	18,740	17,443	8,638	1	0		
G 78,064	74,528	68,320	48,219	33,274	31,977	23,172	14,535	14,532	0	
Er 92,536	89,000	82,792	62,691	47,746	46,449	37,644	29,007	29,004	14,422	0

What this does is give us a big pile of numbers to compare. The idea is to find consistent, parallel, and hopefully symmetrical figures that show us beyond a shadow of a doubt *what is going on*. And whatever is happening must *keep* happening; it must lead us to an understanding of how to proceed through the numerics and geometry of Scripture. So we come up with a list of relationships as follows:

Chart 5: List of All Significant Numerical Relationships in the Torah by Simple Arithmetic (Charts 3 and 4 combined in Ascending order)

1	18,740	42,551	62,691	90,877	124,151
1,297	19,488	44,790	63,529	92,174	127,038
3,536	20,101	45,148	63,530	92,536	127,059
6,208	23,172	46,087	64,636	93,374	127,060
7,072	25,047	46,449	67,065	93,375	132,956
8,637	26,309	47,746	67,066	96,072	137,326
8,638	29,004	48,219	68,320	99,682	138,623
8,805	29,007	48,326	73,273	100,979	141,594
9,744	29,845	49,623	74,528	102,280	141,595
10,102	31,977	51,356	74,635	107,909	147,428
13,280	33,274	53,785	75,274	108,319	156,065
14,422	33,381	53,786	75,932	108,320	156,066
14,532	33,694	54,892	78,064	109,616	156,128
14,535	33,685	55,831	81,600	109,617	170,600
14,945	35,046	58,070	82,792	109,784	185,072
16,242	36,343	58,428	84,737	118,421	
17,442	37,644	59,690	87,808	118,422	
17,443	39,589	59,993	89,000	122,328	
18,739	41,254	59,994	89,580	122,854	

And after several thousand back-and-forth figurings, this tells us nothing. There are, of course, amazing coincidences popping up all over the place, but completely disorganized. We could excitedly show how the letters in Deuteronomy, 54,892, minus 53,785 (Exodus minus the reverse of Leviticus), equals 1107, which is equal to an Array read by anti-diagonals, considered a doubly infinite chessboard with squares labeled (i,j), i in Z, j in Z; T(i,j) = number of king-paths of length max{i,j} from (0,0) to (i,j), but this does not relate symmetrically to any other figures. Furthermore it's just too complicated.

The key to the solution is that it must be self-referential. God tends to set up these arrays in such a manner that the answer is embedded in the original figures. All we have proven so far is the fact that *something* amazing is going on and we have no idea what it is. Time to step back, take these figures, and rethink. Ironically, the literal meaning of 'rethink' is 'repent' from the Greek.

Time to reconsider.

One thing that i noted when doing the meaning of numbers (Appendix II) is that there is always a 'filter' applied to a given subject. For example, i was puzzled by the fact that the meaning of the first 22 numbers did *not* match the meaning of the 22 Hebrew letters. Then i realized that the 'filter' that one must apply is that of 'mankind' (the fact that many of the letters refer to the human body was a good clue). There are many traditions of the meanings of each Hebrew letter (including my own), yet none of them serve the seventh Hebrew letter, ז (Zayin), as 'perfection' per se, but almost all of them make sense as *the perfection* (or perfecting) *of mankind*. Each letter in the Hebrew alphabet must be taken through the filter of 'mankind'. This realization allows us to project the idea that every mystery has a 'filter' which must be discovered. A key. And the key must be hidden in the text itself.

So thank you, gentle reader, for putting up with this chapter: it represents an enormous amount of time spent exploring. Next we find the key, and proceed accordingly.

And why have i gone ahead and included this first chapter of dead ends in this book? Two reasons: one is that i am writing in the style of a diary so that we can share the journey. Secondly, and more importantly, it emphasizes the fact that **simply juggling numbers around <u>does</u> <u>not</u> work**. The Bible is not a crosswords puzzle or a Sudoku game. We need to know what we are doing and why we are doing it in that manner. For this, methodology and the knowledge that come of wisdom (as opposed to out of books and classrooms) must be applied. And for *that*, perseverance is required. So once again, let's forge ahead.

Approaching the Solution

II Approaching the Solution

I don't recall what kind of night it was (though i do remember some lightning), only that i had been working with the magic and inexplicability of the Pentateuch for longer than would normally be considered healthy. The idea of a 'filter' was bouncing around the room. But what kind of filter? Well it turns out that there are many of them. Let us start with **21,618**. This number is found by taking the amount Genesis is above the average of **60,961**, (**17,103**), adding how far Leviticus is below the average (**16,171**), and adding again how far Deuteronomy is below the average (**6,069**). This gives a new average of all five books at **39,343**, which is **21,618** lower than the previous average of **60,961**. The chart below shows both.

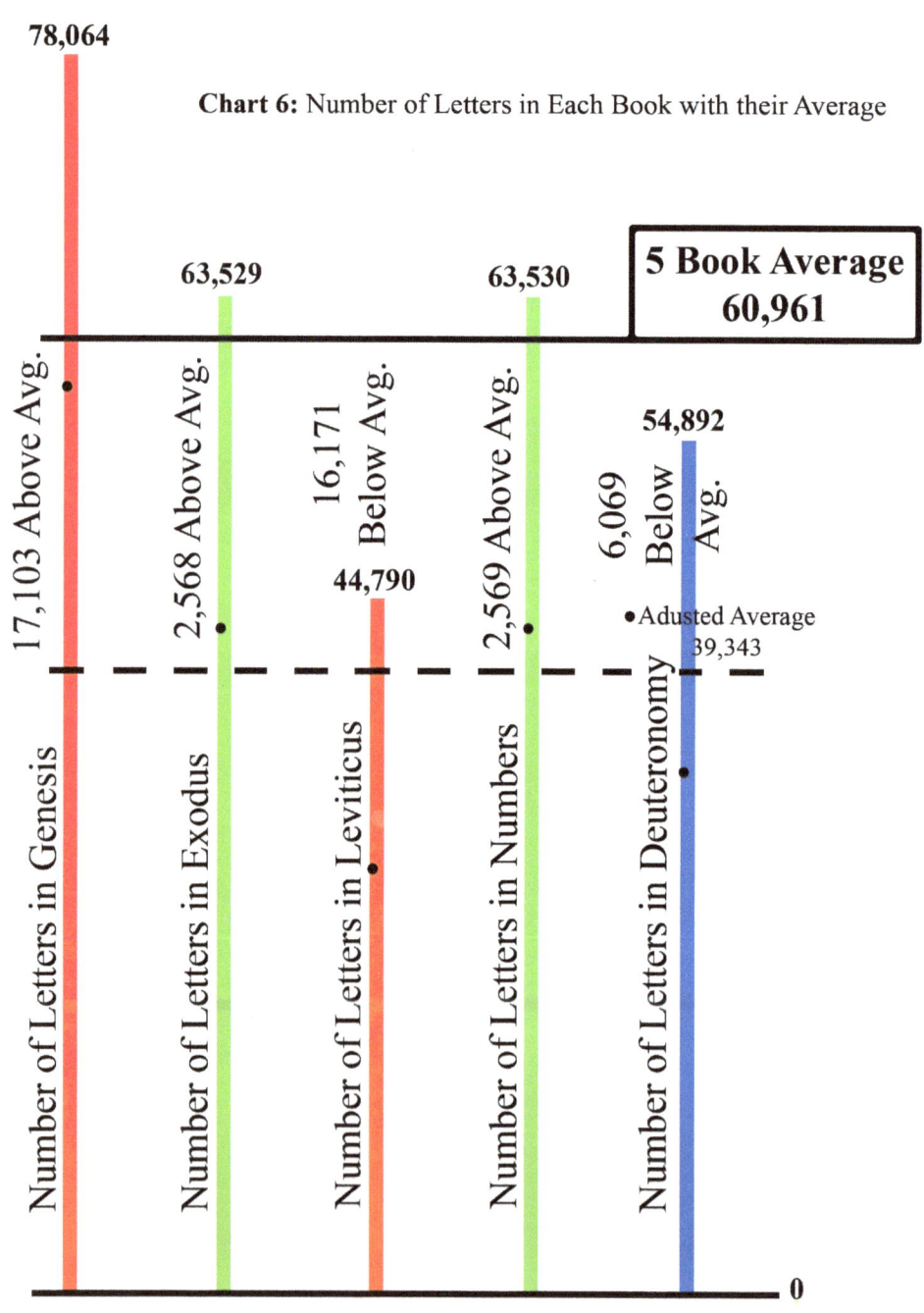

Chart 6: Number of Letters in Each Book with their Average

This shift has the advantage of showing that Genesis minus Leviticus equals Deuteronomy, to the letter.

Chart 7: Number of Letters in the Pentateuch Adjusted Down by 21,618					
	Genesis	**Exodus**	**Leviticus**	**Numbers**	**Deuteronomy**
	78,064	63,529	44,790	63,530	54,892
minus 108,090 $(D - (7 \times 11^2)) \times 2$	- 21,618 $(2 \cdot 3^2 \cdot 1201)$	- 21,618	- 21,618	- 21,618	- 21,618
New Totals 196,715 5 x **39,343** (prime)	56,446 $(2 \cdot 13^2 \cdot 167)$	41,911 (Prime)	23,172 $(2^2 \cdot 3 \cdot 1931)$	41,912 $(2^3 \cdot 13^2 \cdot 31)$	33,274 $(2 \cdot 127 \cdot 141)$
	56,446 → minus →		23,172	→ equals →	33,274
21,618 is the number of ways that 37 can be divided into 3 or more pieces to equal 37. Example: 6 has 7 ways as follows: (4+1+1), (3+2+1), (2+2+2), (3+1+1+1), (2+2+1+1), (2+1+1+1+1), (1+1+1+1+1+1)					

This is wonderful. We have finally found some internal consistency. We shifted the values according to the differences between the values, and found that three of the books are perfectly proportional. But again, *where does this go?* Why are not Exodus and Leviticus part of this proportion? The obvious answer is that we did not include them in the sum of amounts shifted. An obvious *objection* is that this relationship could have been found by simple algebra: A–X–B–X = C–X gives us the value of **39,343** that we used as the new average. Yet does algebra explain why X should be found at A+B+C? Actually, it does. If we were to do a graph of how far any three numbers need adjusted to meet that relationship, we will find that that X *always* will be found at A+B+C.

So while this *does* give us additional information about the relationships, as well as a manner of discovering new relationships, it does *not* answer the question of whether the number of letters in the Pentateuch is perfect, as similar relationships could be found if there were a different amount of letters.

So far we have found that examining the average of the five books and the difference of each from that average has value. Before we begin a new approach to taking this further, let us look at some more charts which give us information when we shift the average up or down. In other words, we are not yet at our goal, but let's look around a bit before proceeding to the next chapter. Supposing we *added* the **21,618** to the average instead of subtracting it?

Chart 8: Number of Letters in the Pentateuch Adjusted Up by 21,618					
	Genesis	**Exodus**	**Leviticus**	**Numbers**	**Deuteronomy**
	78,064	63,529	44,790	63,530	54,892
plus 108,090 $(2 \cdot 5 \cdot 3^2 \cdot 1201)$	+ 21,618 $(2 \cdot 3^2 \cdot 1201)$	+ 21,618	+ 21,618	+ 21,618	+ 21,618
New Totals 412,895 5 x **82,579** $(7 \cdot 47 \cdot 251)$	99,682	85,147	66,408	85,148	79,510
	Genesis (99,682) = Leviticus (66,408) + 1/2 Leviticus (33,204) +70 **13 x 6,069 + 613 = Deuteronomy (79,510)**				

This produces a relationship between Genesis and Leviticus by exactly 70, as well as giving us 13 times Deuteronomy's difference from average (6,069) by exactly the number of laws given, 613.

Now the idea of deviations is interesting. What if it was not static over various adjustments, but grew as the average grew? In other words, if there were one letter in each book, there would be no deviations from the average amount of letters. If there were half as many letters in each book as there are, the deviations would be half the actual sum that they are now, which at **44,480** is **73%** (72.96%) of the average of **60,961**. If the difference kept growing as we adjust the average up, at what point would the deviations from the average equal the average?

As it turns out, we would have to add **22,593** letters to each book, adjusting the differences from average accordingly, before the deviations perfectly equaled the average. Let's look at that:

Chart 9: Number of Letters in the Pentateuch Adjusted Up by 22,593 plus Differences from Average Adjusted Proportionally					
	Genesis	**Exodus**	**Leviticus**	**Numbers**	**Deuteronomy**
Original Amounts	78,064	63,529	44,790	63,530	54,892
Averaged to + 22,593	83,554	83,554	83,554	83,554	83,554
Original Difference + 27%	+ 21,728	+ 3,262	− 20,544	+ 3,264	− 7,710
New Total 417,770 Average **83,554**	**105,282**	**86,816**	**63,010**	**86,818**	**75,844**
Sum difference of the books = 83,554, same as the average of the totals.					

The only factors for **83,554** are **2** and **41,777**, which is prime. Of course, 2 x (5 books) = 10, which times **41,777** equals **417,770**; but the fact that it is the only factor (with 2) indicates another internal consistency to explore.

Using the differences from the average seems to keep producing results. Deuteronomy is **6,069** below the average, and bumping everything up by that amount results in the following:

Chart 10: Number of Letters in the Pentateuch Adjusted Up by 6,069					
	Genesis	**Exodus**	**Leviticus**	**Numbers**	**Deuteronomy**
	78,064	63,529	44,790	63,530	54,892
plus 30,345	+ 6,069 ($3 \cdot 7 \cdot 17^2$)	+ 6,069	+ 6,069	+ 6,069	+ 6,069
New Totals 335,150 5 x 67,030	**84,133**	**69,598**	**50,859**	**69,599**	**60,691**
	Exodus / Genesis = .8272 and Deuteronomy / Numbers = .8720				

This gives a very close figure between the relationship between Exodus and Genesis and the relationship between Deuteronomy and Numbers, but not yet exact.

If we add **310** (which figure keeps coming up for some reason in these calculations) to the Leviticus shortfall of **16,171**, we get **16,481** which provides this:

Chart 11: Number of Letters in the Pentateuch Adjusted Down by 16,481					
	Genesis	**Exodus**	**Leviticus**	**Numbers**	**Deuteronomy**
	78,064	63,529	44,790	63,530	54,892
minus 82,405	- 16,481	- 16,481	- 16,481	- 16,481	- 16,481
New Totals 222,400 5 x 44,480	**61,583**	**47,048**	**28,309**	**47,049**	**38,411**
	This average (44,480) of each book's letter total *also* equals the total sum of deviations of the five books.				

16,481 is the Catalan $\frac{2x!}{(x+1)!x!}$ of 7: $\frac{87,178,291,200}{203,212,800}$ (= 429) with its squares concatenated ($4^2, 2^2, 9^2 = 16, 4, 81$ then combined to 16,481).

16,481 is also part of an amusing mathematical problem: if ten men checked their hats at a restaurant and the hats were returned in random order, what is the probability that none of the men get the right hat. The answer is about $\frac{1}{3}$, and more precisely .367879464286 which is gotten by the dividing $\frac{16,481}{44,800}$, which is accurate to four decimal places to $\frac{16,481}{44,790}$, the number of letters in Leviticus.

For example, look how **310** pops in when we adjust everything down by Chart 11's average of **44,480**, reversing the new average and the amount dropped down:

Chart 12: Number of Letters in the Pentateuch Adjusted Down by 44,480 to 16,481					
	Genesis	**Exodus**	**Leviticus**	**Numbers**	**Deuteronomy**
	78,064	63,529	44,790	63,530	54,892
minus 222,400	- 44,480	- 44,480	- 44,480	- 44,480	- 44,480
New Totals 82,405 5 x 16,481	**33,584**	**19,049**	**310**	**19,050**	**10,412**
	Genesis $\frac{33,584 + 310 + 310}{\text{Deuteronomy } 10,412 + 310 + 310} = \frac{310}{100}$				

And adjusting the last four digits of **44,480** by half to equal **42,240** produces another strange result:

Chart 13: Number of Letters in the Pentateuch Adjusted Down by 42,240 to 18,721					
	Genesis	**Exodus**	**Leviticus**	**Numbers**	**Deuteronomy**
	78,064	63,529	44,790	63,530	54,892
minus 211,200	- 42,240	- 42,240	- 42,240	- 42,240	- 42,240
New Totals 93,605 5 x 18,721	**35,824**	**21,289**	**2,550**	**21,290**	**12,652**
	Genesis / Exodus = 1.6827 equals Numbers / Deuteronomy = 1.6827				

And another 450 added to 39,343, the average in chart 7, gives us yet another item to add to our list:

Chart 14: Number of Letters in the Pentateuch Adjusted Down by 38,893 to 22,068					
	Genesis	**Exodus**	**Leviticus**	**Numbers**	**Deuteronomy**
	78,064	**63,529**	**44,790**	**63,530**	**54,892**
minus 194,465	- 38,893	- 38,893	- 38,893	- 38,893	- 38,893
New Totals **110,340** **5 x 22,068**	**39,171**	**24,636**	**5,897**	**24,637**	**15,999**
	55,170 = (Genesis + Deuteronomy) = (Exodus + Leviticus + Numbers)				

Now this **21,618** adjustment we first made in Chart 7 is an odd one; add three **7's** to him to get **21,637** and we get:

$$\text{Genesis } 78{,}064 + \text{Exodus } 63{,}529 - \text{Numbers } 63{,}530 - \text{Deuteronomy } 54{,}892 = \text{Leviticus } 44{,}790 - 21{,}637$$

This is somewhat better; it includes all five books without the confusion that comes in from Exodus and Numbers being only one letter off. Yet as we have seen, this is not enough; it must be done far more gracefully. Let us explore this offset filter in greater detail and see what comes. We subtract **27,687** from the totals so that Leviticus has the same value (**17,103**) as the amount that Genesis (**78,064**) was over the average (**60,691**). The chart that emerges opens things further:

Chart 15: Number of Letters in the Pentateuch Adjusted Down by 27,687					
Original Number of Letters	**Genesis**	**Exodus**	**Leviticus**	**Numbers**	**Deuteronomy**
	78,064	**63,529**	**44,790**	**63,530**	**54,892**
minus 138,435	- 27,687	- 27,687	- 27,687	- 27,687	- 27,687
Total 166,370 **Average 33,274**	**50,377** (Prime)	**35,842** (2 · 17,921)	**17,103** (3 · 5701)	**35,843** (73 · 491)	**27,205** (5 · 5441)
+ 50,377 G = Base Line Shift → for this Relationship	→ 100,754 − **22,690** 78,064	86,219 − **22,690** 63,529	67,480 − **22,690** 44,790	86,220 − **22,690** 63,530	72,582 − **22,690** 54,892
+ 35,842 E = Base Line Shift → for this Relationship	→ 86,219 − **8,155** 78,064	71,684 − **8,155** 63,529	52,945 − **8,155** 44,790	71,685 − **8,155** 63,530	63,047 − **8,155** 54,892
+ 17,103 L = Base Line Shift → for this Relationship	→ 67,480 + **10,584** 78,064	52,945 + **10,584** 63,529	34,206 + **10,584** 44,790	52,946 + **10,584** 63,530	44,308 + **10,584** 54,892
+ 35,843 N = Base Line Shift → for this Relationship	→ 86,220 − **8,156** 78,064	71,685 − **8,156** 63,529	52,946 − **8,156** 44,790	71,686 − **8,156** 63,530	63,048 − **8,156** 54,892
+ 27,205 D = Base Line Shift → for this Relationship	→ 77,582 + **482** 78,064	63,047 + **482** 63,529	44,308 + **482** 44,790	63,048 + **482** 63,530	54,410 + **482** 54,892

Note that the number of books themselves added again into the total make **166,375**. This is a perfect cube (**55³**) as well as the 11th in the series of Fibonacci cubes. At this point it is important to look for **11** (as in 11 × 5 = 55) as it has been conspicuously absent. 11's appearance will be the signal to tie in the number of distinct letters in the Pentateuch. Also, **166,375 – 666 = 165,709**, which is the natural logarithm *e* (**2.718281828...**) times the original average of number of letters in the five books (**60,961**).

The new average in this chart, **33,274**, is precisely Genesis, **78,064** minus Leviticus, **44,790**. It is also how far Genesis is above the average, **17,103** plus how far Leviticus is below the average, **16,171**. If **6,069** (the number of letters in Deuteronomy below the average) is added to this **33,274**, we get **39,343**, the average of the five books in Chart 7. So the charts are linked. Genesis in Chart 7 (**56,446**) minus the average of Chart 15 (**33,274**) equals Leviticus on Chart 7 (**23,172**). Genesis on Chart 7 minus Genesis on Chart 15 equals **6069**, how far below the average Deuteronomy is.

What is happening is the numerical structure behind the scriptures revealing itself. We have not yet proven or demonstrated anything conclusive, but we have demonstrated that more is going on than one could expect. Chart 15 reveals 5 new number shifts that are... well, *something*. What are they? The 5 **base line shift numbers** from Chart 15 appear to be corrections of some sort. So we take a *third* adjustment of the letter totals, shifting them down the same amount as previously. There is **6,069** between **21,618** and **27,687** so we subtract that number again to arrive at **33,756**. This puts our new average at **27,205**.

Chart 16: Number of Letters in the Pentateuch Adjusted Down by 33,756					
Original Number of Words	**Genesis**	**Exodus**	**Leviticus**	**Numbers**	**Deuteronomy**
	78,064	**63,529**	**44,790**	**63,530**	**54,892**
minus 168,780 ($2^2 \cdot 3 \cdot 5 \cdot 29 \cdot 97$)	- 33,756 ($2^2 \cdot 3 \cdot 29 \cdot 97$)	- 33,756	- 33,756	- 33,756	- 33,756
Total 136,025 ($5^2 \cdot 5,441$) Average 27,205 ($5 \cdot 5,441$)	(22,690) 44,308 ($2^2 \cdot 11 \cdot 19 \cdot 53$)	(8,155) 29,773 ($19 \cdot 1,567$)	(-10,584) 11,034 ($2 \cdot 3^2 \cdot 613$)	(8,156) 29,774 ($2 \cdot 14,887$)	(-482) 21,136 ($2^4 \cdot 1,321$)

Shown in parentheses above the totals, our **base line shift numbers** from Chart 15 are the amounts that this chart is adjusted from *the distance Chart 7 was adjusted down from the original totals*, **21,618**. If we were to do a 4th shift down, **21,136** of our current value for Deuteronomy would be the new average for that chart. Let's look at that:

Chart 17: Number of Letters in the Pentateuch Adjusted Down by 39,825					
Original Number of Words	**Genesis**	**Exodus**	**Leviticus**	**Numbers**	**Deuteronomy**
	78,064	**63,529**	**44,790**	**63,530**	**54,892**
minus 199,125 ($3^3 \cdot 5^3 \cdot 59$)	- 39,825 ($3^3 \cdot 5^2 \cdot 59$)	- 39,825	- 39,825	- 39,825	- 39,825
Total 105,680 ($2^4 \cdot 5 \cdot 1,321$) Average 21,136 ($2^4 \cdot 1,321$)	38,239 (Prime)	23,704 ($2^3 \cdot 2,963$)	4,965 ($3 \cdot 5 \cdot 331$)	23,705 ($5 \cdot 11 \cdot 431$)	15,067 ($13 \cdot 19 \cdot 61$)

Also for use in the next chapters are included the square roots of both the number of letter totals and the number of letters that deviate from the average. And because we will be looking at these somewhat extensively, Chart 18 will give the square roots of the Pentateuch. Note that when taking and using the square root of a book, we are not using decimals. The nearest whole square that fits into the number is found, and the remainder carefully noted.

	Chart 18: Pentateuch Square Roots of the Variations from Average					
	Genesis	**Exodus**	**Leviticus**	**Numbers**	**Deuteronomy**	Totals
Letters	78,064 (2⁴ · 7 · 17 · 41)	63,529 (17 · 37 · 101)	44,790 (2 · 3 · 5 · 1,493)	63,530 (2 · 5 · 6,353)	54,892 (2² · 13,732)	304,805 (5 · 60,961)
Average Letters 60,961 (Prime)	+ 17,103 (3 · 5,701)	+ 2,568 (2³ · 3 · 107)	− 16,171 (103 · 157)	+ 2,569 (7 · 367)	− 6,069 (3 · 7 · 17²)	Sum Variations 44,480 (2⁶ · 5 · 139)
Total Square Root + Remain.	279 223	252 25	211 269	252 26	234 136	1,228 679
Variation Square Root	130	50	127	50	77	434 (2 · 7 · 31)
Remainder	203	68	42	69	140	522 (2 · 3² · 29)
Square Sizes	16,900	2,500	16,129	2,500	5,929	43,958 (2 · 31 · 709)

* * *

Frankly, this chapter had way too many numbers in it, and it is a fraction of the material actually explored. The first chart (Chart 6) provides the only visual that helps us to hold in our mind's eye what is happening. I like pictures. Furthermore, pictures force us to organize what otherwise has so many relationships that it is ridiculous to be expected to put them all together.

The two chart listed the square roots. The advantage of a square root is that it allows you to easily draw it (it's a square) and visually compare it to other squares without doing any calculations. So having dragged my dear reader (and myself) through numerical mud, let's wash off and begin anew using what we have found, but translating to a much more pleasing medium.

Descent Into the Vault

III Tripping Over the Solution

Our initial questions were these:
- Is every letter significant, and if so, how?
- Do sections of scripture act as units, and if so, which ones and how?
- Do the same patterns carry over from the Old to New Testament, or are they 'worlds apart'?

We saw that there are **304,805** letters in the Pentateuch. The average for the five books is thus **60,961**, not surprisingly a prime number, meaning that **304,805** is only divisible by **5** and **60,961**. As far as clues as to how to proceed this one could not be plainer. Five books adding up to a number only divisible by five and one other huge prime number tells us to examine this further.

Each book has a certain amount of letters that is either higher or lower than the average of **60,961**. For example, Genesis has **78,064** letters which is **17,103** more. Leviticus has **16,171** less than **60,961**, What we want to do is visually represent these differences from the average, both higher and lower. We do this by making them into squares, and also noting how many extra letters there are left over from that square. Thus with Genesis, a square **130** letters high and **130** letters wide holds **16,900** letters. There are **203** letters left to add up to **17,103**. We then put these squares either above the Average Line (if they have more letters than the 5-book average) or below the Average Line (if they have less letters). This can be represented visually as follows:

Chart 19: Deviation from Average, Squares, and Remainders of the Pentateuch

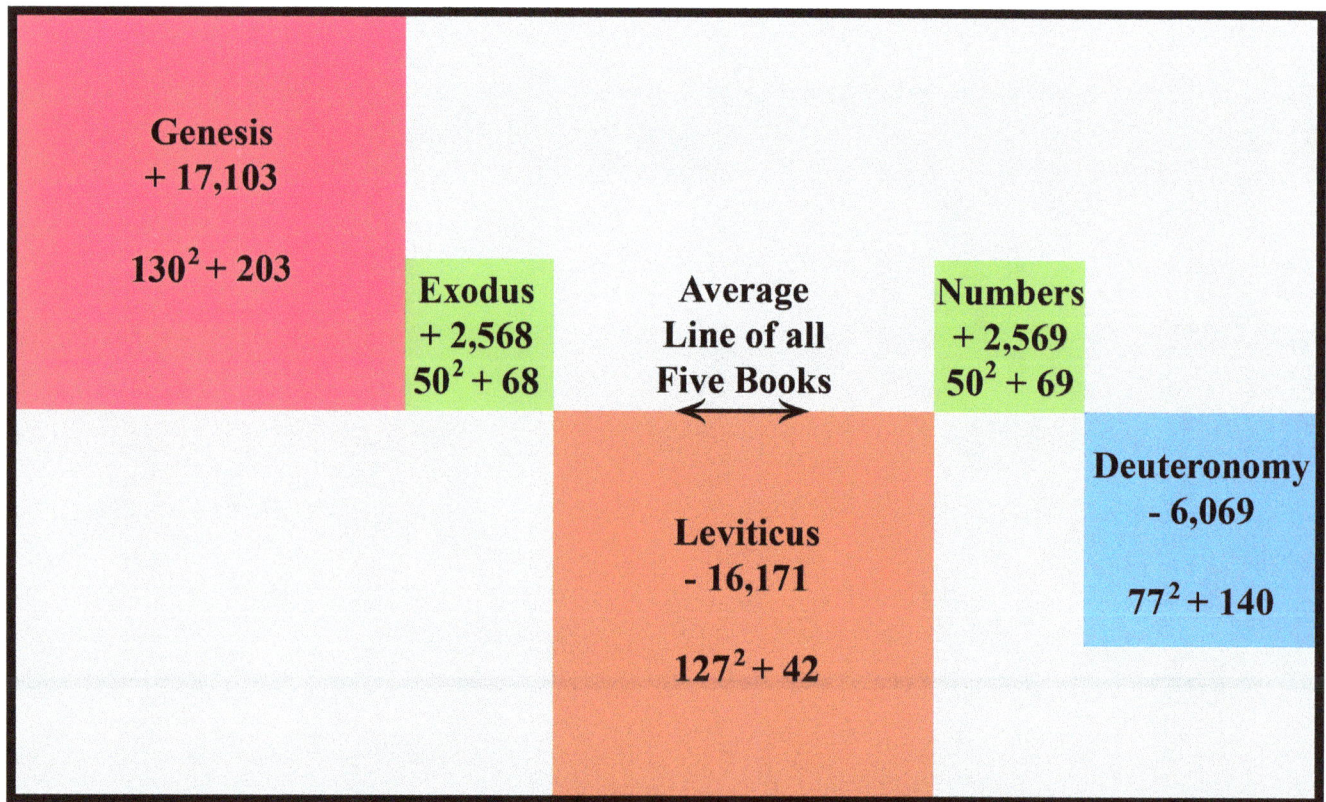

With the accuracy that Photoshop provides us, we can represent these to the letter, or in this case, the pixel. They exist in a "Field" that is **257** units high by **434** units wide that can hold **111,538** letters.

Because none of the amounts make perfect squares, we have **522** letters left over. In addition there are in Numbers 10, two reversed Nun's mentioned in Chart 2 that act as marker letters that are not always counted with the rest. <u>These **524** letters surround Genesis exactly</u>, making it two units larger in height and width. This makes the "Field" (the grey rectangle surrounding everything) one unit higher and one unit wider on the two sides it touches Genesis to become **258 x 435**, or **112,230**, previously **111,538**.

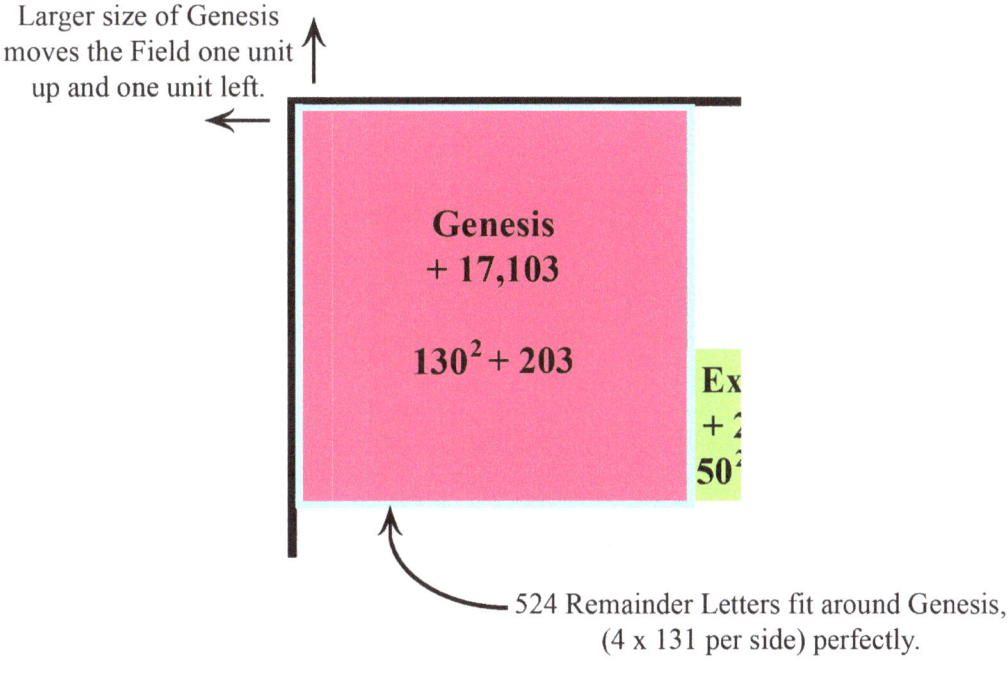

Chart 20: Positioning the Squares' Remainder Letters

One perfect coincidence deserves another, so i sat back and stared at the picture for a while. The next one that caught my attention was the fact that Deuteronomy, Exodus and Numbers all fit perfectly in Leviticus.

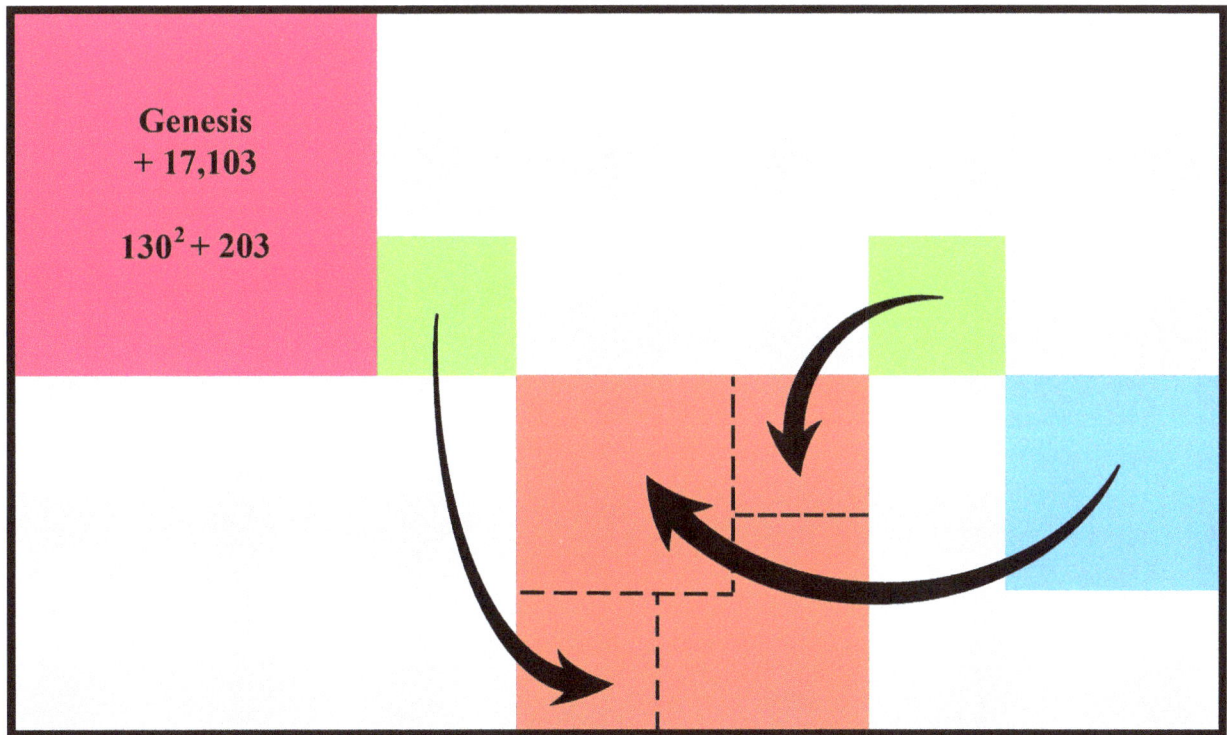

Chart 21: Geometric Self-Reference of the Proportions of Exodus through Deuteronomy

So I put them there.

Chart 22: Exodus through Deuteronomy Arranged by Proportion

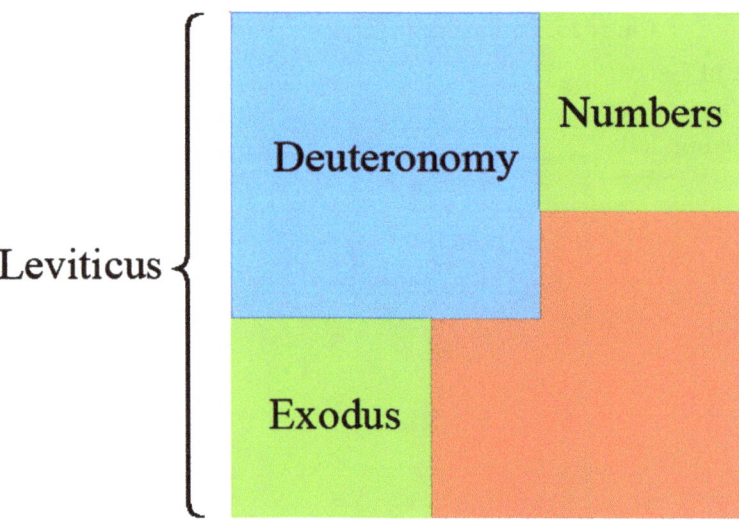

This brings up the question of the significance of the middle square formed between the corners of Numbers and Exodus.

Chart 23: Exodus through Deuteronomy Arranged by Proportion with Projected Middle Square

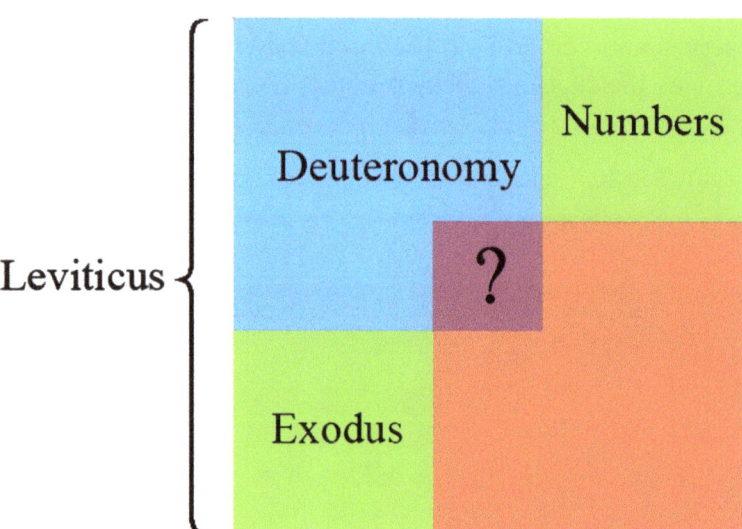

This new square in the middle is 27 x 27, the number of Hebrew letters including the final forms. It is also where Deuteronomy would overlap itself if it were orange and placed in the opposite corner. If this odd little pattern is going somewhere, that middle square is significant. And because we cannot add outside elements (the key to the pattern must be found within the text itself), let us continue the pattern by placing the little square within Numbers (or Exodus) the same way Deuteronomy was placed in Leviticus above.

What we are doing is repeating the same pattern suggested by the fact that Exodus and Numbers fit up against Deuteronomy inside of Leviticus so perfectly. Note that this is mostly the result of curiosity and simple continuation of what we have already done.

Chart 24: Repeating the Pattern on a Smaller Scale Using the New Square

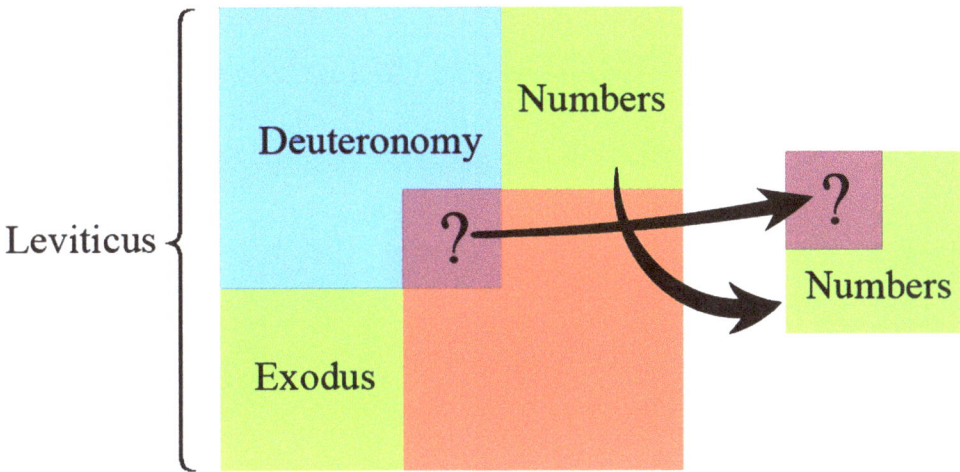

This new proportion is remarkably similar to the larger original. What happens when we fill in two more squares in the same way that Numbers and Exodus were filled in against Deuteronomy? Let's see:

Chart 25: Extension of Squares Series to its Conclusion

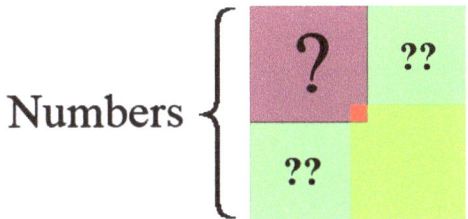

The new squares (marked with two question marks) are 23 x 23. The tiny square produced in the middle is 4 x 4 and marks the end of this progression as it is too small to continue the pattern. Since we have reached the end of the process, let's lay out all these squares in the original configuration and see what we have:

Chart 26: Arrangement of the New Squares into the Original Five-Book Pattern

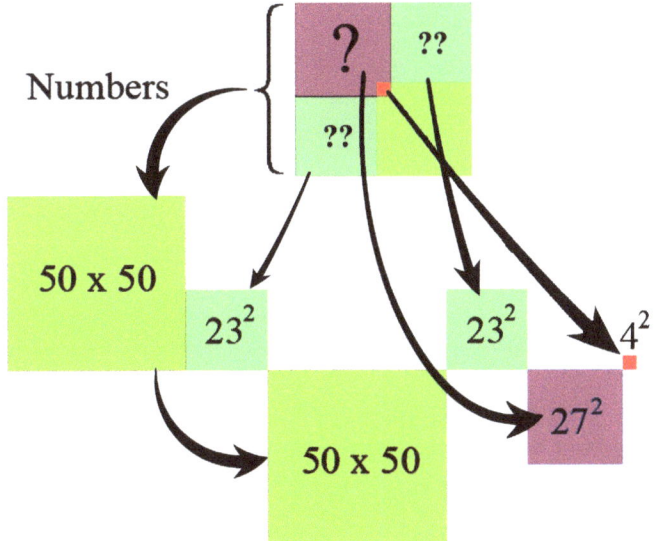

And we find that they make a new smaller model of the original. This is rather odd. The proportions have all shifted slightly, but the pattern is unmistakable, and I'll make it easier by using the colors of the original five. In relation to Leviticus, all three of Exodus, Numbers, and Deuteronomy have shrunk by the size of the new tiny square at the end, and Genesis has shrunk by one pixel (or letter). And we have an additional tiny square at the end.

Chart 27: Arrangement and Sizes of Self-Generated Series of Squares

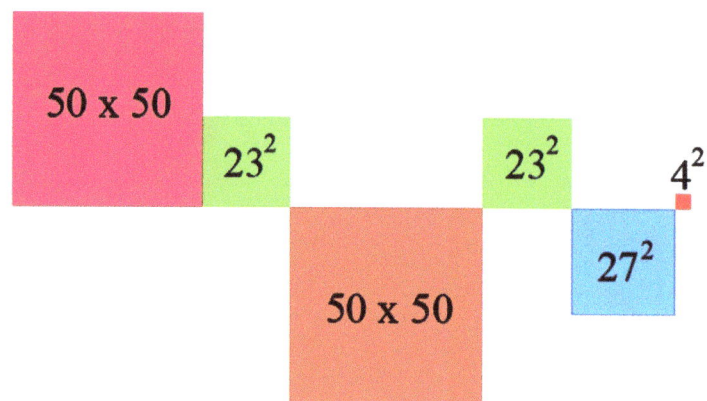

Now we have a new smaller model of the original. Because Genesis was not included in the generation of this series, the first experiment was to place this new pattern on its side and place it back in the larger picture with the new smaller 'Genesis' overlapping the original one.

Chart 28: Arrangement of Self-Generated Series of Squares Within the Original Squares

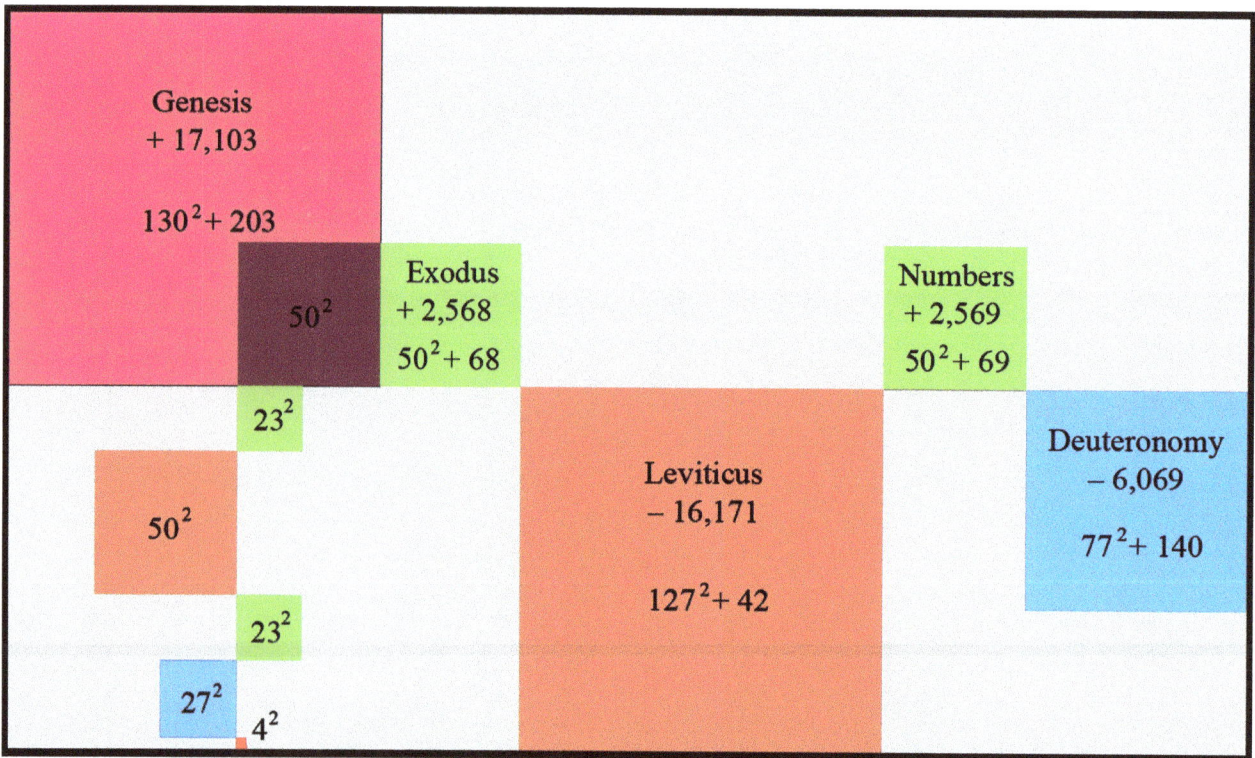

It fits perfectly to the pixel. While this might be expected of a series of squares fitting within one another, it would *not* be expected that the form would be preserved so perfectly. Peculiarly, it fits perfectly when that last little block is included. What is that last block? We will hold off from guessing until more information is forthcoming.

So let's step back and look at what we have now. Way back in Chart 6 we showed the relationships between five (possibly arbitrary) numbers, the number of letters in each book of the Pentateuch, and found their average to be **60,961**.

Taking the various deviations from that average, we produced five squares containing a total of **43,958** letters. Then we took the **522** left over from making the squares, added the **2** 'Nun' backward letters from Numbers and fit them perfectly around Genesis.

This gave us a total of **44,482**.

We noted that drawing a large grey rectangle that encloses all these blocks measures **258 x 435** and holds **112,230** units.

Then we added to this picture five small squares produced from an internal progression of relationships. The total of this small model of the larger one adds up to **6,787**.

So the border around Genesis (**524**) plus the large squares (**44,482**) and small squares (**6,787**), add up to **51,269**.

Chart 29: Arrangement of All Spaces Relevant to the Pentateuch's Self-Verification

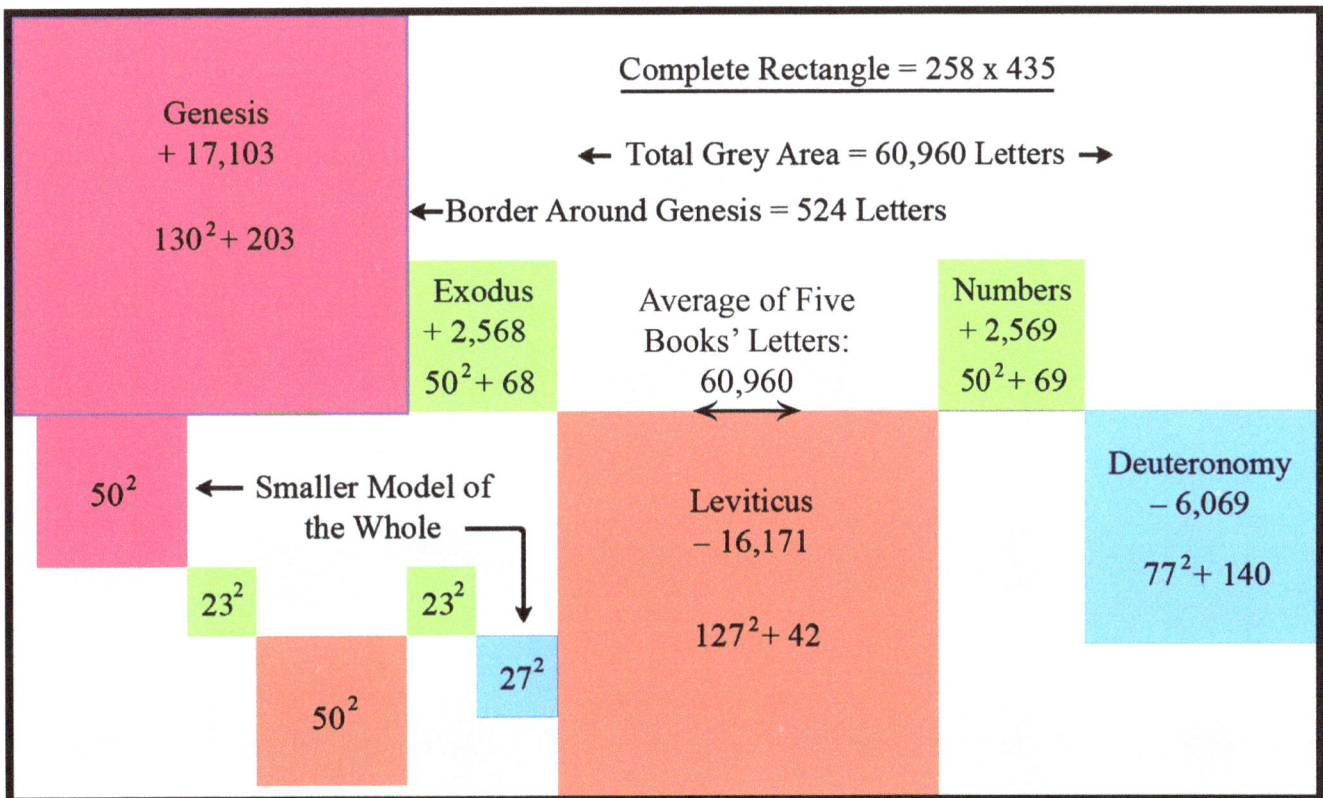

Note that in the new arrangement of the small squares above, there is exactly **4** spaces under the orange square to the bottom, again the size of that strange **4 x 4** square that had popped up.

The question of this chapter is: How much space is left over in the "Field", the large grey rectangle? What ties together all 10 of these shapes produced in so many different ways?

112,230 (the Field) − 51,269 (the Squares) = 60,961 (the Average)

60,961 is the average of the number of letters in each of the five books that we started with. It is *also* the number of letter spaces left over in the grey area. To the pixel.

<u>If one letter were added or taken away from any of the first five books of Moses, this would not work.</u>

I must mention here how this was discovered. I had *no idea* that anything like this would or could work out. I was merely looking for another figure to include in the calculations, and was curious as to how many grey spaces were available for any extra letters. So i subtracted the colored squares from **112,230** and my calculator said "**60,961**". "Oh," says i, "I must have typed in the Average by accident." So i did it again. And again. Then i stared long and hard at what had just happened. The magic of the proportions between the first five books had just fallen into my lap without a hint of a warning. Lesson to be learned: amazing discoveries do not telegraph their punches.

To put it into another picture:

Chart 30: Field, Squares, Background, and Average

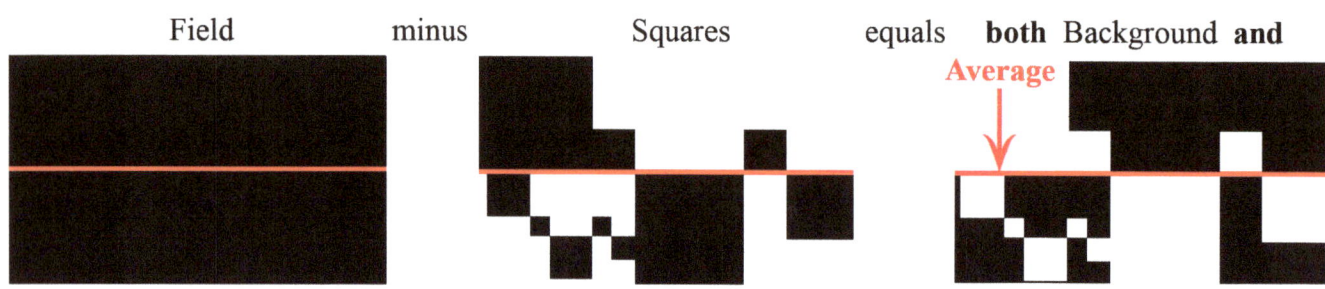

We have just achieved our first demonstration; that there is an internal consistency and interrelationship between the 5 books of the Pentateuch that verifies itself to the letter.

And we've barely started.

Piet Mondrian Attempts to turn the Old Testament into Fine Art

IV Exploring the Unthinkable

The discoveries of the previous chapter were made exactly as the chapter unfolds; in fact, most of it was written before the final demonstration was discovered. This chapter, in contrast, was exhaustively researched with no results until quite simply it was time to give up and start something more fruitful. There is something about that "I give up" point that seems to allow a breakthrough.

The idea that the self-validating element of the Pentateuch includes a geometric extension of itself raises far more questions than it answers. It is too straightforward to be accidental, yet too intricate to have been arranged for just one purpose. The choices for the next step were: Expand the Pentateuch pattern until it is better understood, or Determine if that pattern appears elsewhere and compare notes.

The trouble with the latter step is that so much new homework has already been produced by the previous discovery that an additional one of a similar magnitude would create more than can be accomplished if sleeping is to be a regular activity. Yet the attraction of simultaneously making a second discovery and confirming the first finally won out.

Time to turn the lamp to the New Testament.

Now unlike the Hebrew of the Old Testament, the Greek of the New is highly disputed in more ways than most scholars could hope to investigate. How can we start working with the number of letters of a *book* when no one even agrees on the number of letters in any single *chapter*? So noting that i only have one lifetime, i deemed it best to research if anyone else had worked on this problem, and assess their work.

It turns out that there was a certain Ivan Panin (1855-1942) who spent his life doing precisely what we would need someone to spend their life doing if this research is going to go anywhere. I had already immersed myself for some years in his work, transcribing his writings into publishable formats, checking his figures, learning Greek and Hebrew, checking his figures again, and generally becoming familiar enough with his approach to determine that it *might* be exactly what he said it was: a mathematical validation of every letter of the New Testament.

Note i said *might*. Jumping to conclusions may help find the occasional new discovery, but even then it can be tricky to jump back to where you belong and continue the requisite grind of research. So if my patient reader wishes to explore his work further (recommended), get *Ivan Panin's Numerics in Scripture* and either his *Numeric English New Testament* or his *Numeric Greek New Testament* if you can read Greek. For now, it was found to be solid enough for a start. After all, no one else has ever *claimed* to do what he claims to have done, and his credentials and methodology were found to be relatively impeccable. And both his Greek text and English translation are in the top five of any that i have encountered for accuracy of translation, textual criticism, and readability.

So then; the Old Testament has five large books at its start, considered to be independently significant as a unit. The New Testament also has five large books at its start, considered to be independently significant as a unit. Already knowing what approach we would like to take was supposed to be an enormous time-saver. It wasn't. But rather than lay out the all the neat half-discoveries as we did in blue in chapters I & II, let us go directly to the pictures and figures. This time the average of the five books is **82,129**, somewhat higher than the Pentateuch. Here is our chart of figures that Mr. Panin was so kind as to spend his life's work laying the groundwork for:

Chart 31: Letters in the Gospels and Acts with Averages and Square Roots						
	Matthew	**Mark**	**Luke**	**John**	**Acts**	Totals
Letters	90,512 ($2^4 \cdot 5657$)	56,687 (Prime)	96,091 ($307 \cdot 313$)	71,515 ($5 \cdot 14,303$)	95,840 ($7 \cdot 13,687$)	410,645 ($5 \cdot 82,129$)
Variation from 82,129 Average (Prime)	+ 8,383 ($83 \cdot 101$)	− 25,442 ($2 \cdot 12,721$)	+ 13,962 ($2 \cdot 3 \cdot 13 \cdot 179$)	− 10,614 ($2 \cdot 3 \cdot 29 \cdot 61$)	+ 13,711 (Prime)	Sum Variations 72,112 ($2^4 \cdot 4,507$)
Total Book Sq. Root + Remain.	300 512	238 43	309 610	267 183	309 226	1,423 1,574
Variation Square Root	91^2	159^2	118^2	103^2	117^2	588
Remainder	102	161	38	5	22	328
Square Values	8,281	25,281	13,924	10,609	13,689	71,784

And we find that <u>just like the Pentateuch, the total number of letters is only divisible by **5** and a large prime number, **82,129**</u>.

And we can note in passing the numerical sequences that produce the number of letters in each book:

Matthew = $8(7^5) - 8(6^5) + 8(5^5) - 8(4^5) + 8(3^5) - 8(5^3) + 8(4^3)$ = **90,512**
   and $2^4 \times (7(3^9) - 6(4^8) + 5(3^7) - 4(6^6) + 3(7^5)) + 9(2^5) - 8(2^4) - 7(2^3) - 6(2^2) - 5(2^1)$
   and $2(5^9) - 2(4^9) - 2(3^9) - 2(2^9) - 2(1^9) + (100 \times 73) + 37 + 37 = 37 \times$ Matthew (3,348,944)

Mark $9(6^1)+8(6^2)+7(6^3)+6(6^4)+5(6^5)+4(6^6)+3(6^7)+2(6^8)+1(6^9)$ = ($2^8 \times$ Mark) − 2 (14,511,870)
   and $5^7 - 4^7 - 3^7 - 2^7 - 1^7 - (37(37+37))$ = **56,687**

Luke = $((1^2 + 2^2 + 3^2 + 4^2 + 5^2) + (5^2 + 6^2 + 7^2 + 8^2 + 9^2) + 3)$
         $\times$ $((1^2 + 2^2 + 3^2 + 4^2 + 5^2) + (5^2 + 6^2 + 7^2 + 8^2 + 9^2) - 3)$
         = **96,061**

John = $5 \times (-1(7) - 1^7 + 2(7) + 2^7 - 3(7) - 3^7 + 4(7) + 4^7 - (5)7)$ = **71,515**
   and $5 \times [\quad (3^1 + 3^2 + 3^3 + 3^4 + 3^5) + (3^5 + 3^6 + 3^7 + 3^8 + 3^9) \quad - 703]$
   and $5 \times [8(5^3)+8(6^3)+8(7^3)+8(8^3)+8(9^3) - (8(5^3)+8(4^3)+8(3^3)+8(2^3)+8(1^3)) + 703]$

Acts = $3(1(9^4))+3(2(8^4))+3(3(7^4))+3(4(6^4))+3(5(5^4))+3(6(4^4))+3(7(3^4))+3(8(2^4))+3(9(1^4))$
         $- [((1 \times 9^2)+90) + ((2 \times 8^2)+80) + ((3 \times 7^2)+70) + ((4 \times 6^2)+60) + ((5 \times 5^2)+50)]$
         $- [((9 \times 1^2)+10) + ((8 \times 2^2)+20) + ((7 \times 3^2)+30) + ((6 \times 4^2)+40) + ((5 \times 5^2)+50)]$ = **95,840**

Average = $9(6^5) + 8(6^4) + 7(6^3) + 6(6^2) + 5(6^1) + 3(7) - 4(6) + 5(5) - 6(4) + 7(3) = $ **82,129**

Note that with John, in the latter two examples we had to utilize the 'magic' number 703; something that we will find necessary later in Chapter V (yes i came back and added this paragraph). Page 47 begins a section that begins to explain the significance of this strange number. I said "begins", so don't expect a doctoral dissertation.

And again, each book has a certain amount of letters that is either higher or lower than the average. This is visually represented as follows:

Chart 32: Arrangement of the Squares of the Number of Letters Variant from the Average in the Gospels and Acts

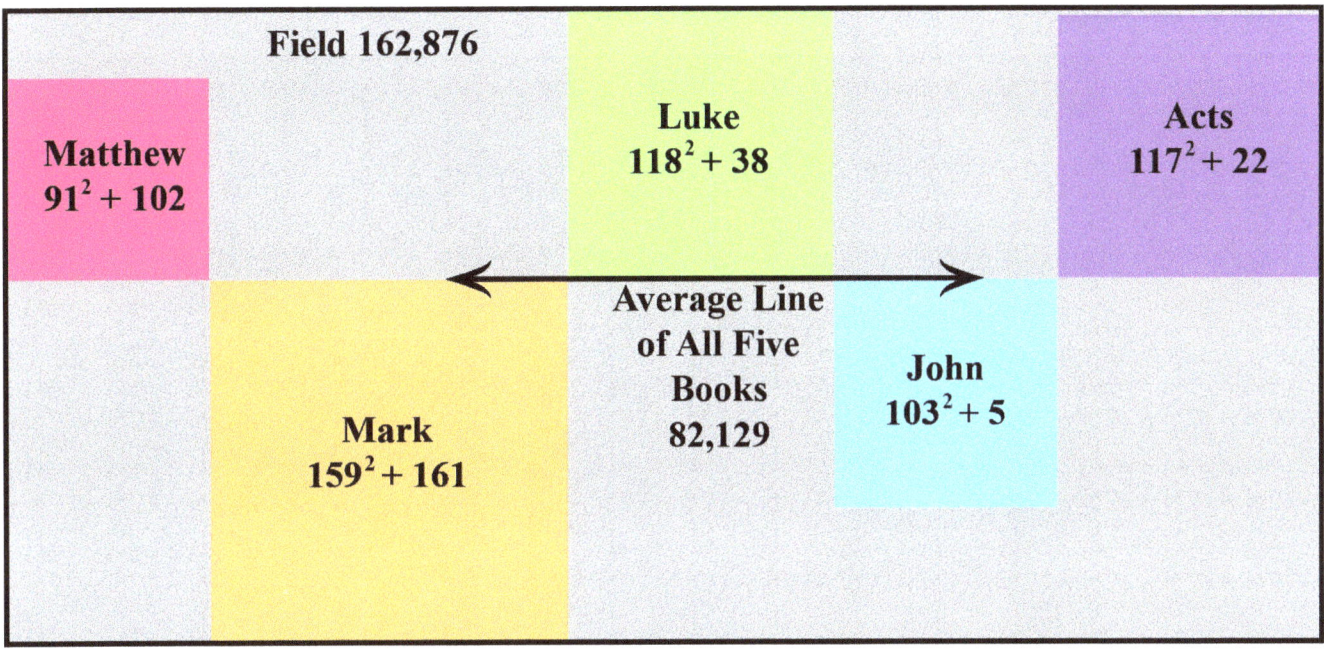

The 'Field' that holds the squares measures **277 x 588**, giving us a Field total of **162,876**.

The Squares themselves hold **71,784** letters with **328** Remainder Letters.

We proceed in the same manner as before. The 'remainder' letters equal **328** we want to fit around Matthew, but we are **39** short. What goes? Is there obvious place to find this 39, or are we to look for an alternative method?

Here is our visual of the Remainder Letters being used for the border, with the thickness exaggerated:

Chart 33: Arrangement of the Remainder Numbers Around Matthew

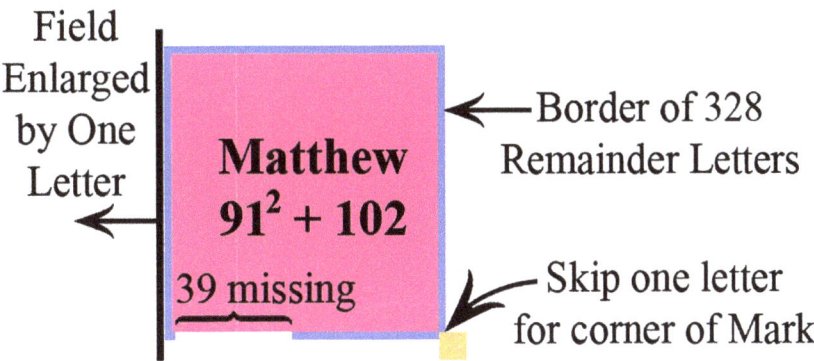

Because Greek is read the opposite direction from Hebrew, we would look to put the smaller version of the *last* book (Acts) nestled inside Matthew instead of the first as we did with the Pentateuch. So how does **39** relate to Acts? It is precisely ⅓ of **117**, the size of Acts. This nicely even proportion tells us how to size the rest of the squares, as follows:

32

Chart 34: Series of Smaller Squares Proportional by one-third to their Larger Counterparts

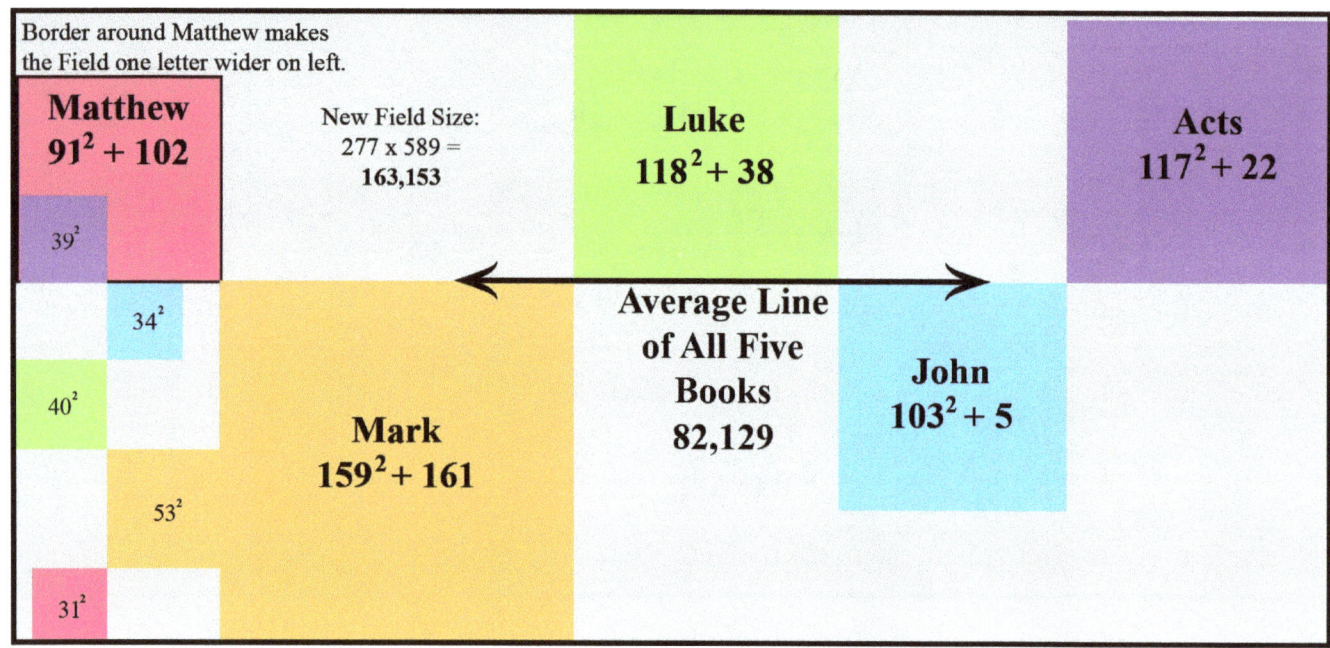

When we nestle the smaller Acts inside Matthew, we block exactly **39** letters of the border so that we require precisely **328** (the Remainders) for the rest of the border. This shoves the Field size out to the left one letter, giving us a new Field size of **277 x 589 = 163,153**.

Does the pattern follow through? Yes, perfectly. When the rest of the books are reduced to ¹/₃, *they fit precisely both vertically and horizontally in the space to the left of Mark and below Matthew.*

Matthew is now **93** letters wide. The small Luke touches the Field edge and the small Mark overlaps by one to stay aligned with Matthew; this is **53 + 40 = 93**. The space is **158** letters high (it was 159, but we enlarged Matthew on all sides by **1**) and Matthew through John are **31 + 53 + 40 + 34 = 158**.

Now let us pause for just a moment. The first Appendix in this book (Page 75) talks about the reciprocal numbers **37** and **73**. They are highly significant, one of the many reasons being that the letters in the first verse of Genesis add up to **2,701**, which is **37 x 73**. Here, our first clue was the **39** letters missing from the border, which then produced a smaller model that is **93** letters wide. Hm, reciprocal numbers again.

Do the two sets of reversed numbers play the same role? Genesis 1:1 says *"In the beginning God created the heavens and the earth"* which adds up to **37 x 73**. John 1:1 says *"In the beginning was the Word, and the Word was with God and the Word was God"* which adds up to **39 x 93**, 3,627. We have a perfect match. As we will find in the appendixes, these numbers are key players, not just in scripture but in mathematics and geometry.

So do we stop there? Of course not. Taking the content of each smaller square (they came out almost perfectly; Luke and John had remainders, so we took John's remainder off to make him 34, and added it to Luke to make him 40 to keep whole numbers), we have from top to bottom, Acts **1,521** + John **1,156** + Luke **1,600** + Mark **2,809** + Matthew **961** = **8,047** for the smaller set of squares. So now we can add up what we have so far.

Book Square Values:	71,784
Square Remainders Bordering Matthew:	+ 328
Small Square Values :	+ **8,047**
	80,159

And a unique feature here in the New Testament is that we need to add to this group the *Length of the Average Line* (**588**) from Matthew to Acts, and the *Added Left Side* (**277**) that we put on to make room for the border around Matthew. Another way to put this would be the *height* (**277**) and *width* (**588**) of the original Field. Either way we have:

		80,159
Length of the Average Line		+ **588**
Added Left Side		+ **277**
	Total	**81,024**

Subtracting this from the Field total of **163,153**, we get **82,129**. <u>This is precisely the Average</u>.

Again, we have:

Field 163,153 minus Letter Group 81,024 equals Average 82,129

And here is our summary in visual form:

Chart 35: Visual Summary of Geometric Proportions within the Gospels and Acts

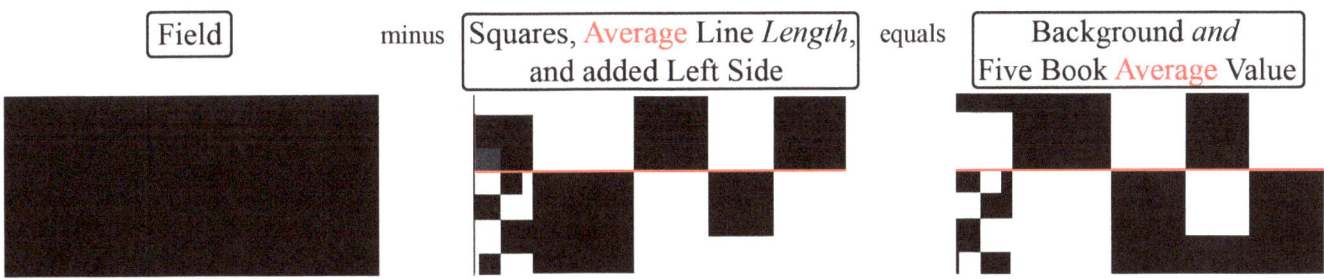

If one letter were added or taken away, this would not work. We have achieved our second demonstration; that there is an internal consistency and interrelationship between the 5 books of the New Testament that verifies itself to the letter.

That last point is important. *Even if you kept the same total number of letters for the five books, but took 5 out of Luke and put them into Mark, you would ruin the pattern.*

This also attests to the enormous amount of work that Panin put into finding the exact letters of the Greek text. His work appears to be vindicated by both this and the other patterns that work with his mathematical studies. None of the other critical texts, whether Westcott & Hort a century ago or the NA28 we have today, have so far been able to produce these results.

And it is a strange way of achieving closure to the patterns. What is that smaller version of squares supposed to be? Is it a hint as to how we proceed next? Are we to consistently expect these in groupings of books? How about groupings of chapters? Is it a phenomena of letter count only, or might we find it in gematria?

As i ask these questions, the next chapter is blank. I do not know the answers yet, or if they will ever be found. At the beginning of this journey, i said that i would be writing while discovering, and having gotten this far, i have less idea than you as to what is coming next. I say 'less' because you can simply turn the page. I have hours in front of me.

Greek Institute of Higher Learning

V Integration

The discoveries of the previous two chapters suggest a new possibility: If the first five books of both the Old and New Testaments are self-consistent according their geometrical and mathematical properties, what about *both of them together*?

What if we put all ten books into the same construct to see if two rather different languages, Hebrew and Greek, will work together and produce a unified structure?

On the next page is the initial set-up to investigate this; i have had to put it sideways on the page. The squares have been placed exactly as the Old and New Testament would be placed together, since Hebrew is read right-to-left and Greek left-to-right. Perhaps significantly, the Bible starts in the middle and goes both directions.

The total letters of these ten books is **715,450** is divisible by the number of books, ten. It is also **John ((71,515) + (2^9–2^8–2^7–2^6–2^5) – (2^5–2^4–2^3–2^2–2^1)) x 10** which seems appropriate. So our new average for this chart is **71,545**. The Gospels with Acts had an average of **82,129** which was prime, and the Pentateuch had an average of **60,961**, also prime. This puts both the differences between the averages at exactly **10,584** with quite a few significant numbers (**11**, **13**, **22**, **37**) in its factors as well as being found associated with Leviticus in Chart 15.

John in the chart is virtually invisible, being only **5** units wide because he is almost exactly the same number of letters as the average of all the books. Leviticus has the greatest variation, having **26,755** *fewer* letters than the average, with Luke coming in a close second, having **24,546** *more* letters than the average. Note also that the New Testament squares total **81,796** which is itself a perfect square (**286^2**). And 286 is the 11th Tetrahedral number; in other words, if we stacked cannon balls in a perfect tetrahedron (three sided pyramid), at 11 layers we would have **286** cannon balls. If we stacked them 7 layers high to get the 7th Tetrahedral number we would have **84** cannon balls… which when added to the Old Testament squares total of **65,452** equals **65,536** which is far more than a perfect square or even a perfect cube or even the 4th power… it is 2^{16}. Yes, the Old Testament half of our chart minus a perfect tetrahedron of 7 layers is 2 x 2 x 2 x 2 x 2 x 2 x 2 x 2 x 2 x 2 x 2 x 2 x 2 x 2 x 2 x 2. Incidentally, **84** also makes a perfect *dodecahedron* of three layers.

The rectangle enclosing everything is **319** units high and **1,124** units wide, containing room for **358,556** letters. I won't mention that this number is a perfect 3-layer octahedron plus $3(5^5) + 3(6^5) + 3(7^5) + 3(8^5) + 3(9^5)$. If it were folded between Genesis and Matthew, the new one would contain precisely **175,450** fewer units with **183,106**. I'll also try not to complicate matters by mentioning that the height (**319**) plus the width (**1,124**) equals **39 x 37 (1,443)** while the Remainders equal **38 x 37 (1,406)**.

These **1,406** 'remainder' letters are to be placed somewhere so that every letter is included. As well as **37** less than two sides of the Field, they are also $37^2 + 37$. The squares of the books add up to **147,248**. Adding in the **1,406** 'remainder' letters give us **148,654**. This leaves us with unused spaces in the background (the Field) of **209,902**.

Average:	**71,545**
Field:	**358,556**
Background:	**209,902**
Remainder Letters:	**1,406**
All Squares:	**147,248**

Chart 7A: Number of Letters in the Gospels and Acts and the Pentateuch

	Matthew	Mark	Luke	John	Acts	Genesis	Exodus	Leviticus	Numbers	Deuteronomy	Totals
Letters	90,512 (2⁴·5657)	56,687 (Prime)	96,091 (307·313)	71,515 (5·14,303)	95,840 (2⁵·7·13,687)	78,064 (2⁴·7·17·41)	63,529 (17·37·101)	44,790 (2·3·5·1,493)	63,530 (2·5·6,353)	54,892 (2²·13,732)	715,450 (10·71,545)
Average Letters 71,545 (5·41·349)	+18,967 (13·1,459)	−14,858 (2·17·19·23)	+24,546 (2·3·4,091)	−30 (2·3·5)	+24,295 (5·43·113)	+6,519 (3·41·53)	−8,016 (2⁴·3·167)	−26,755 (5·5,351)	−8,015 (5·7·229)	−16,653 (3·7·13·61)	Sum Variations 148,654 (2·11·29·233)
Total Square Root + Remain.	300² 512	238² 43	309² 610	267² 226	309² 359	279² 223	252² 25	211² 269	252² 26	234² 136	2,651 2,429
Variation Square Root & Remainder	137² 198	121² 217	156² 210	5² 5	155² 270	80² 119	89² 95	163² 186	89² 94	129² 12	1,124 (2²·281) 1,406 (2·19·37)

Chart 36: Average, Deviations, and Squares of the Ten Books Together

Deuteronomy 129² · Numbers 89² · Leviticus 163² · Exodus 89² · Genesis 80² · Matthew 137² · Mark 121² · Luke 156² · John 5² · Acts 155²

Chart 32: Squares of the Gospels, Acts, and Pentateuch in Proportional Relation to Each Other

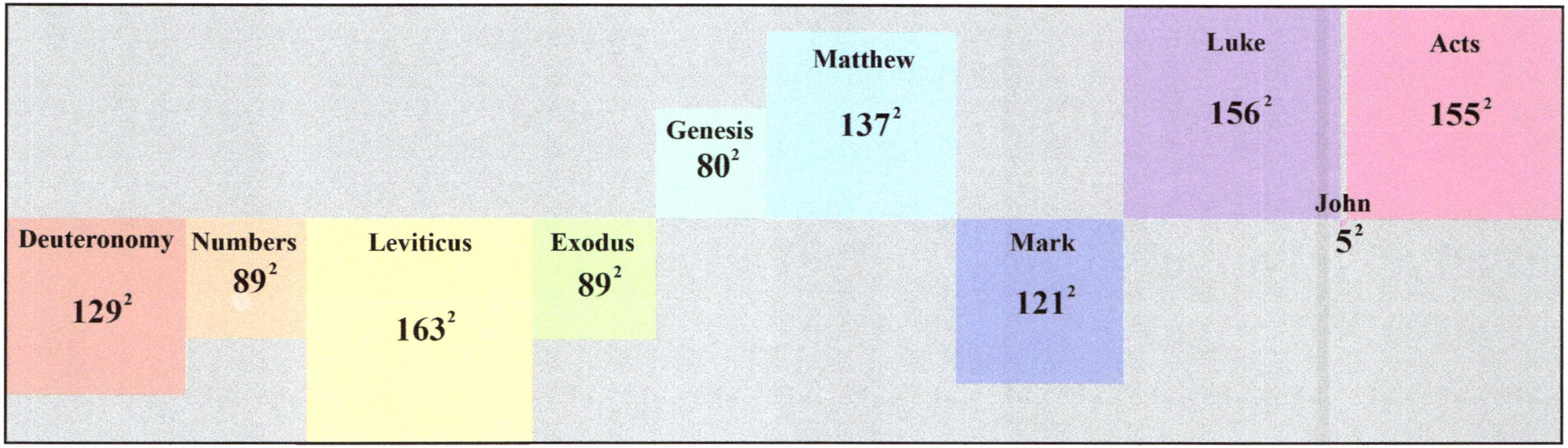

That is our raw data. The task now become a question of whether we can apply a similar method of placing a scaled duplication into the picture that will demonstrate an internal consistency which depends on there being precisely *that* many letters, no more, no less, in precisely that arrangement. At this point we go pour a large cup of coffee.

The visually obvious place to start is that big empty space in the top left quadrant. If we were to place a duplicate of the whole there, we would want it to fit exactly between the top of those first four books (which is the Average line) and the top of the whole chart. This is not difficult to calculate; the space is **156** units high (the height of the largest book above the line, Luke) so we take the height of the entire structure (**319**) and divide **156** by it, getting **.489028**. This is the number we multiply each book by to determine its new size in the smaller scaled duplicate.

Since we know the height is **156**, we add them up to determine the length. Deuteronomy **63.084639** + Numbers **43.523512** + Leviticus **79.7115987** + Exodus **43.523512** + Genesis **39.122257** + Matthew **66.996865** + Mark **59.172414** + Luke **76.288401** + John **2.445141** + Acts **75.799373** = **549.6677127**. We now must decide whether we are going to round off to the nearest whole number and take remainders like we did in chapter IV, or find some other way to make the squares whole so that we can actually draw them.

However, there is something strange about the answer we summed. The length of the whole picture we are working with is **1,124** and can divide between Old Testament (**550**) and New Testament (**574**). Our sum of **549.6677116** is less than half a letter away from the length of the Old Testament.

Is there a reason why this should be? There will always be a relationship between the height and the length since everything above the line must balance everything below the line, measured by the sides of squares which are equal in height and length. But why should it divide exactly between the Old and New Testaments? If Acts and Deuteronomy switched places, everything else would stay the same, but our model would be nowhere near the dividing line.

So to test this, we make a different model, *under* the line this time. It must fit in the space that is the height of Leviticus, so we divide **163** by **319**, getting **.5109718**, and multiply it by the total length of the construct (**1,124**) getting **574.332288** as the ideal length for our new model. This is less than one-third of a letter from the length of the New Testament. The above total is **35,214.2**..., and below is **38,445.3**...

Together the new model above the line plus the new model below the line equal **1,124** in length, matching the **1,124** total length. Here is our visual for these, with the new models in black:

Chart 37: Arrangement of Two Smaller Series Proportional to their Larger Counterpart in Height and Length

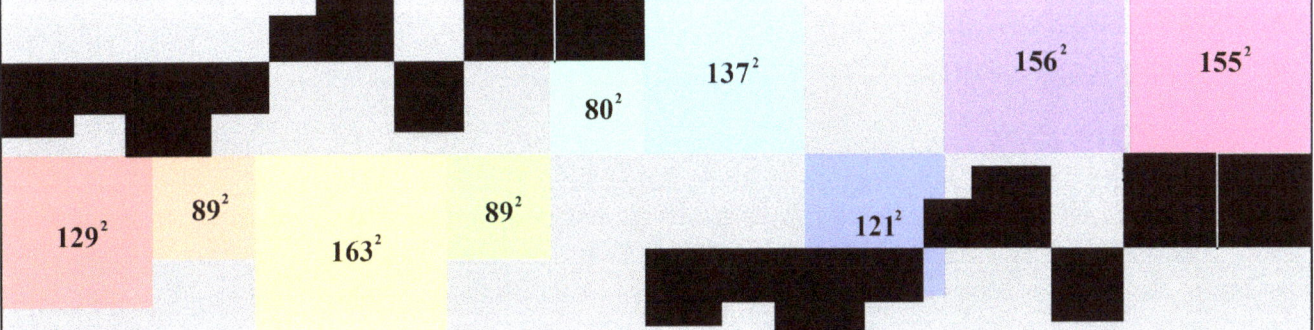

The units in black are both the same pattern at two slightly different scales. The one overlapping the Old Testament was scaled from Luke in the New Testament, and the one overlapping the New Testament is scaled from Leviticus in the Old Testament. They stretch from end to end of the rectangle.

While this diversion gives a very good clue that internal consistency is hidden in here, it does not solve it, nor is it specific enough to use with confidence. <u>When one calculates a proportion, one cannot then present it as anything *other* than something which has been calculated</u>, however impressive it might be. The idea here is to use the same method the ancients used: stick with whole numbers. If the construct is self-validating, there is always a way, and the key is embedded in the layout.

When we started, we noted that if we folded the rectangle enclosing everything between Genesis and Matthew, the new one would contain precisely **175,450** fewer units with **183,106**.. Let us look at that.

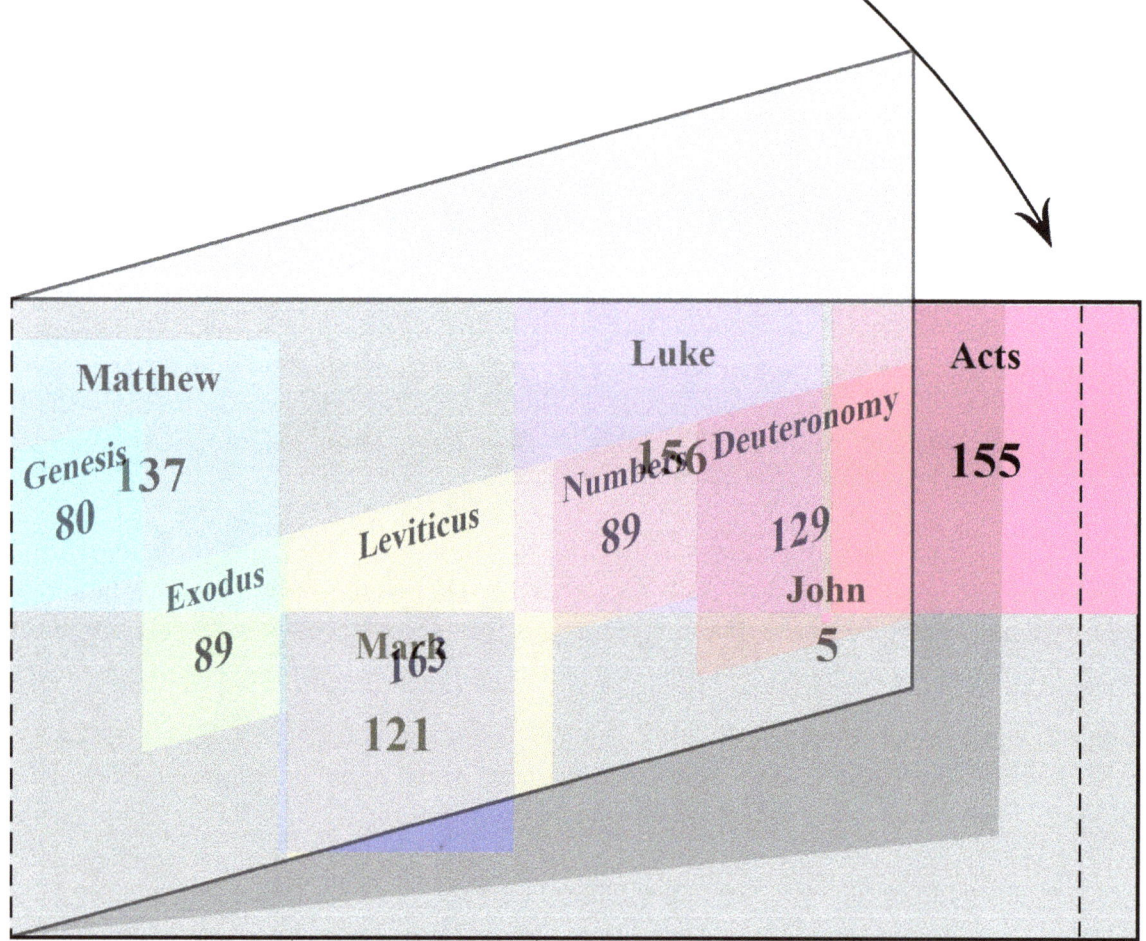

Chart 38: Folding the Pentateuch and Gospels Between Genesis and Matthew

When note that the edges on the left do not line up exactly, so we're going to end up with a Field that is ever so slightly larger than exactly half of the original.

The resulting **319 x 574** rectangle comes out with a total area of **183,106**, one more than a perfect octahedron with 65 layers, and a wealth of interesting clues. The idea that we must respect here is that it is *folded*; that is, we will be looking at two layers, not one. Thus the primary areas of interest are going to be those which overlap. Notice on the folded version (next page) the little **32 x 32** square that appears in the lower left hand corner of Mark. It holds **1,024** letters, which is **100** less than our **1,124** overall length before folding. An **89 x 89** square placed catty-corner to it would fill to the opposite corner of Mark, and peculiarly enough, we have two such squares on the board.

We have a total of **127,206** units which are colored, and **55,900** of white background. Of these colored units, **107,164** are single-layer, and **20,042** are overlapped books or section of books. These include **6,400** where Matthew overlaps Genesis, **2,848** where Exodus overlaps Mark, **10,769** where Leviticus overlaps Mark, and **25** where Numbers completely eclipses little John.

Chart 39: The Pentateuch and Gospels Folded Between Genesis and Matthew to Overlap

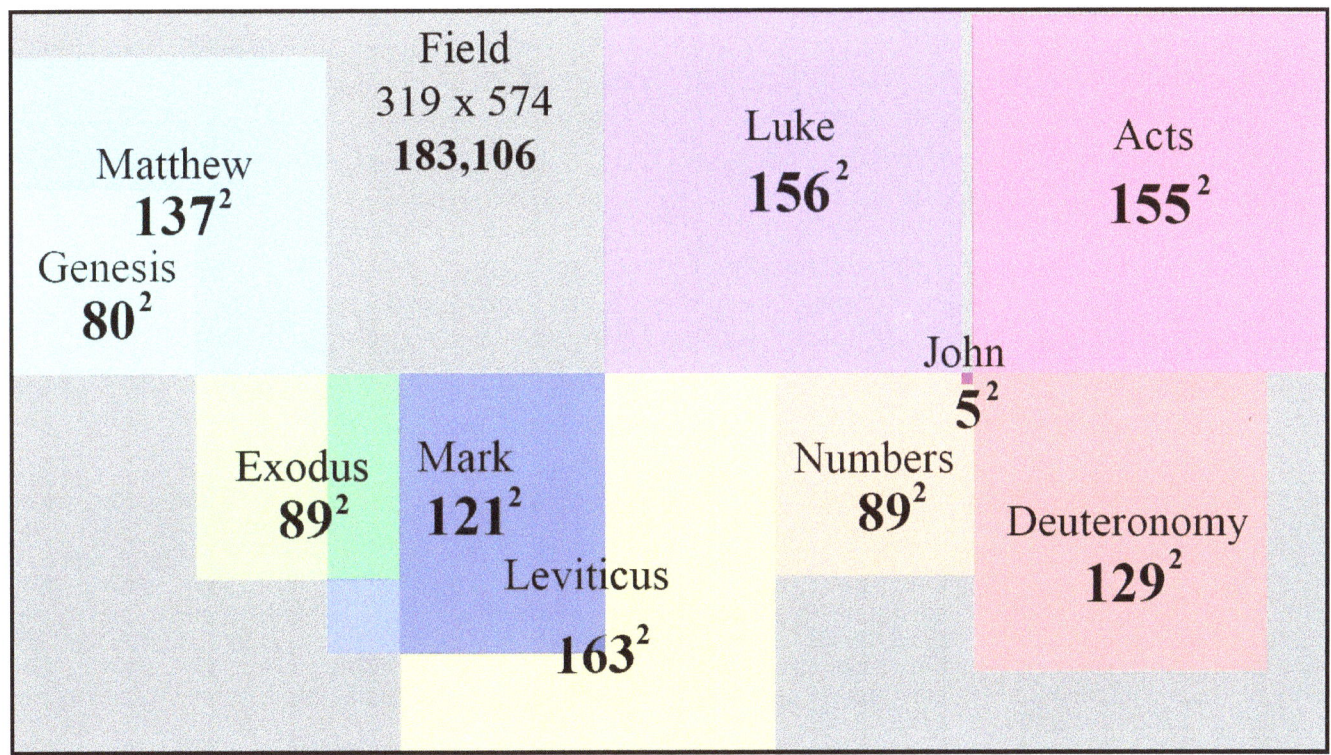

Average:	71,545
Field:	183,106 (319 x 574)
All Squares:	127,206
Single Layers:	107,164
Double Layers:	20,042
Background:	55,900
Remainder Letters:	703

We have folded in half the **1,406** remainder letters left over from making perfect squares, giving us **703**, which turns out to have two and only two very significant factors, **19 x 37**, which you can see diagrammed throughout the last half of Appendix **I**. One thing it does not mention there is that while we call **1,406** "remainder" letters, **1,406 x 7 = 9,842** *which just happens to be the exact number of Greek words in the book of Revelation.* But back to Appendix I, let's look at an abridged version of that discussion here (in blue):

What we are looking for here here are are the numbers **73** and **37** that make up Genesis 1:1 when multiplied together. . . and how they unfold from **Creation** into the rest of the Scriptures.

40

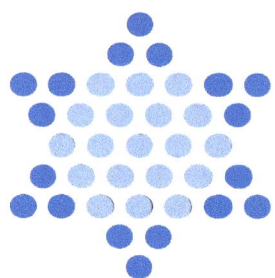

It so happens that the **73rd** Triangle Number is **2,701**, the very value of the first verse, which is **37 x 73**.. Here we have a star of **37** pennies nesting a hexagon of **19** pennies by putting an inverted **28** triangle (there are **28** letters in the first verse) upon itself. The Hebrew word for the *heart* is "הלב". The ordinal value of these letters (they are the 5th, 12th, and 2nd letters respectively) equals **19**. Their cardinal value (5, 30, and 2) equals **37**. And our star above has **19** pennies in the center hexagon, and **37** pennies altogether. Does this relate to Genesis 1:1? The phrase "*and the earth*" has a value of **703**, which is **19 x 37**. And **703** is also the **37th** triangle number.

Now counting from **1** to **1,000,000,000,000,000** (one quadrillion) there are only **12** numbers that can make both a star and a hexagon, and there is only **one** under **1,000**. If you guessed **37** you were right. We have already seen the **37** star; here is the **37**-hexagon embedded in a star:

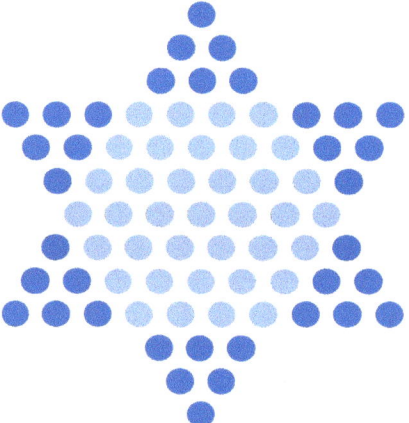

And how many pennies do we have altogether? **73.**

And because **37** is one of the very few numbers that can be both a star and a hexagon, what happens

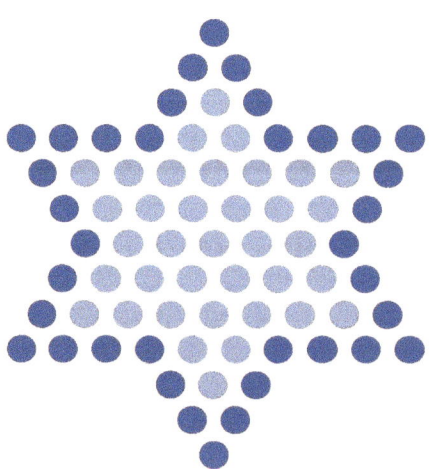

when we take the **37** star, and surround it with a larger star?

Again, our **37** star is embedded in a star of **73**. This all seems so simple and natural except for the fact that *these are the only numbers that this works for*. And they're the numbers we find in Genesis 1:1.

Here is our **73rd** (**73** layers) triangle number, which as we have mentioned, has **2,701** 'pennies' (the value of Genesis 1:1) units, as follows:

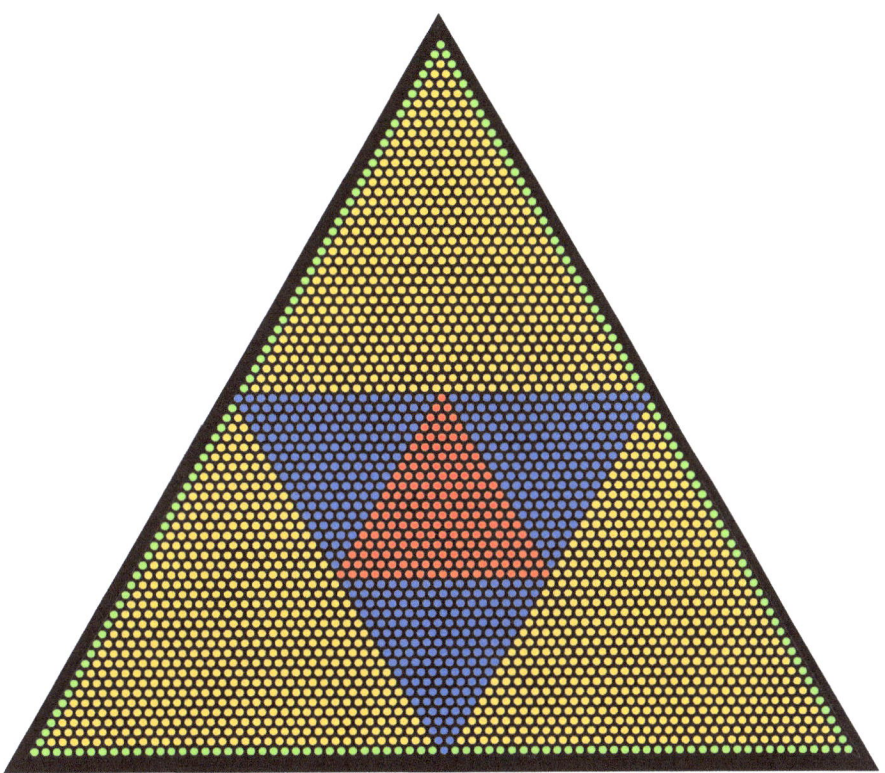

The middle blue triangle is the **37**th triangle number and holds **703** letters, which is **37 x 19**. When we put a red triangle fitted into the blue one, it turns out to be the **19**th triangle number, which is quite reminiscent of our earlier **37**-star with a **19**-hexagon in its center.

And if we combine **Genesis 1:1** (**2701**) and **John 1:1** (**3627**) we get **6,328** which turns out to be the **112th** Triangle Number. And what is **112**? It happens to be the value of

יהוה אלהים

...which we know as "Jehovah Elohim". It is also the value of "pure" and "think". . . something to think about. While we are on **112**, we might note that in our study of the letters in Mark, we found **6,862** Alphas and **1,314** Omegas. We are familiar with the verse, "I am the Alpha and the Omega". The two letters add up to **8,176**, which is **112 x 73**.

[End of Abridged Quote from Appendix I]

If this all seems strange, it gets stranger. The value of the **112**th triangle number, as mentioned above, is **6,327 + 1**. This **6,327** is **9 x 703**. When we divide this **6,327** by our 'magic' (or seemingly so) number of **37**, we get precisely **171**. What is so special about **171**? Aside from being the **18**th triangle number (and **37 x 18 = 666**), we will soon see that we can't solve our current puzzle without it.

The Remainder Letters in the past two chapters have been found to fit perfectly on the perimeter of the first book; here we have *two* first books. Investigating their perimeters, we discover that Matthew has exactly **544** places for letters if we put them *inside* his perimeter instead of adding another layer on the outside.

The remaining **159** Remainder letters fit perfectly around the outside of the the remaining two sides of Genesis. These add up up to our requisite **703** letters.

Chart 40: The Placement of the 703 Remainder Letters Around Matthew and Genesis

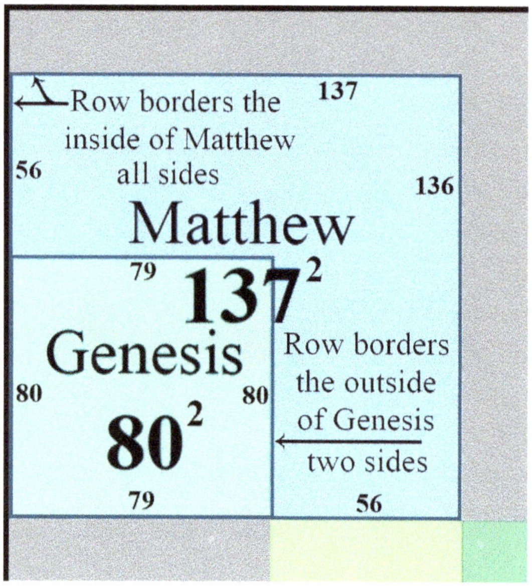

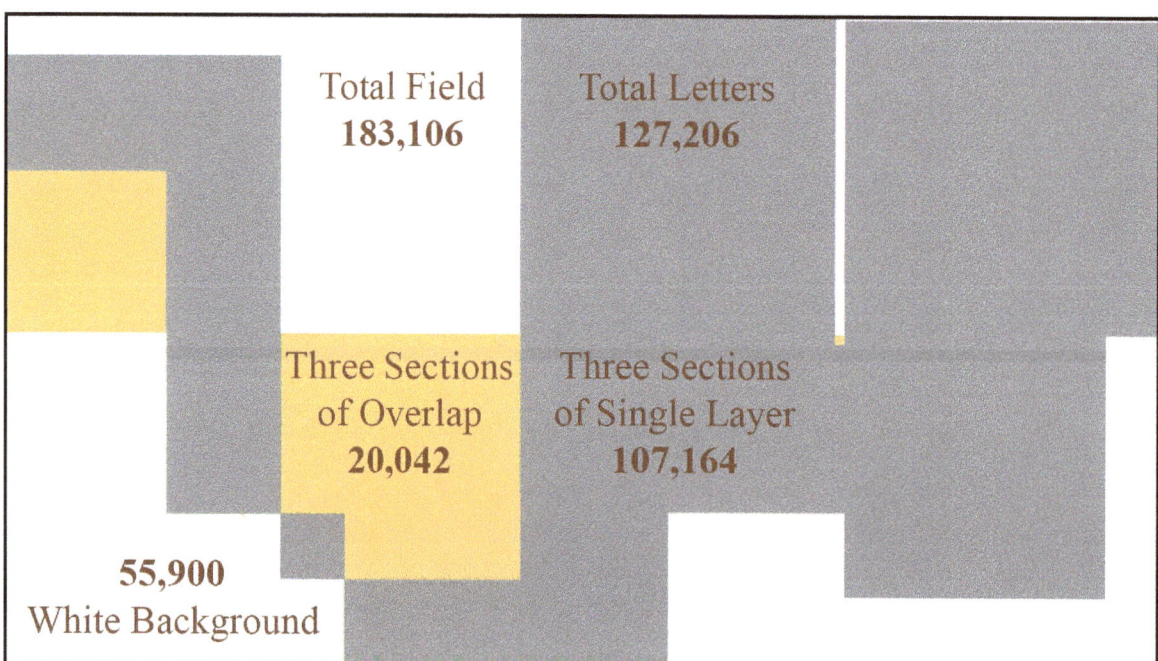

Now every letter is accounted for. Do we find any correlation between the doubled areas totaling **20,042**, the white background of **55,900**, and the average of **71,545** that generated all this? Of course not, that would be too easy. Those numbers do not seem to want to cooperate. Here again is a summary of the folded chart:

Chart 41: Space Totals of the Pentateuch and Gospels Folded Between Genesis and Matthew

Yet we note that it is a *folded* diagram. If our calculations for the area of color that are from two different books are to work, they must be unfolded. This is going to give us three sets of figures: the original ten books as laid out, the folded version, and the *unfolded* version which will be larger than the original. Let's color code them so that we can keep track:

Original Layout		Folded Version		Unfolded Version	
Average:	71,545	Average:	71,545	Average:	71,545
Field (319 x 1,124)	358,556	Field: (319 x 574)	183,106	Field: (319 x 1,148)	366,212
All Squares:	147,248	All Squares:	127,206	All Squares:	254,412
		Single Layers:	107,164	Unfolded Single Layers:	214,328
		Double Layers:	20,042	Unfolded Double Layers:	40,084
Background:	209,902	Background:	55,900	Background:	111,800
Remainder Letters:	1,406	Remainder Letters:	703	Remainder Letters:	1,406 – 171

Here is the visual for the unfolded version:

Chart 42: Space Totals of the Pentateuch and Gospels Folded then Unfolded

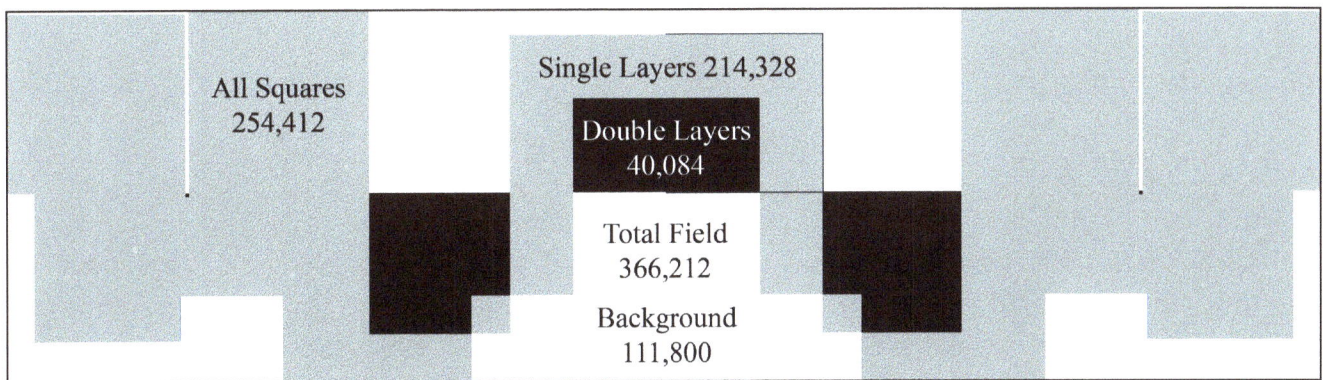

The key of the figures above is the "**171**" Remainder Letters under "Unfolded Version". This is **703** times **9** (**6,327**) then divided by **37** (**171**). Why? To keep the flow going, i'll lay it out at the end of the chapter. Meanwhile we are finally ready for some self-referential proportions:

First Proportion
(Chart 43)

Background minus Unfolded Double Layers minus Remainders equals **Average**

or

111,800 − 40,084 − 171 = 71,545

or

44

Second Proportion
(Chart 44)

Unfolded Field minus twice the Original Squares minus Remainders equals **Average**

or

366,212 − (2 x 147,248) − 171 = 71,545
     (294,496)

or

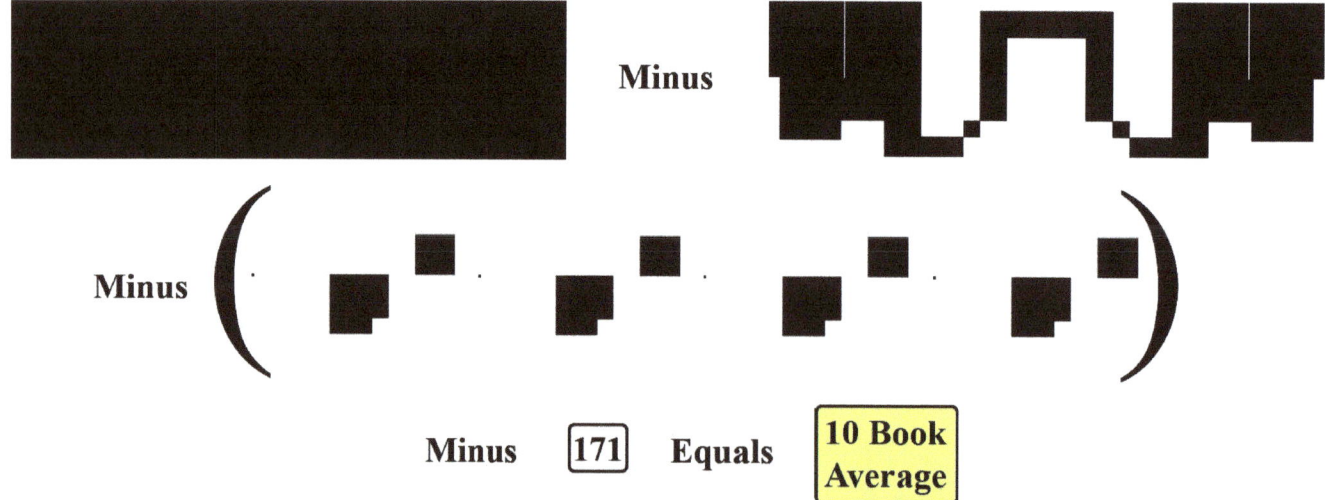

Third Proportion
(Chart 45)

Field minus Unfolded Single Layers minus Four Folded Double Layers minus Remainders equals **Average**

or

366,212 − 214,328 − (4 x 20,042) − 171 = 71,545
                    (80,168)

or

And again we arrive at the Average by using nothing but the proportions handed to us in the letters. We have added nothing apart from the letters, and we have taken nothing away apart from the letters. Of course, there are plenty of other oddities, such as the Unfolded Single Layers (**214,328**) added to the *reverse* of the Folded Remainder Letters (**307**) equaling the **3 x** The **71,545** Average (**214,635**), but i think that these are best left for the Reader to explore.

At this point it is high time to take a break and consider what **171** is all about.

Visual Break

What's with subtracting 171 every time?

Believe it or not, the function of **171** is *completely different* each time it is used. Recall how we first place the **703** Remainder Letters. I'll put in the number of letters that fit on each line:

Chart 46: The Placement of the 703 Remainder Letters Around Matthew and Genesis

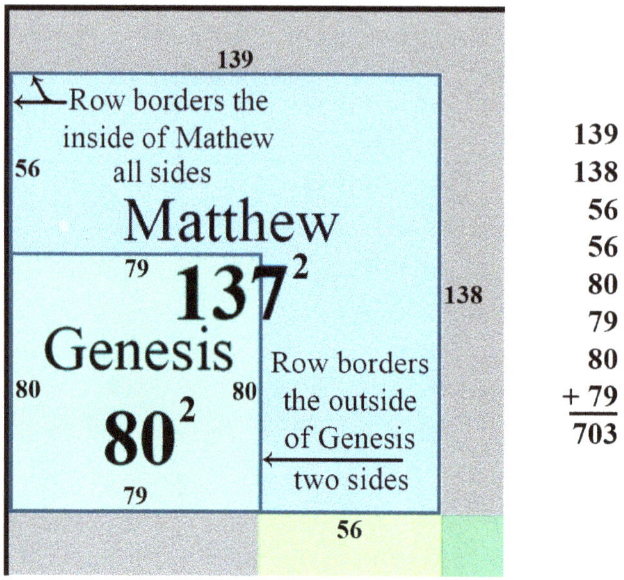

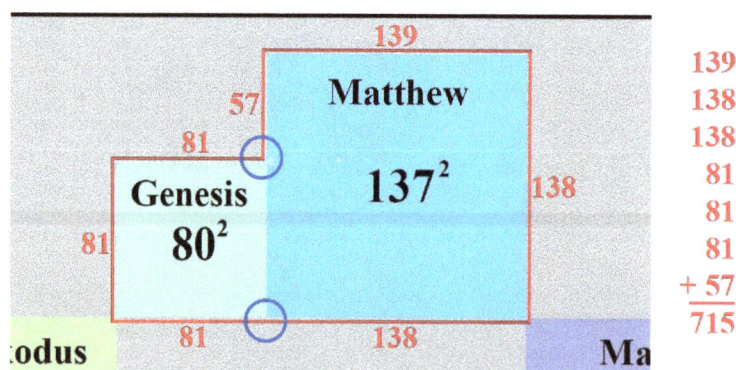

This is all fine and dandy, but what happens to these positions when we unfold the squares? In fact, where are these positions on the *original unfolded* arrangement?

It turns out that the positions on the unfolded arrangement were the enormous hint in the first place that it had to be folded. Before folding, there were **1,406** Remainder Letters to be placed, not the **703** above that represents half of that figure.

In Chapter 3, the Remainder Letters fit around the outside of Genesis. In chapter 4, the Remainder Letters fit around the outside of Matthew, but had 39 missing, which space was filled in by the smaller model of the books. Here we proceed similarly and see what happens; we'll need to exaggerate the lines so that we can keep track of the smaller details.

Chart 47: Placement of an Outside Border of Remainder Letters Around Matthew and Genesis

715 is close to **703**, but nowhere near **1,406**. Note also that the two blue circles show where the Genesis–Matthew borders overlap, as if we are considering them to be distinct borders. Because the **703** initially fit using both inside and outside borders, and because we need another **691** more letters or so to use all **1,406** Remainder Letters, we apply an additional border inside. Yet the fact that the **703** initially fit without an extra line for Genesis on its left or bottom border in chart 46 gave me pause. *It was as if it was anticipated that the picture would be folded.* With this in mind, we leave room when placing the inside border for overlap *of the inside border of Genesis only.*

Chart 48: Placement of an Inside Border of Remainder Letters in Matthew and Genesis

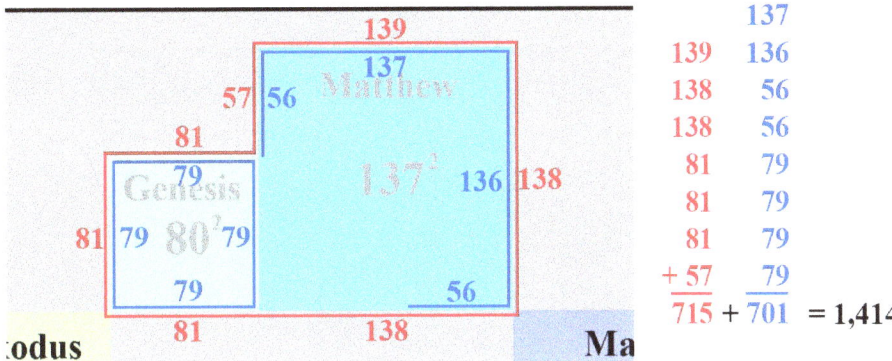

Well so far so strange. Now if this outside (red) border does *not* mind overlapping, while the inside (blue) one *does*, we are going to have a bit of a mess when we fold it, and stray significantly from the **1,414** just achieved, which is so tantalizingly close to the **1,406** we need. It is tempting to add one letter to each leg of **56** to make the inside border equal our **703** target, but that is against the rules as they're being laid out. So we proceed along the path of logic, and starting with the red, begin to place the lines as they demand. And guess who begins popping up as soon as we do so?

Chart 49: Placement of Remainder of Inside Border in Anticipation of Folding

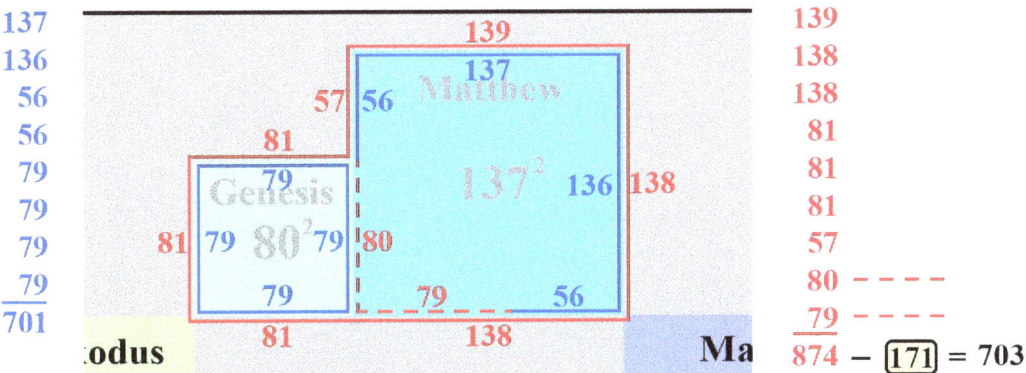

It's our friend **171**. If we had hovered around **1,415** trying to twist it into **1,406** we never would have seen this. So now we have no choice but to look at *all* the ramifications of folding the picture.

Chart 50: Placement of Remainder of Outside Borders in Anticipation of Folding and Unfolding

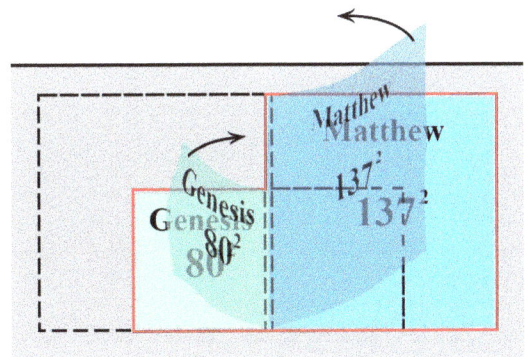

The next illustration shows the <u>outside</u> borders first. From Charts 48 and 49 we see that Genesis has three sides bordered while Matthew has four. This leads to a number of oddities, such as the doubling, tripling, and quadrupling of layers of border as they cross each other and stack up when folded, as we saw in chart 47. Note the circles drawn with a small number beside some of them; this indicates how many redundant layers are in that particular spot.

Chart 51: Placement of Outside Borders after Folding and Unfolding

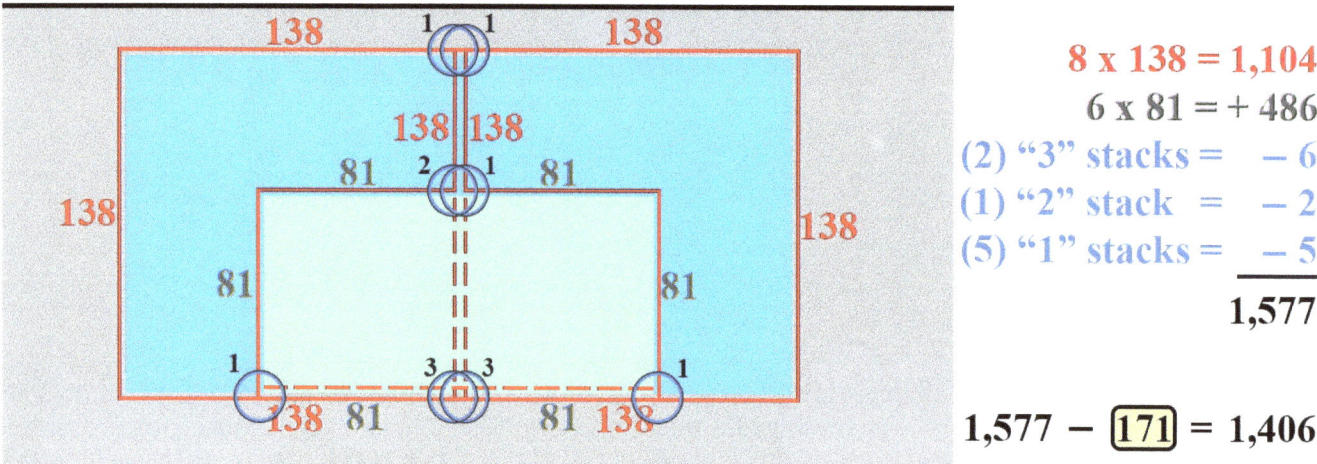

And once again, our friend **171** is there to bring us back to the precise figure of **1,406**.

If the stacking up of border spots seems confusing, remember that at the fold line, an *outside* border also stacks onto the *inside* border when folded. This only occurs immediately adjacent to the fold line; the more remote lines only stack outside on outside and inside on inside. It is very important to know precisely where our lines are before we start folding and unfolding.

Chart 52: Folding and Stacking Protocols

In addition to 'stacking' when dealing with the relationship between the inside and outside lines, their 'crossing' points are significant. For example, if we take the inside and outside borders from Chart 49:

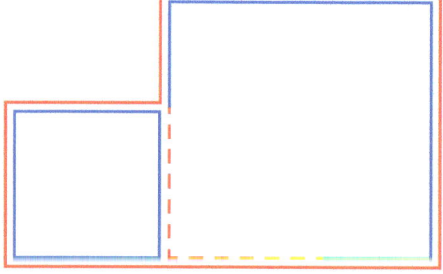

49

...and fold then unfold (as if it were made of wet ink) we find that there are four and only four places where the inside line crosses with the outside line.

Chart 53: Crossover Locations Between Inside and Outside Borders

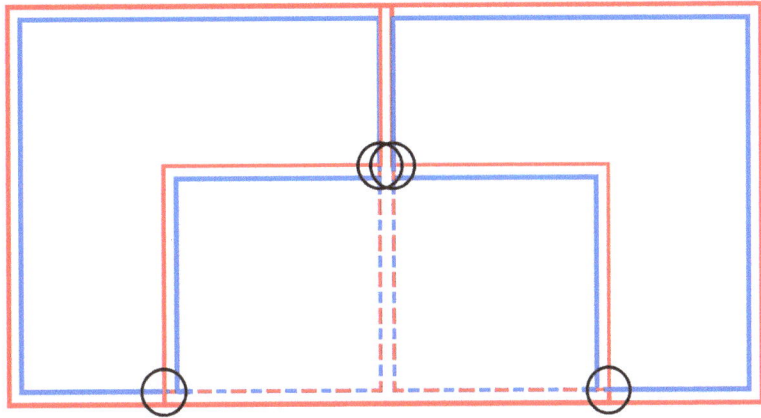

These are significant and must be counted differently from mere 'stacking'. as they *reverse the order of inside and outside*. In this arrangement we have **4** crossovers, and **432** double stacks (two of which are crossovers.)

When counting up inside borders like we did with outside borders in Chart 51, we *add* the crossovers rather than subtract them as they represent a switching point from outside to inside; the letter at that spot is 'inside' two different spaces at once. Here is the count of inside borders:

Chart 54: Placement of Inside Borders after Folding and Unfolding

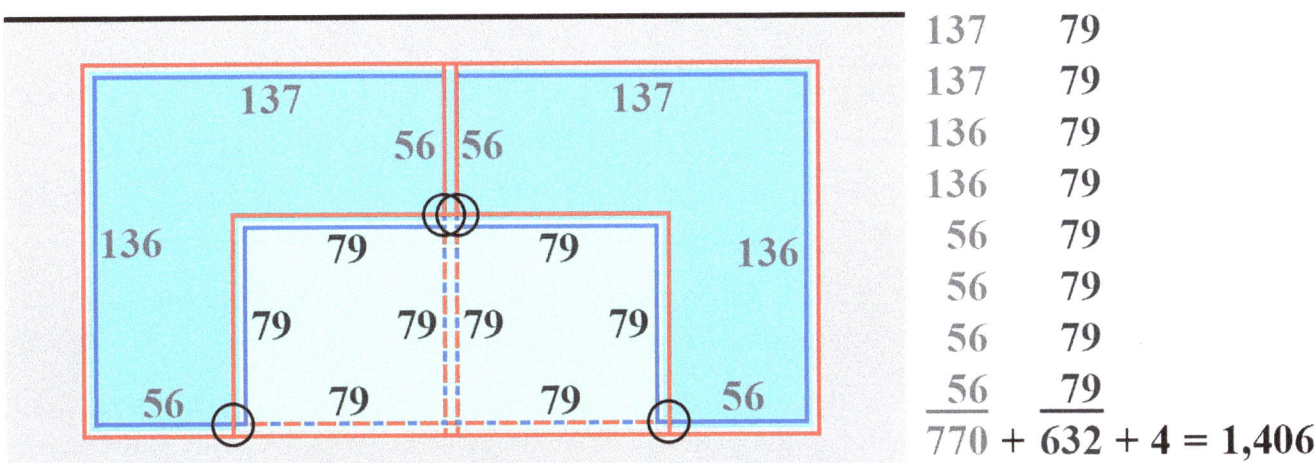

And oddly enough, this time we *don't* need our friend **171** to arrive at the perfect Remainder Number figure of **1,406**. Perhaps once he has given the message that it gets folded, **171** takes a break.

So you say to me, "Mark, this is all too complicated. How many *actual letters* do we have inside and outside with no special rules, no overlap, nothing but a simple count of each space." Okay, let's do that.

Genesis has **632** inside (79 x 8).
Matthew has **770** inside (see chart 54).
Genesis has **318** outside that are still inside Matthew.
Matthew has **826** on its full perimeter.

So altogether we have 2,546 non-overlapping places that are taken up on our picture. A nice happy insignificant number. If you hear low warning music in the background, pay it no mind.

Now remember when we started with **703** and **171**? We found all sorts of strange connections, the main one being that **9 x 703 = 6,327** which happens also to be **37 x 171**. So with our new number of 2,546, let's try that again. **9 x** 2,546 = **22,914**, which is **134 x 171**. What on earth?

And the two numbers, **37** and **134** that were both multiplied by **171** to get our figures? Add them together and see what we get. You guessed it: **37 + 134 = 171**. Are all these numbers in some sort of secret society together? Take **134 x 703**. We get **94,202** which just happens to be 2,546 **x 37**.

And it doesn't help to find out that **171**, **703**, 2,546, **and 6,327** are all divisible by **19**. **134** isn't divisible by **19**, but **19 x 134** *is* 2,546. And **67** less than that is **2,479**, which is **67 x 37**. And of course, **19 x 37** is **703** and **2 x 67** is **134**.

And of little consequence, but interesting, Average **71,545 - 1001 +** 2,546 **= 70,000**. Or for that matter, the difference between the New Testament and Old Testament halves of the chart is **16,344**, which when added to the Average **71,545**, and multiplied by **4** equals **351,556** which is **7,000** *under* the unfolded Field **358,556**.

While all this is fun, we need closure. The three elements of a full self-referential system are the Field, the Common, and the Unique. The figures on this page so far have been limited to the Unique... we need the figures for the Common and the Field. So let's find them and lay them out.

Unfolded Version

Average:	71,545
Field: (319 x 1,148)	366,212
All Squares:	254,412
Unfolded Single Layers:	214,328
Unfolded Double Layers:	40,084
Background:	111,800
Remainder Letters:	1,406 – 171

So it should be a simple matter of putting our nice 'unique' **171** into the relationship between Unique (the squares), Common (the average) and the Field (the whole rectangle). Here we go:

Average (71,545) + **Unique** (171) + **All Squares** (254,412) + **Double Layers** (40,084)
equals **Field** (366,212)

Looking back over this chapter, i see that this is just another version of **Proportion 3** on chart 45. It is nice, however, to have arrived at through a completely different method, somewhat to my surprise, as i didn't get it figured out until i typed out the above two paragraphs.

As to the *Original* Field and how the Remainder itself has been morphing, we can now note that:
       Field **358,556** + (1,406 + 19 + 19) = **360,000** (**600²**)
and   Field **358,556** =   + 19 + 19 + (3 x 703) + **597²**

And remember those two smaller models of the Large Squares in black on chart 37? The subsequent discovery of **171** gives us this:

(((1,406 + 171) x 41) + 41) + 1,406 + Avg. **71,545** + Large & Small Squares **220,907**
= Field **358,556**.

And now i believe it is high time to move along to whatever turns out to be next.

VI Regrouping:

The <u>Common</u>, the <u>Unique</u>, and the <u>Field</u>

We have now explored three separate discoveries and found each one of them to work perfectly to the letter. The method for each was similar, yet each one required investigation into its own particular character to solve. Before going further, it would be valuable to establish just what it is that we have and have not discovered.

Let us take the Pentateuch with which we started. The questions were:

- Is the length of each of these five books a necessity down to the letter?
- Does the number of letters in each book interconnect with the number of letters in the other books?
- Does the length of all the books together work as a self-consistent unit?

To solve this, we first found what all five books had in <u>common</u>. So we took the number of letters in each book, added them all together and divided by five. The average of the five books turned out to be the prime number **60,961**. This is a <u>common</u> number that all five books share equally.

This **commonality** became our base line. Now we could look at each book individually and determine what was <u>unique</u> about it by measuring how far it deviated from the <u>common</u> average. Combining Chart 6 and Chart 19 here give us a visual of the <u>unique</u> length of each book in relation to the <u>common</u> average that they all share:

Chart 55: Each Book of the Pentateuch Sized According to its Deviation from the Average

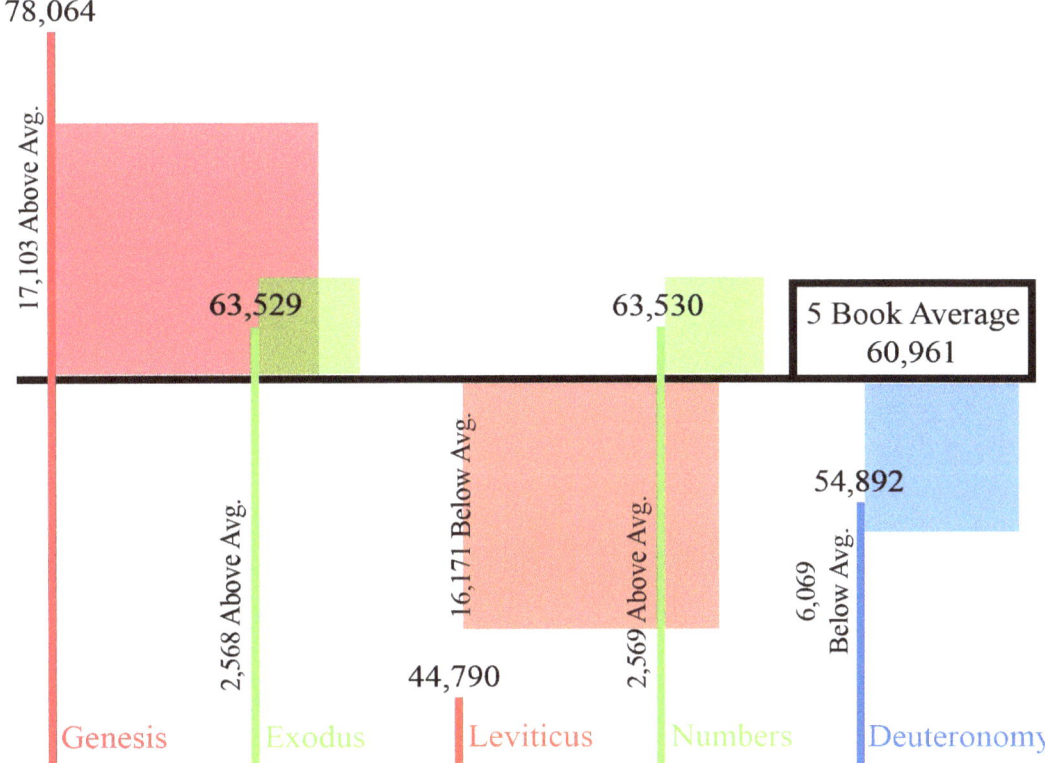

For this we took the excess or lack of each line above or below the **average** and made it into a square. Mathematically, this meant taking the square root of each number. This gave us an <u>accurate visual and geometric representation of each book in relation to the others</u>.

Once we had both the **commonality** and the **uniqueness** of the books of the Pentateuch, we needed to put them together into one context. We will call this context the **field**. This is simply the rectangle into which everything fits.

Chart 56: Common and Unique Properties of the Pentateuch in One Context, or Field

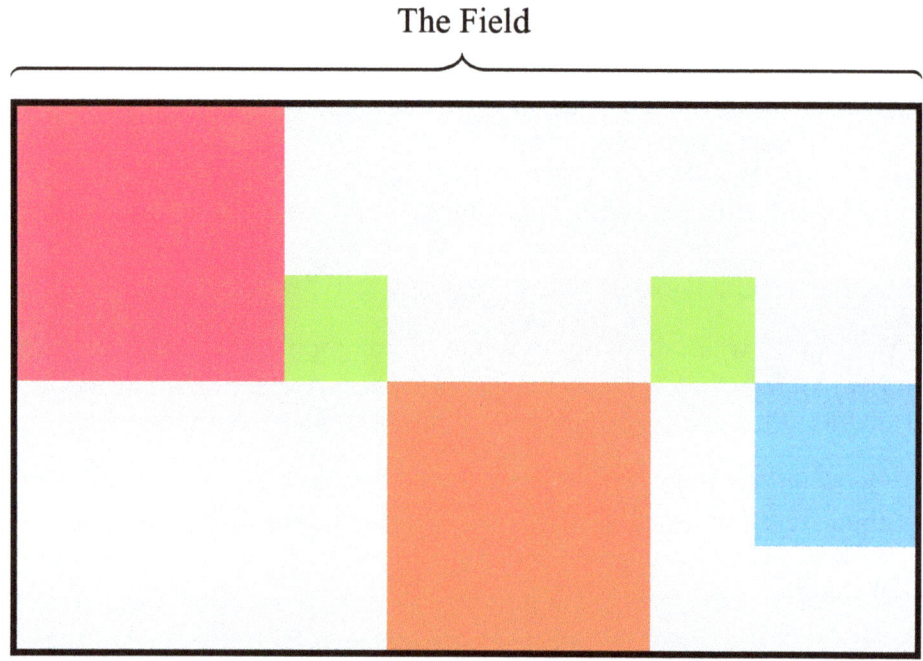

We then included every letter that was left over from making the squares, since none of the numbers made perfect squares by themselves. These leftover letters fit around Genesis perfectly and made the **field** one letter higher and one letter wider.

Once this was done, we went through an intricate process of building a smaller model that was proportional to the larger one (Charts 21 through 27). Initially this process was simple exploration into the fact that Exodus, Numbers, and Deuteronomy all fit into Leviticus perfectly. However, it was discovered (and quite a surprise it was) that once this smaller model was included in the picture, that the **Commonality** (the average) plus the **Uniqueness** (all the colored squares) equaled the **Field** (the whole picture).

However, we might include an additional element that is part of the **Unique**: and that is the role that the smaller sets play in chapters 3 and 4, and the doubled letters when folded play in chapter 5... as well as the morphing from **1,406** to **171** in chapter 5. We can call this the **Key**. It appears that the **Unique** always has a **Key**. And this Key must be discovered anew for each scenario; otherwise we could simply subtract the Unique from the Field and get the Common. In our current picture, the inclusion of the Smaller Model of the Whole is the **Key**.

And thus we got our first confirmation that a powerful pattern ties together every letter:

60,961 (the Average) + **51,269** (the Squares) = **112,230** (the Field)

This can be represented as follows:

Chart 57: Common, Unique, and Field Amounts in the Pentateuch

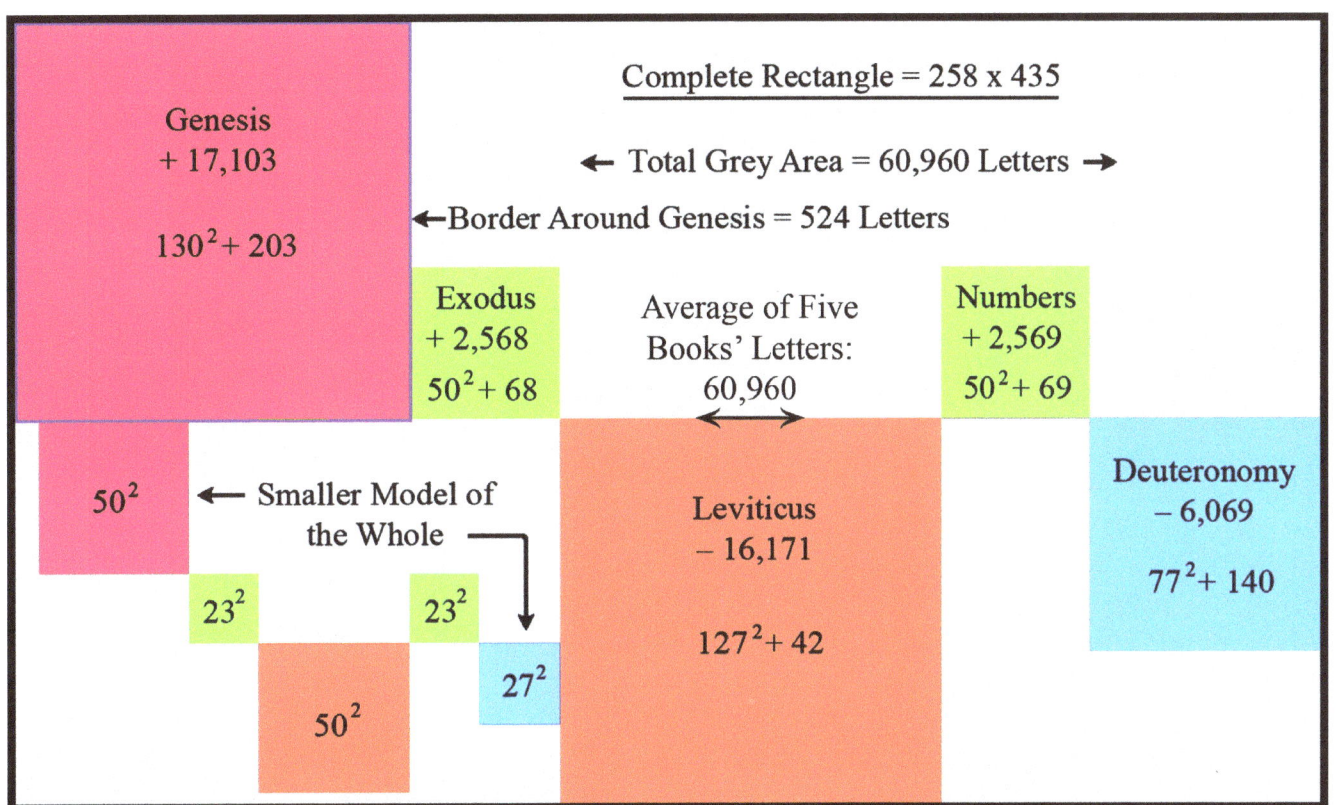

Chart 58: Summation of Common, Unique, and Field areas of the Pentateuch				
Common Area (All Grey Parts)	**Unique Area** (All Colored Parts)		Left Over	**The 'Field'** (The Whole Rectangle)
as well as ———— The Average of the Number of Letters in All Five Books **60,961**	Genesis	130 x 130 = **16,900**	203	258 x 435 = **112,230**
	Exodus	50 x 50 = **2,500**	68	
	Leviticus	127 x 127 = **16,129**	42	
	Numbers	50 x 50 = **2,500**	2 Nun + 69	
	Deuteronomy	77 x 77 = **5,929**	140	
	Smaller Genesis	50 x 50 = **2,500**	The 'Key'	
	Smaller Exodus	23 x 23 = **529**		
	Smaller Leviticus	50 x 50 = **2,500**		
	Smaller Numbers	23 x 23 = **529**		
	Sm. Deuteronomy	27 x 27 = **729**		
	Totals	**50,745**	+ **524**	
	Total Unique Area = 51,269			
Common Area (The Average) **60,961** + Unique Area (The Letters) **51,269** = Total Area **112,230**				

We then proceeded in Chapter IV to discover a similar design in the Gospels and Acts. Once again, we found that the **common** element (the average of the 5 books), the **unique** elements (the books along with a smaller model of them) and the **field** were perfectly proportional. In both cases, a single letter can not be added or removed; the patterns are tight and internally consistent.

The Gospels and Acts can be summarized with this picture:

Chart 59: The Common, the Unique, and the Field Balanced in the Gospels and Acts

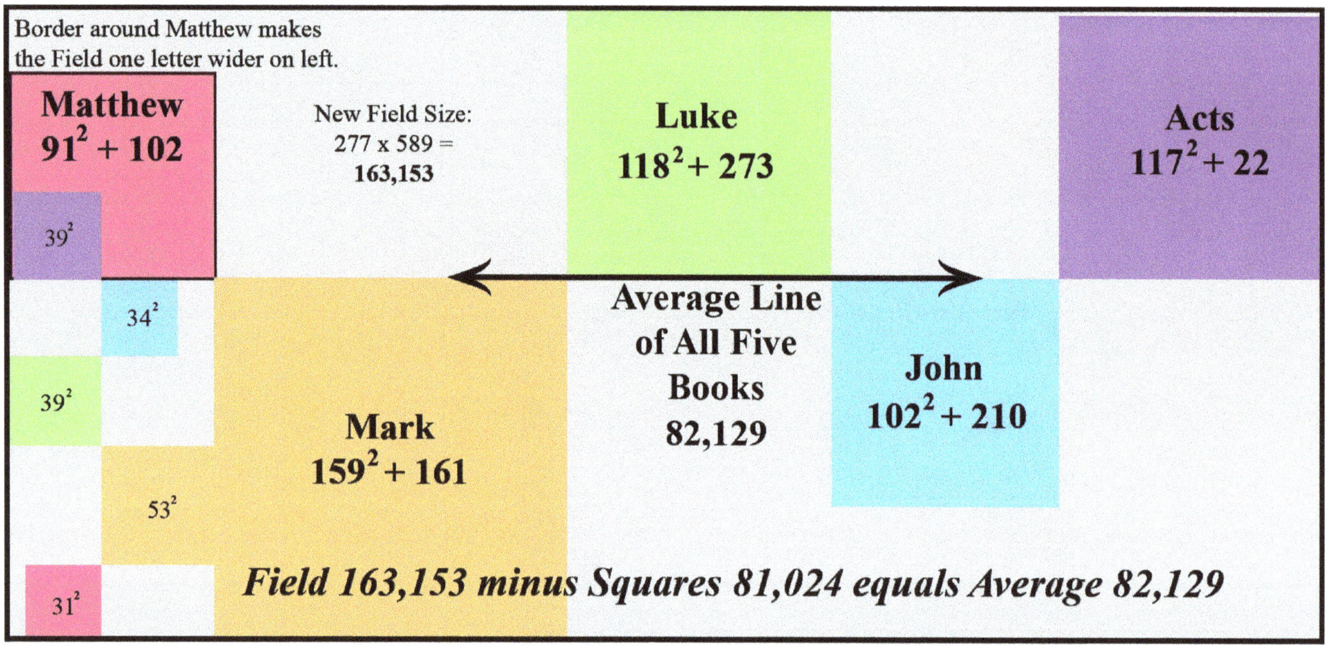

Border around Matthew makes
the Field one letter wider on left.
Matthew
91² + 102
39²
New Field Size:
277 x 589 =
163,153
Luke
118² + 273
Acts
117² + 22
34²
Average Line
of All Five
Books
82,129
John
102² + 210
39²
Mark
159² + 161
53²
31²
Field 163,153 minus Squares 81,024 equals Average 82,129

Once again, we have the **Common** (Average 82,129) and the **Unique** (plus Squares 81,024) equal to the **Field** (163,153). The **Common** again has a smaller model as its **Key**.

Then in Chapter V we analyzed both groups together as one group. This became fairly complex, and the attempt to introduce smaller models to balance the picture were met with only limited success. It was not until we folded the picture that the perfection was discovered; and we found that it is the areas where books overlap each other which is crucial. No smaller model was needed as in the previous chapters; it seems that the overlapped areas replace that peculiar element.

Thus we found that in the first case the unfolded overlapping areas became the **Unique**, the background to the letters became the **Field**, and the average, as always, became the **Common**. Let's look at that as addition rather than subtraction:

Chart 60: The Common, the Unique, and the Field in Gospels and the Pentateuch Together

Common
+
Unique
=
Field
10 Book Average
Plus
171
Plus
Equals
71,545
+
171
+
40,084
=
111,800

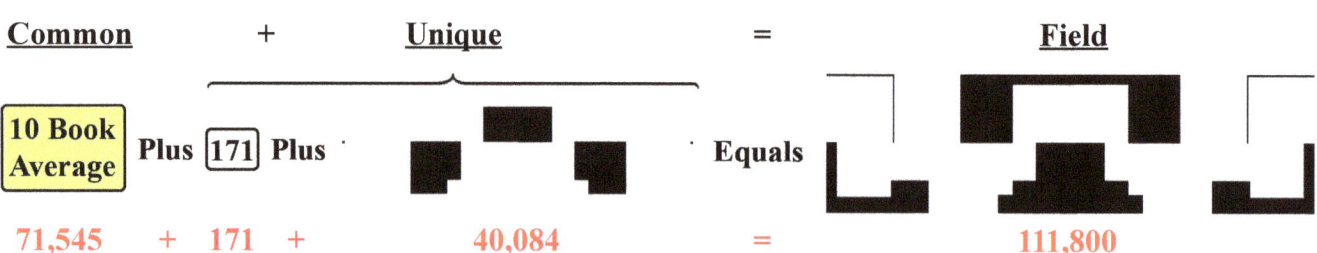

In the second case we found that the <u>total original number of letters</u> became the **Unique**, the <u>entire field</u> became the **Field**, and the <u>average</u>, as always, became the **Common**. Again, let's look at that as addition rather than subtraction:

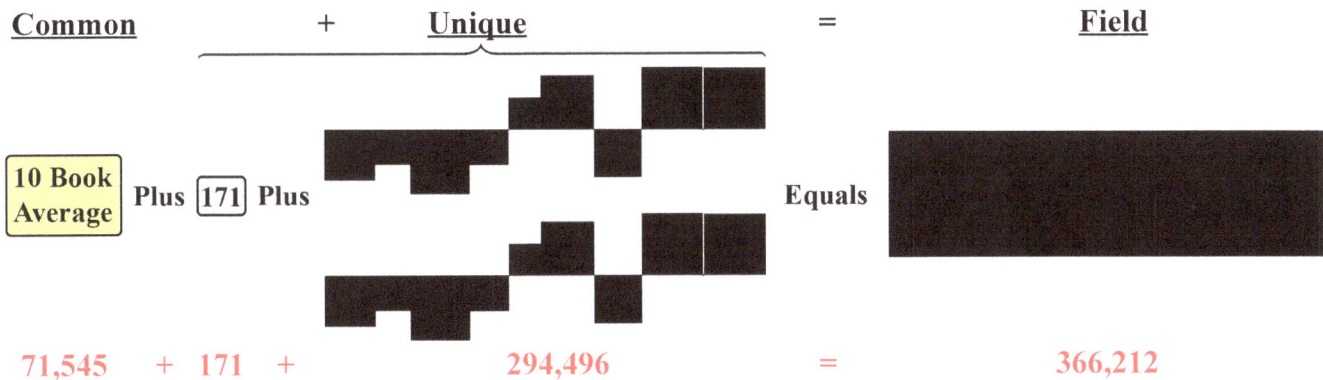

Chart 61: The Common, the Unique, and the Field in Gospels and the Pentateuch Together

In the third case we found that the <u>unfolded **non-**overlapping areas</u> **and** <u>the folded double (overlapping) areas</u> became the **Unique**, the <u>entire field</u> became the **Field**, and the <u>average</u>, as always, became the **Common**. We can, for the **Unique**, use twice the <u>unfolded overlapping areas</u> instead of four times the <u>folded overlapping areas</u> as they amount to the same thing. Once again, let's look at this as addition rather than subtraction:

Chart 62: The Common, the Unique, and the Field in Gospels and the Pentateuch Together

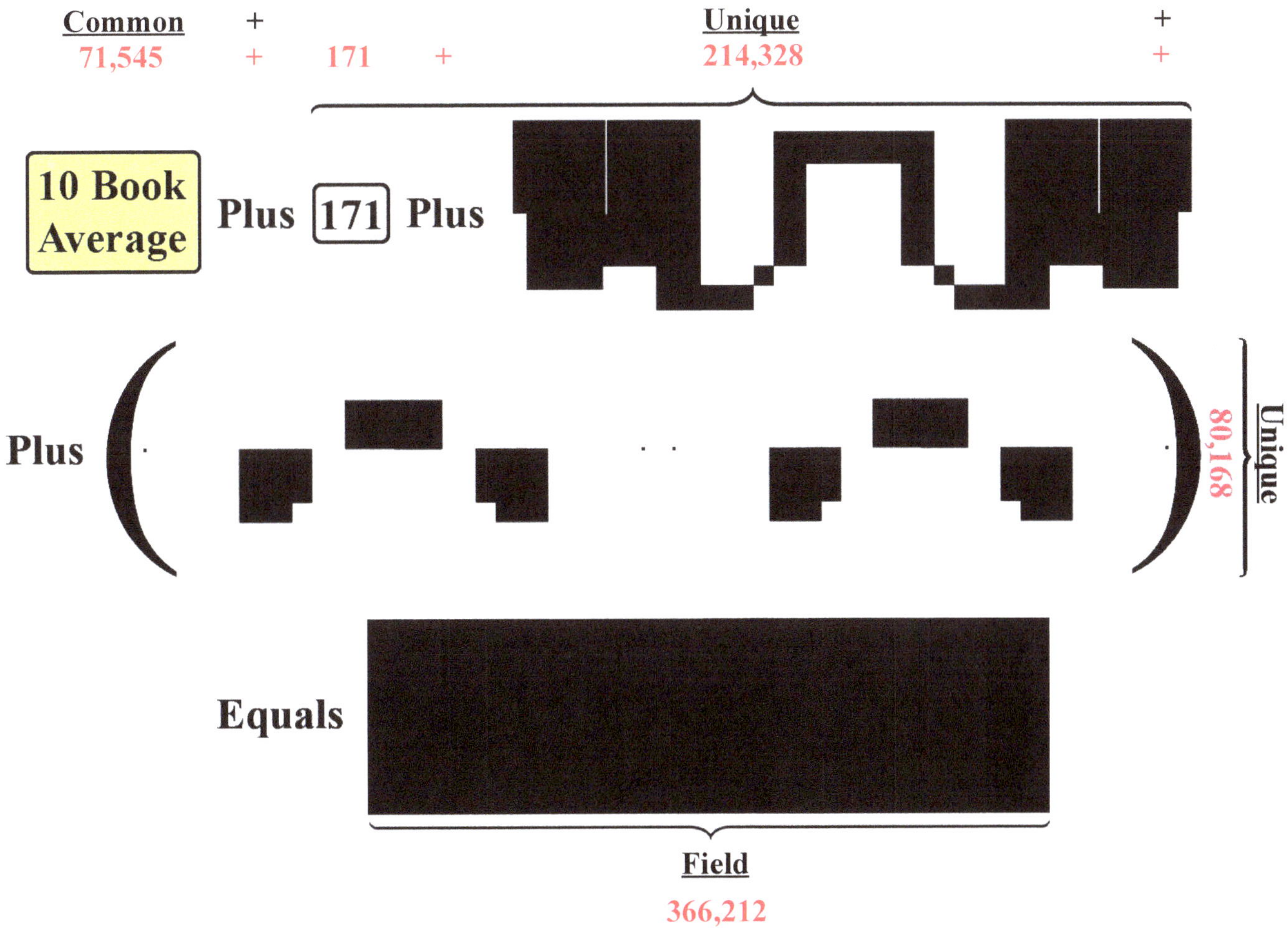

Summarizing with the next picture, the white minus black equals the average of all books. Also, the whole picture minus the grey minus twice the black equals the average of all books.

Chart 63: The Gospels and the Pentateuch Unfolded Showing Single and Double Layers

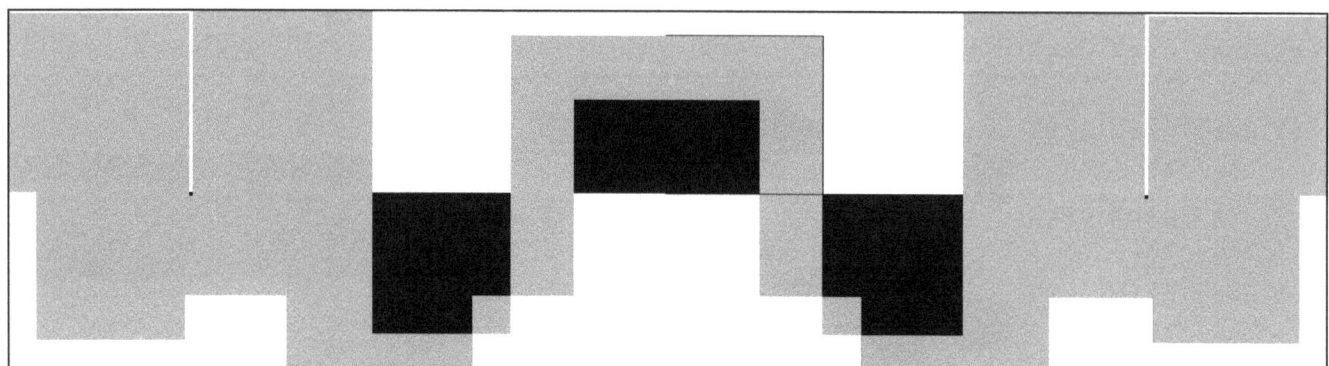

That was the first and third steps. The second one shown in the next picture is simply: the whole thing minus twice the black equals the average of all the books.

Chart 64: The Gospels and the Pentateuch Sized According to Deviation from the Ten-Book Average

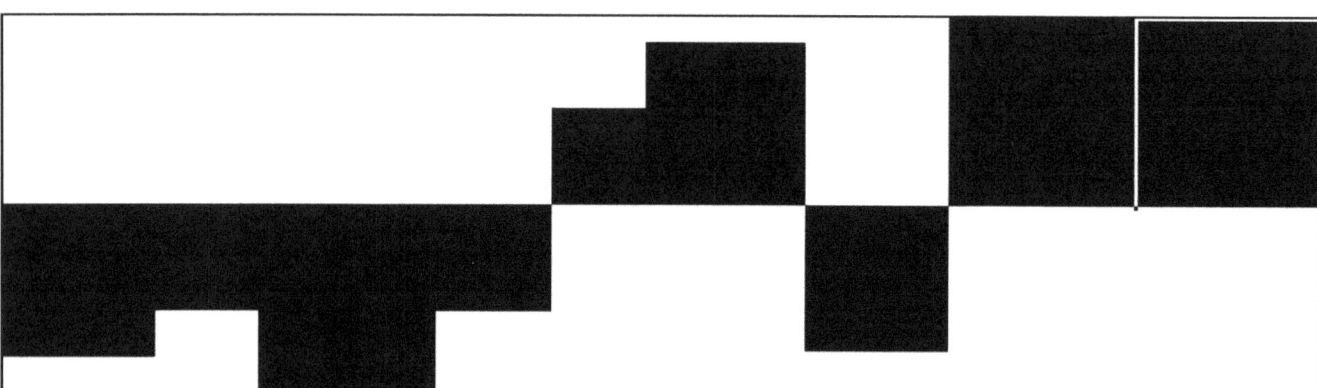

So here we have a strange scenario. In order to find the consistency of the 10 books together, we had to *fold* and then *unfold* the picture, which gave us **366,212** spaces with the proportions of each book working together to the very letter.

In the final comparison of this picture from Chapter V to the previous two chapters, it is the *overlapping sections when folded* which become what in the other pictures is the smaller version of the books. There are still many oddities which want exploring; for now let us concentrate on what we have learned and hopefully apply it to further exploration. That is, there is the **Field**, the **Common Element**, and the **Unique Element**; these three have consistently emerged as the carriers of the perfect relationships for which we are searching. Note that these are the 3 necessary <u>dimensions</u> to solve the puzzle. In Appendix II on pages 91-93 where we consider how to discover the meanings of numbers, we find that they also utilize the 3 dimensions of numbers (cyclic, cardinal, and ordinal) to complete the pattern.

We will find that <u>any</u> thorough endeavor must by necessity include all three dimensions of which it is composed. Mere lists or endlessly adding numbers together and hoping for something magical to happen is never enough. In mechanics we have stroke, position, and timing; in a motor we have electricity, magnetism, and motion; in architecture we have form, function, and aesthetics. These dimensions tend to operate at right angles to their other two companions, which is why the Cartesian Coordinate System is useful for setting up a model. Because they always operate three-dimensionally, linear thinking—no matter how thorough—can never achieve what must be a comprehensive approach to our understanding and discovery. Suppose your windshield-wipers are bumping against each other… mechanical systems have stroke, position, and timing. You adjust the length of the stroke and now it doesn't clear the whole windshield. So you adjust its position and now it bumps against the side of the window instead. Finally, you adjust timing by replacing the worn gear on the left side, and you've finally fixed the problem. Even genius adjustments of stroke and position are not going to help if it's a timing problem. Likewise with numbers, looking for a cardinal (amount) solution to an ordinal (order) or modular (cyclic) problem will never be found; all three dimensions must contribute.

Placing that Last Piece of the Puzzle

VII Opening Up the Game

We have now demonstrated that the Bible is letter-perfect, numerically perfect, and of a logical order that is beyond the power of investigation. Those who want this to be true will cheer, those who don't will check their facebook accounts, and all those in between (probably most of us) will kind of wonder what to do with it.

So let's change the tune. It's time for me to stop searching for crystal-clear cases and open this up for participation. I have added a few Appendixes to stimulate ideas; in face, i've already *removed* a dozen that seemed too far adrift of the subject; it's tricky to 'Keep It Simple' in this line of investigation. Like someone handing you a dictionary and saying, "Can you shorten this for readability?" "Um… which words would you like me take out?" But fortunately for us, this is not a dictionary; it's a journey.

So i'm going to relax a bit and present new directions at face value without loading up the queue past what can be presented easily, the sheer weight of which could be impractical.

Moses Decides to Implement Carry-On Weight Regulations for the Red Sea Crossing.

Let's start by looking at the *individual separate* letters of the Torah.

Chart 65: Number of Letters in the Entire Torah with their Factors, Deviations from Average (**13,854** Remainder **17**), Squares of Deviations & Remainders

א	ב	ג	ד	ה	ו	ז	ח	ט	י	כ
27,057	16,344	2,109	7,032	28,052	30,509	2,198	7,187	1,802	31,522	11,960
(3·29·311)	(2³·3²·227)	(3·19·37)	(2³·3·293)	(2²·7013)	(Prime)	(2·7·157)	(7·13·79)	(2·17·53)	(2·15,761)	(2³·5·13·23)
13,203	2,490	−11,745	−6,822	14,198	16,655	−11,656	−6,667	−12,052	17,668	−1,894
114²	49²	108²	82²	119²	129²	107²	81²	109²	132²	43²
207	89	81	98	37	14	207	106	171	244	45

ל	מ	נ	ס	ע	פ	צ	ק	ר	ש	ת
21,570	25,078	14,107	1,833	11,244	4,805	4,052	4,694	18,109	15,592	17,949
(2·3·5·719)	(2·12,539)	(Prime)	(3·13·47)	(2²·3·937)	(5·31²)	(2²·1013)	(2·2347)	(7·13·199)	(2²·1949)	(3·31·193)
7,716	11,224	253	−12,021	−2,610	−9,049	−9,802	−9,160	4,255	1,738	4,095
87²	105²	15²	109²	51²	95²	99²	95²	65²	41²	63²
147	199	28	140	9	24	1	135	30	57	126

Totals Added Straight Down, Combining the Two Sets of Eleven (Average **27,709** Remainder **6**)										
48,627	41,422	16,216	8,865	39,296	35,314	6,250	11,881	19,911	47,114	29,909
20,918	13,713	-11,493	-18,844	11,587	7,605	-21,459	-15,828	-7,798	19,405	2,200
144²	117²	-107²	-137²	107²	87²	-146²	-125²	-88²	139²	46²
20,736	13,689	11,449	18,769	11,449	7,569	21,316	15,625	7,744	19,321	2,116
182	24	44	75	138	36	143	203	54	84	84

This begins to open up a world of possibilities. It also contributes to our workload significantly, so let's maintain a sense of what we are doing. With 22 letters, we can only divide them up into two sets of 11, which we have done, and they are added together in the bottom section of the chart.

Note that we have remainders to the Averages for the first time (**13,854** Remainder **17** and **27,709** remainder **6**). So let's look at an illustration of the last section of the chart in which the two sets of eleven letters have been added to each other:

Chart 66: Squares of the Deviations from Average of the Two Sets of Eleven Letters in the Torah Added Together

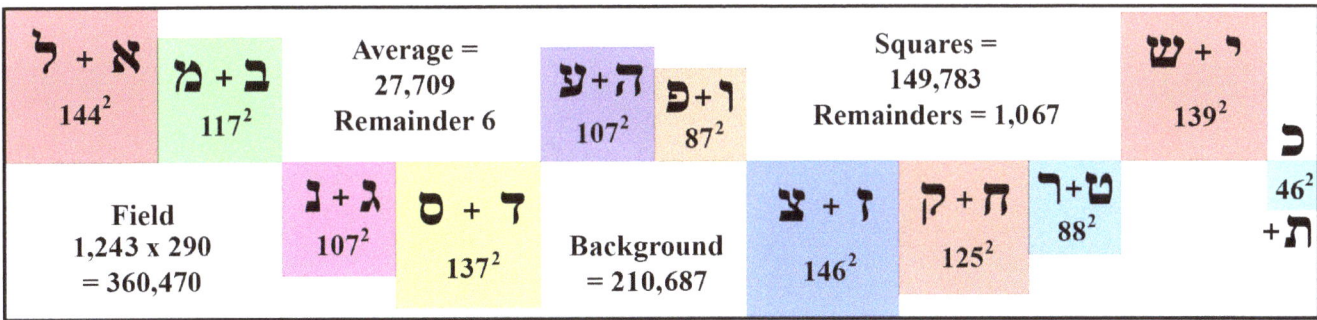

These are squares of the deviations from average. In other words, the amount of times each pair of letters occur in the Pentateuch were added up and divided by 11, arriving at **27,709**, with a remainder of **6**. Then each pair was added or subtracted from this average to arrive at the deviation from average. This deviation is shown by the size of the square; in the chart, if the square is above the middle line, it has more than the average, and if it is below the middle line, it has less than the average.

Lining the squares up gives us an accurate visual representation of the proportions between the amounts of different letter pairs.

The large rectangle that borders them we call the **Field**. In this case, the field can hold **360,470** letters. Yet the colored squares which represent the actual letters only use up **149,783** spaces in the field. In addition, there are **1,065** remainder letters left over from when we made the squares, that did not fit into the squares. Together they equal **150,848**. So we have:

Field   360,470 ($2 \times 5 \times 7 \times 61^2$ *or* 70×61^2) (**1,243** width **x 290** height)
Letters   149,783 (101×1483)
Letter Remainders   1,067 (11×97)   **Letters + Letter Remainders = 150,850** ($2 \times 5^2 \times 7 \times 431$)
Background   210,687 ($3 \times 70,229$)   **Background – Rem. = 209,620** ($2^2 \times 5 \times 47 \times 223$)
Average   27,709 ($11^2 \times 229$)   **B – Rem. – A Rem. = 209,614** ($2 \times 311 \times 337$)
Average Reminders   6   **LR + AR = 1073** (29×37)

[The fact that the Average has 11^2 in it and the Field has the very unusual 61^2 in it made me go look at Psalm 119, as 61 is characteristically in texts (like Psalm 119) that deal with the subject of 'law'. In fact, Psalm 119 has seven verses including the first one with 61 as a factor in their gematria, and $2 \times 61 = 122$ (11^2+1), 122 being the only of the 176 verses that has no mention of 'law' in any of the the ten forms used; every other one does. It turns out that the total gematria value of Psalm 119 is **333,245** which has both **11** and **73** as factors. Adding the Average above of **27,709** we get **360,954**, which is exactly $2^2 \times 11^2$ (**484**) over the Field value of **360,470**. Why $2^2 \times 11^2$? I'm not sure, but **2 + 1067**, our Letter Remainders, equals **1069**, which is the number of words in Psalm 119. In addition, there are **4476** letters in the psalm, which is $11^2 \times 37 - 1$. Furthermore, just as there are five books of the Pentateuch, there are five books of the Psalms and their gematria average is **15,147** ($11 \times 3^2 \times 153$), remainder **11**.]

Other than strange paragraphs in blue pointing out distracting side-tangents, i discovered very little that immediately jumped out at me. And in this chapter i'd like to be free from the constraints of having to find the key to how it all works together and look around for other kinds of things that can be discovered. So let's try folding it to see how it affects the data.

    Chart 67: Squares of the Deviations from Average of the Two Sets of Eleven Torah Letters Added, Folding

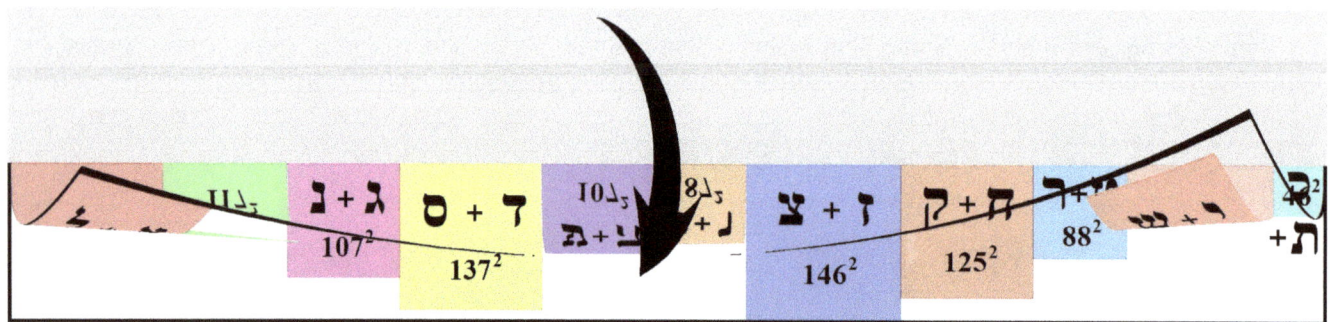

And once again we get something a great deal more compact.

Chart 68: Squares of the Deviations from Average of the Two Sets of Eleven Torah Letters Added then Folded

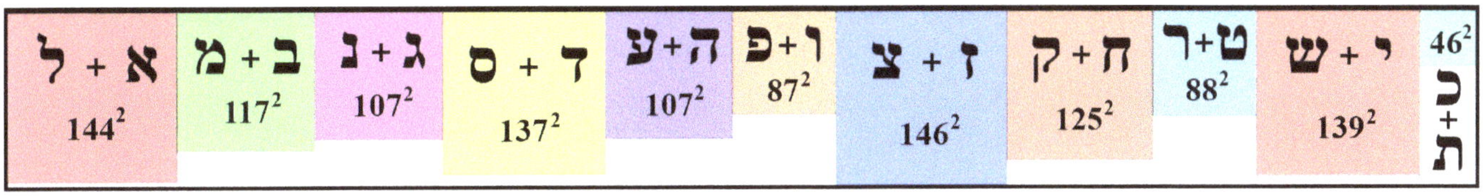

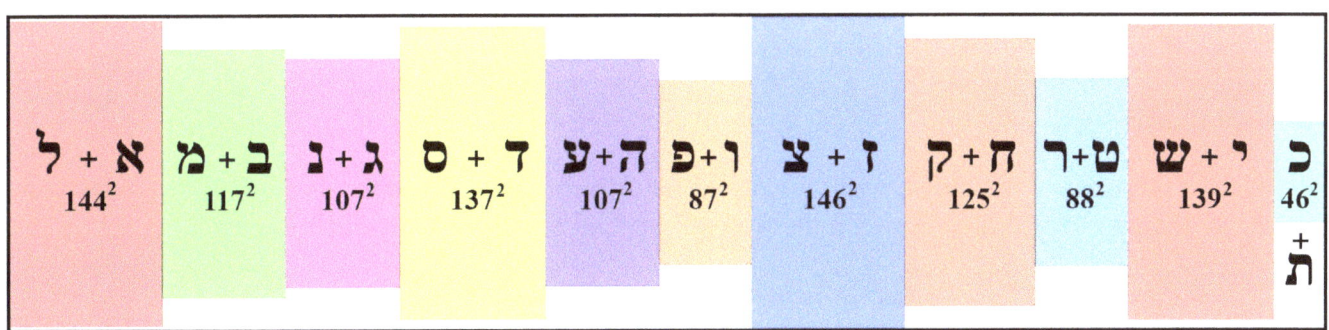

Field	181,478 (2 x 11 x 73 x 113) (**1243 Width x 146 Height**)
Background	31,695 (3 x 5 x 2113)
Squares	149,783 (101 x 1483)
Remainders	1,067 (11 x 97)
Average	27,709 (11^2 x 229)
Average Rem.	6

We're getting lots of 11's and 73's popping up, which is great. And the connection between the Average and the Background is emerging: **B – A – 2R – AR = 1,852**, a number that will be popping up a *lot* in the charts to come in which we take the simple number of each letter without adding the two sets of eleven together. I'm going to leave this as is for now with the data just sitting there for you to play with. Let's unfold it again and get that set of figures.

Chart 69: Squares of the Deviations from Average of the Two Sets of Eleven Torah Letters Added then Folded then Unfolded.

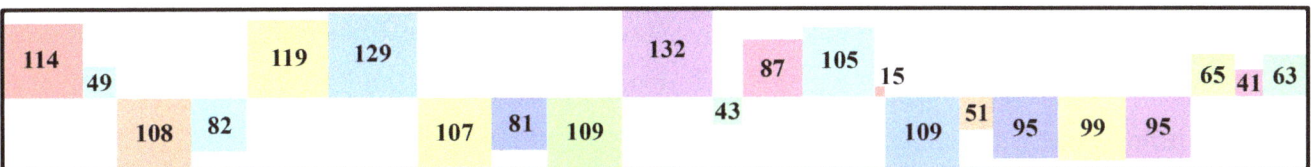

Field	362,956 (2^2 x 11 x 73 x 113) (**1,243** (11 x 113) **Width x 292** (2^2 x 73) **Height**)
Letters	299,566 (2 x 101 x 1483)
Letter Remainders	1,067 (11 x 97)
Background	63,390 (2 x 3 x 5 x 2113)
Average	27,709 (11^2 x 229)
Average Reminders	6

If found a few things that bear more study but the above charts are largely unexplored. Knock yourself out. Here is the field of *all* of the letters, without adding any together, sized by variation from their average, this time **13,854**, remainder **17**.

Chart 70: Sum of Twenty Two Letters and Deviations from Average

And here is the data we get from it:

Field	**457,418** (2 x 13 x 73 x 241)	**(1,898 Width** (2 x 13 x 73) **x 241 Height** (Prime))	
Outside Perimeter	**4,282** (2 x 2141)	**Inside Perimeter**	**4,074** (2 x 3 x 7 x 97)
Letters	**184,778** (2 x 11 x 37 x 227)		
Letter Remainders	**2,195** (5 x 439)	**Letters + R = 186,973** (181 x 1033)	
Background	**272,640** (2^8 x 3 x 5 x 71)	**Background – R = 270,445** (5 x 7 x 7727)	
Average	**13,854** (2 x 3 x 2309)		
Average Reminders	**17**		

On first impression, there's fewer of all those nice 11's we had last time. The Background and the Average are miles apart, thought twenty Averages minus two Remainders puts us within 50 of the Background. Let's fold it.

Chart 71: Sum of Twenty Two Letters and Deviations from Average Folded

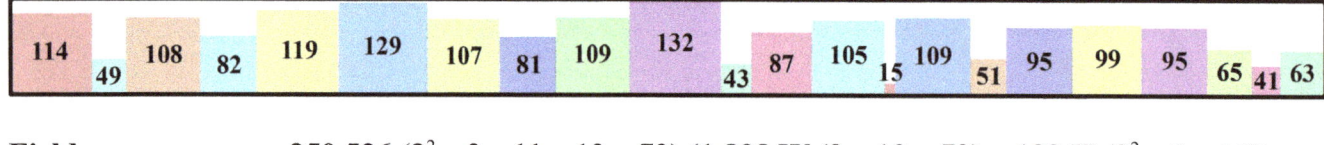

Field	**250,536** (2^2 x 3 x 11 x 13 x 73)	**(1,898 W** (2 x 13 x 73) **x 132 H** (2^2 x 3 x 11))	
Outside Perimeter	**4,064** (2^5 x 127)	**Inside Perimeter**	**4,056** (2^3 x 3 x 13^2)
Letters	**184,953** (3 x 61,651) [690 over 60,961 5 book Average]		
Letter Remainders	**2,195** (5 x 439)	**Letters + R = 187,148** (2 x 3 x 71 x 439)	
Background	**65,583** (33 x 7 x 347)	**Background – R = 63,520** (2 x 3 x 103^2)	
Average	**13,854** (2 x 3 x 2309)	**Background – 2R = 61,325** (3 x 7^2 x 419)	
Average Reminders	**17**		

And since i'm on Disovery Break right now, let's just fold it again. We have several options on how to do this, so here we'll fold it on between the first and second halves of the alphabet.

Chart 72: Sum of Twenty Two Letters and Deviations from Average
Folded then Folded Again at the Alphabetic Midsection

Field	**141,636** (2^2 x 3 x 11 x 29 x 37)	**1,073 Width** (29 x 37) **x 132 Height** (2^2 x 3 x 11)	
Outside Perimeter	**2,414** (2 x 17 x 71)	**Inside Perimeter**	**2,402** (2 x 1201)
Letters	**116,582** (2 x 71 x 821)	**Letters + R = 118,777** (41 x 2897)	
Single Layer	**48,299** (Prime)		
Double Layer	**68,283** (3^5 x 281)		
Letter Remainders	**2,195** (5 x 439)	**Reversed 'Nun's**	**2**
Background	**25,054** (2 x 12,527)	**Background – R = 22,859** (Prime)	
Average	**13,854** (2 x 3 x 2309)	**Background – 2R = 20,664** (2^3 x 3^2 x 7 x 41)	
Average Reminders	**17**		

And let's differentiate between letters that are single-layer and letters that are doubled up on top of each other:

Chart 73: Sum of Twenty Two Letters and Deviations from Average Folded then Folded Again with Layers Differentiated.

And let's unfold it twice since it's been folded twice.

Chart 74: Sum of Twenty Two Letters and Deviations from Average Folded then Unfolded Twice

Here's our new data:

Field (F)	566,544 (2^4 x 3 x 11 x 29 x 37)		
Width	2,146 (2 x 29 x 37) x	**Height**	264 (2^3 x 3 x 11)
Outside Perimeter	4,824 (2^3 x 3^2 x 67)	**Inside Perimeter**	4,816 (2^4 x 7 x 43)
Total Letters (T)	466,328 (2^3 x 71 x 821)	**Letters + R =**	468,523 (11 x 191 x 223)
Single Layer(S)	193,196 (2^2 x 48,299)	**Letters + 4R =**	475,108 (2^2 x 41 x 2897)
Double Layer (D)	273,132 (2^2 x 3^5 x 281)	**4 x R =**	8,280 (2^2 x 5 x 439)
Remainders (R)	2,195 (5 x 439)	**Reversed 'Nun's (N)**	2
Background (B)	100,216 (2^3 x 12,527)	**Background – R =**	98,021 (7 x 11 x 19 x 67)
Average (A)	13,854 (2 x 3 x 2309)	**Background – 2R =**	95,826 (2 x 3 x 15,971)
Average Remainders (AR)	17	**Background – 4R =**	91,436 (2^2 x 22,859)

Now you need to hear a story. Yes, this is an odd place for it, but here's where it happened. Once upon a time i gathered together all the data for these figures, having settled on the Masoretic text as the one most likely to yeild accurate results. But for comparison i listed several other texts such as the Leningrad Codex and its particular letter count, none of which vary significantly for translating purposes; however in patterns every letter counts. So charts were made to compare the differences, which has little to do with what is presented in this book because it's simply part of the requisite background work, but a great deal to do with this story.

Then i began the number crunching. For months. Nothing. I tried every sacred geometry, every vestige of number meanings, gematria nuance, every method i knew and made up new ones to boot. Nothing. Of course, there are always neat things to be found, but the task here is not to list dubious discoveries, but to achieve closure. And there was none. Nowhere nohow.

I have pages of meticulously drawn charts (i do the graphics as i go along) that now have no home. Perhaps the Smithsonian would be interested. Some are very pretty and would make nice wallpaper patterns. So *eventually* i said, "I couldn't possible have made an error with the original data, but i had better go back and check it anyway." That last sentence was a literary device called *foreshadowing*.

Well, you guessed it. Some idiot had used the wrong list of individual letter counts when transcribing from the notes to the charts. And that idiot was me. There were not 25,05**9** Alephs in the Pentateuch, there were 25, 057. There were not 16,34**5** Beths, there were 16,344. Ghimel and Daleth were correct with 2,109 and 7,032 but Hé had four too many. And so on, all through the alphabet. For months i had been using a chart which meticulously recorded the wrong manuscripts, all the while thinking that i was using the Masoretic text. I'll let you figure out how intelligent this made me feel.

So. About two weeks ago as of writing this paragraph i pulled together the proper figures and started All Over. While this story is tragic, no not funny, *tragic*; it has a less than tragic ending. Patterns with closure began spilling out everywhere; it was virtually impossible *not* to find a solid closure anwhere. If i had wanted confirmation of the fact that i wasn't just making things up (yes, i often wonder that too) i couldn't have picked a better experience.

And since this chapter is supposed to be more interactive, let's get to it. Scripture uses every single number, yet it uses particular ones in quite particular ways. For example, Genesis 1:1 is organized around **37** x **73**. John 1:1 is organized around **39** x **93**. Psalm 119 is organized around **16** x **61**, and the letter count of the Pentateuch has several strong characteristics. The Leningrad Codex is organized around **69** x **96** (69 is 3 x 23 and 96 acts as a positive multiplier, being 2^5 x 3), probably because the number **46** (2 x 23) was traditionally used as the base for the number of letters, words, or verses per page; these were three separate but integrated approaches to putting together the physical copies. Not only was **46** used in the ancient scrolls, it was used to maintain the transition from *scroll* to *codex*. They had to insure that not only would no letters be lost, but the integrity of the scroll *including what was on each page* would be preserved across mediums.

The Masoretic Text, however, seems to be based on several powerful schemes simultaneously. For a while i was quite certain it was **17** and **71**, yet **11**, **19**, and a pile of other personalities often take over the stage. So let's see what we get.

Here's our chart again using color to differentiate the areas which we'll use to visualize the patterns:

Chart 75: Sum of Twenty Two Letters and Deviations from Average Folded Twice

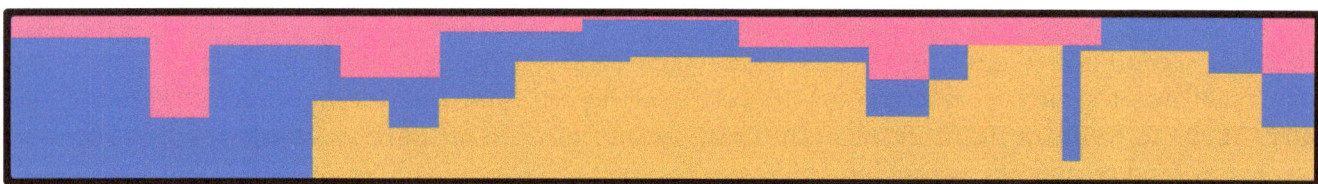

There are a few relationships that don't require a Key, such as the relationship between the Field and the Remainders: One-quarter the Field equals sixteen times the Remainder Letters plus the Average Remainder squared:

$$¼ F = 16 R + AR^2$$
or
$$¼ \times 141{,}636 = 35{,}120 + 17^2$$

As well as an interesting relationship between the Single and Double layers of letters:

$$8A + S + 2B = 3D + 2R$$
or
$$110{,}832 + 48{,}299 + 50{,}108 = 204{,}849 + 4{,}390$$

Which we can visualize as follows:

Chart 76: Two Backgrouinds Plus Single Letters Plus Eight Averages Equals Three Double Letters Plus Remainders.

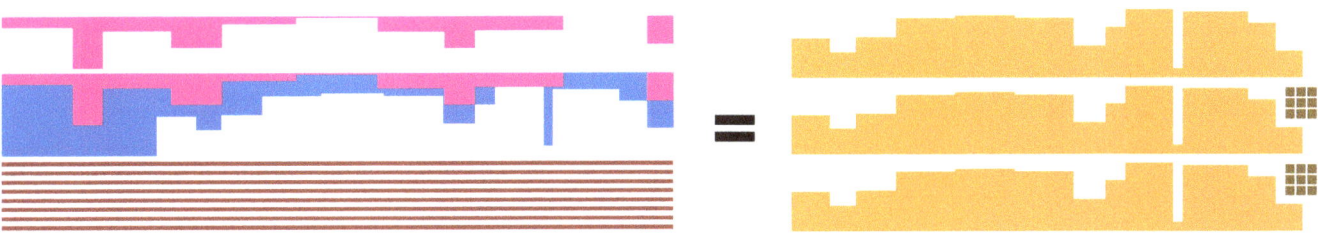

Seeing the picture makes it much nicer than having to break out a calculator. There are the same amount of colored pixels on the left side of the equal sign as on the right, mostly. The 'Average' is represented by a long line with no regard for the pixels in it.

How we depict these can be telling; simpler is not always better. For example, one of the relationships we find is **25B = 39(A + R) + R**, but was actually discovered by a series of **14** to **15** relationships, thus:

$$10B = 14R + 15A + \frac{15B - 15A}{14}$$

...which is the same exact relationship, just not reduced. And while we're on 14's, it's notable that
14R + 5A = 100,000.

Let's look at a couple '**71 Key**' relationships.

$$B + 2A = S + 2R + N + \color{green}{71}$$
or
25,054 + 27,708 = 48,299 + 4,390 + 2 + 71

Which is short for "The Background plus two Averages equals the Single Letters plus two Remainder Letters plus the two 'Nun' markers plus **71**. Visually it appears like this:

Chart 77: Background Plus Two Averages Equals Single Letters Plus Two Letter Remainders Plus the 'Nun's Plus 71.

And again:

$$2B + A + 2R + N = D + \color{green}{71}$$
or
50,108 + 13,854 + 4,390 + 2 = 68,283 + 71

Chart 78: Two Backgrounds Plus Average Plus Two Remainder Letters Plus the 'Nun's Equals Double Letters Plus 71.

The way we folded this letter set (we'll try one other) has two other 'Keys' that kept popping up; **386** and **601**. And this time i have absolutely no idea what they're about. A square pyramid of cannon balls ten layers high would have **385** cannonballs in it, but i like things to be exact, and it's tough to balance that extra one on top. So feel free to solve that one. Here are some examples:

$$S + R = 2B + 386$$
or
$$48{,}299 + 2{,}195 = 50{,}108 + 386$$

Chart 79: Single Letters Plus Remainder Letters Equals Two Backgrounds Plus 386.

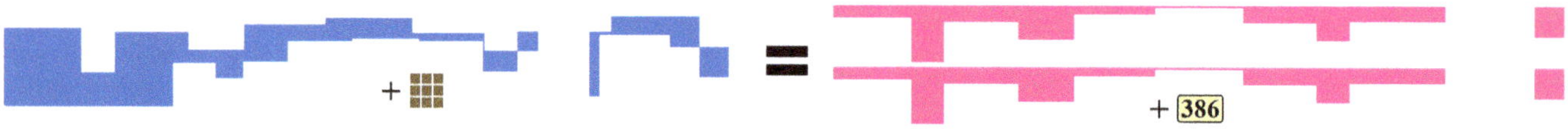

$$F + R = 3B + D + 386$$
or
$$141{,}636 + 2{,}195 = 75{,}162 + 68{,}283 + 386$$

Chart 80: Field Plus Remainder Letters Equals Three Backgrounds Plus Double Letters Plus 386.

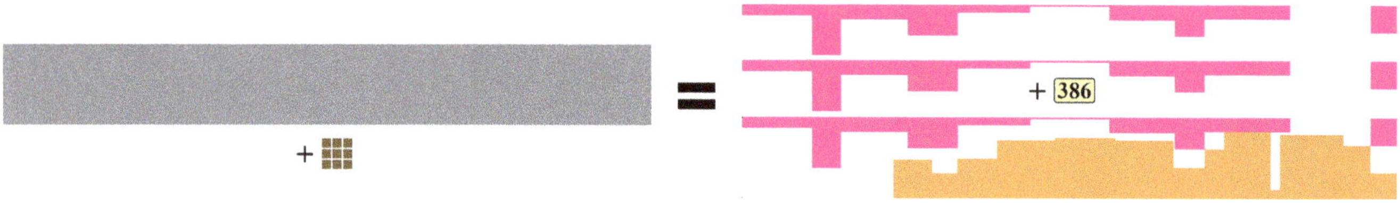

$$5T + 6D + N = 7F + 3(386)$$
or
$$582{,}910 + 409{,}698 + 2 = 991{,}452 + 1{,}158$$

Chart 81: Five Total Letters Plus Six Double Letters Plus 'Nun's' Equals Seven Fields Plus Three 386's.

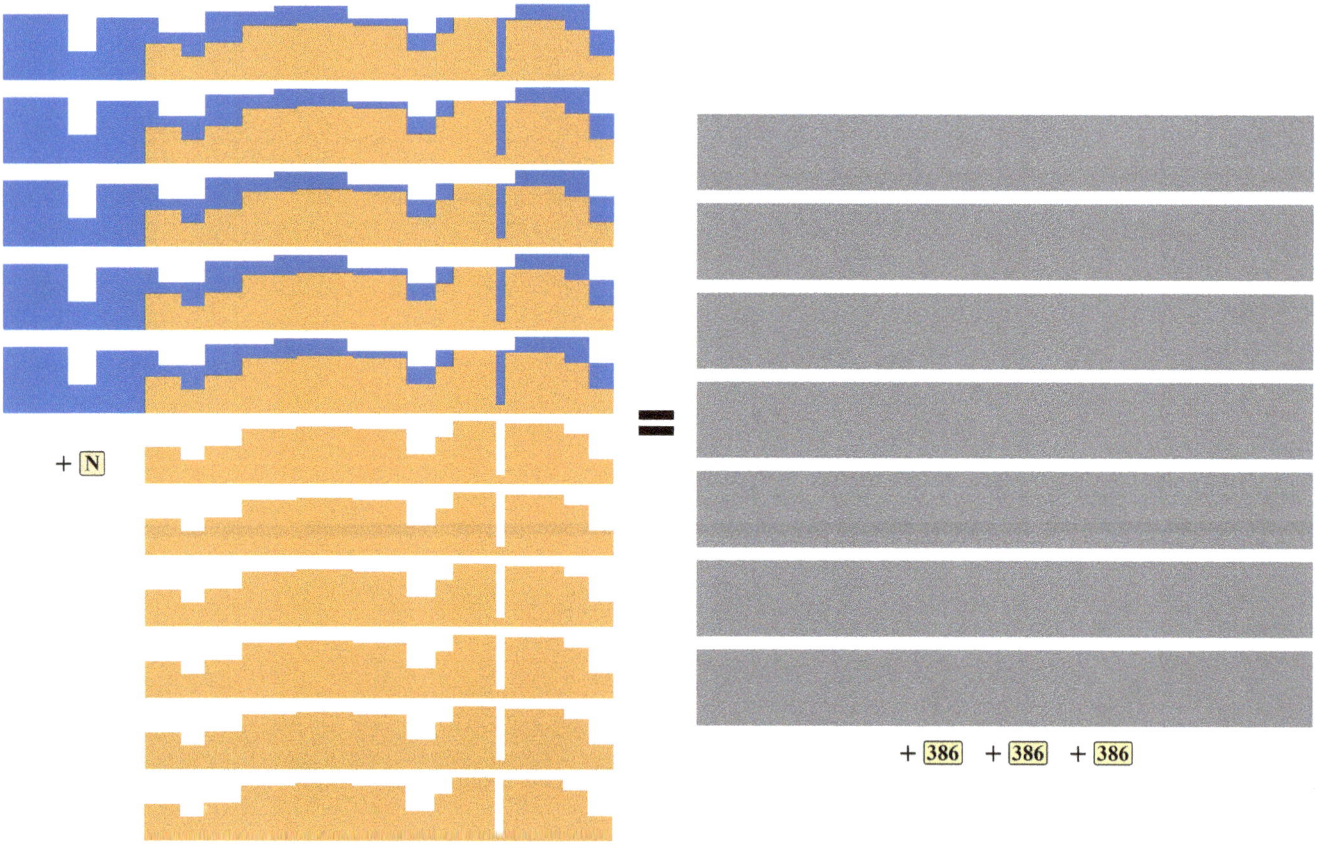

$$F + N = N^6(R) + 3(386)$$
or
$$141{,}636 + 2 = 64(2{,}195) + 1{,}158$$

Chart 82: Field Plus the 'Nun's' Equals Sixty-Four Remainder Letters Plus Three 386's.

And let's look at a couple **601** relationships.

$$2B + 5A = T + R + 601$$
or
$$50{,}108 + 69{,}270 = 116{,}582 + 2{,}195 + 601$$

Chart 83: Two Backgrounds Plus Five Averages Equals Total Letters Plus Remainder Letters Plus 601.

$$4B + 7A = 4S + R + 3(601)$$
or
$$100{,}216 + 96{,}978 = 193{,}196 + 2{,}195 + 1{,}803$$

Chart 84: Four Backgrounds Plus Seven Averages Equals Four Single Letters Plus Remainder Letters Plus Three 601's.

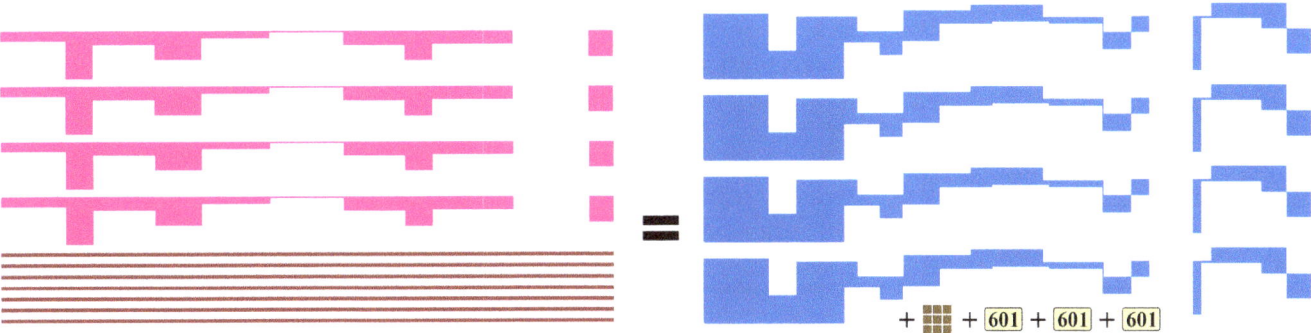

Without knowing for certain what **601** and **386** are supposed to tell us, all i can do is note the fact that they work for some reason, give some examples, and move on. **71**, on the other hand, is exactly what one would expect to see as a 'Key' number, as well as being the reverse of the **17**, the Average Remainder number.

This whole exercise makes me curious as to what would have happened if we had folded the chart, not at the center of the alphabet between Chet (כ) and Lamed (ל), but exactly at the geometric center. So let me get a few more of the patterns down for comparison to that system, and then (hopefully) take a look at the different set of figures that folding geometrically gives us.

$$T + 71 + 71 = 3B + 3A$$
or
$$116{,}582 + 71 + 71 = 75{,}162 + 41{,}562$$

Chart 85: Total Letters Plus 71 Plus 71 Equals Three Backgrounds Plus Three Averages.

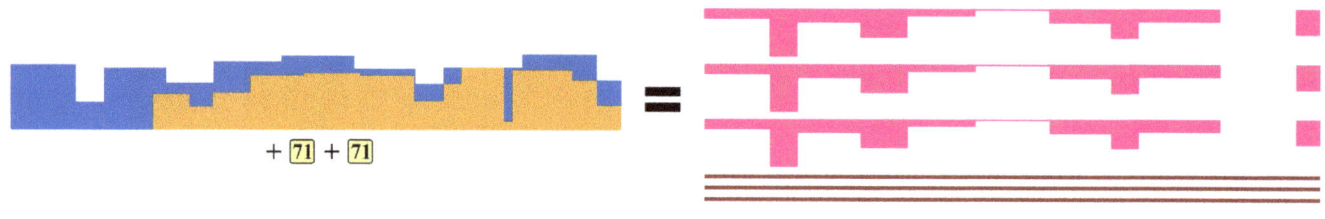

$$7B + A + 2R = 4S + 6(71)$$
or
$$175{,}378 + 13{,}854 + 4{,}390 = 193{,}196 + 426$$

Chart 86: Seven Backgrounds Plus Average Plus Two Remainder Letters Equals Four Single Leters Plus Six 71's.

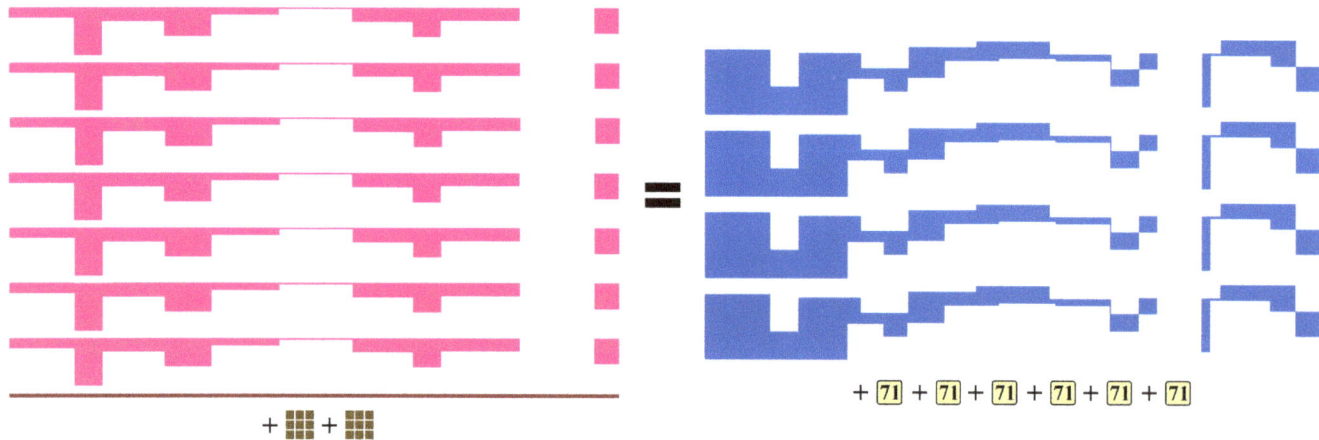

Okay, enough of that kind of fun for a bit, though i might mention that if you want another example of six **71**'s, there's also $7B + 2A + R = 3(D + N) + 6(71)$. We've demonstrated enough to get a sense of what is possible; i've left out a great many other relationships, including $5(B + A + R) = 3D + 666$.

So now let's re-fold our chart at the geometric centerline.

Chart 87: Sum of Twenty Two Letters and Deviations from Average Folded then Folded Again on Centerline.

When i made this chart i was very glad to have taken the trouble. The entire left half is a series of shapes nestled within shapes even while there's a constant 'switch-off' of which set of squares has the prominent one. The Background is unbroken, and the Single Letter path is unbroken. In all the charts i've made (of which only a small portion get into this book) this is one of the most spectacular. Let's look at the figures it procuces.

69

Field	**125,268** (2^2 x 3 x 11 x 13 x 73)		
Width	**949** (13 x 73) **x**	**Height**	**132** (2^2 x 3 x 11)
Outside Perimeter	**2,166** (2 x 3 x 19^2)	**Inside Perimeter**	**2,158** (2 x 13 x 83)
Letters	**105,138** (2 x 3^4 x 11 x 59)	**Letters + R =**	**107,333** (181 x 593)
Single Layer	**25,498** (2 x 11 x 19 x 61)	**Reversed 'Nun's'**	**2**
Double Layer	**79,640** (2^3 x 5 x 11 x 181)		
Letter Remainders	**2,195** (5 x **439**)		
Background	**20,130** (2 x 3 x 5 x 11 x 61)	**Background – R =**	**17,935** (5 x 17 x 211)
Average	**13,854** (2 x 3 x 2309)		
Average Reminders	**17**		

And let's differentiate between letters that are single-layer, the letters that are doubled up on top of each other, and the background:

Chart 88: Sum of Twenty Two Letters and Deviations from Average Folded then Folded Again on Centerline, Blocked Out.

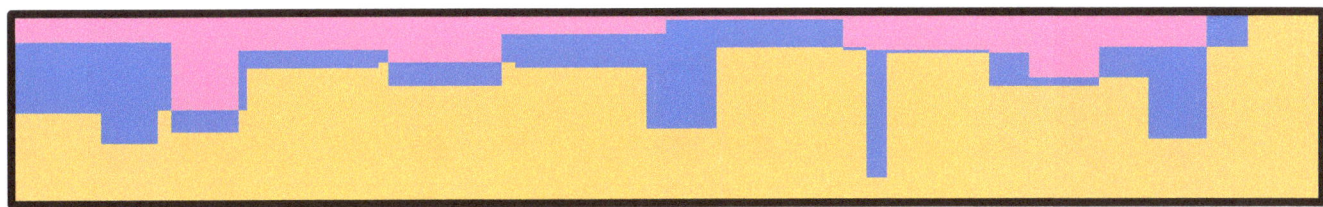

And a quick peek at what it would like like *un*folded once and twice (since it's been *folded* twice):

Chart 89: Sum of Twenty Two Letters and Deviations from Average Folded Twice on Centerline, Unfolded.

Chart 90: Sum of Twenty Two Letters and Deviations from Average Folded Twice on Centerline, Unfolded Twice.

The first thing we do is attempt to find a relationship between the Average and the Background. In this unfolded version, it isn't hard to find.

$$B - A = 66,666$$

Using the initial top *unfolded* version, this would be **4B – 4A = 66,666**. Let's see what else we have.

$$4F + R = 5^2 B + AR$$
or
$$501{,}072 + 2{,}195 = 25(20{,}130) + 17$$

Chart 91: Four Fields Plus Remainder Letters Equals Twenty-Five Single Backgrounds Plus Average Remainder.

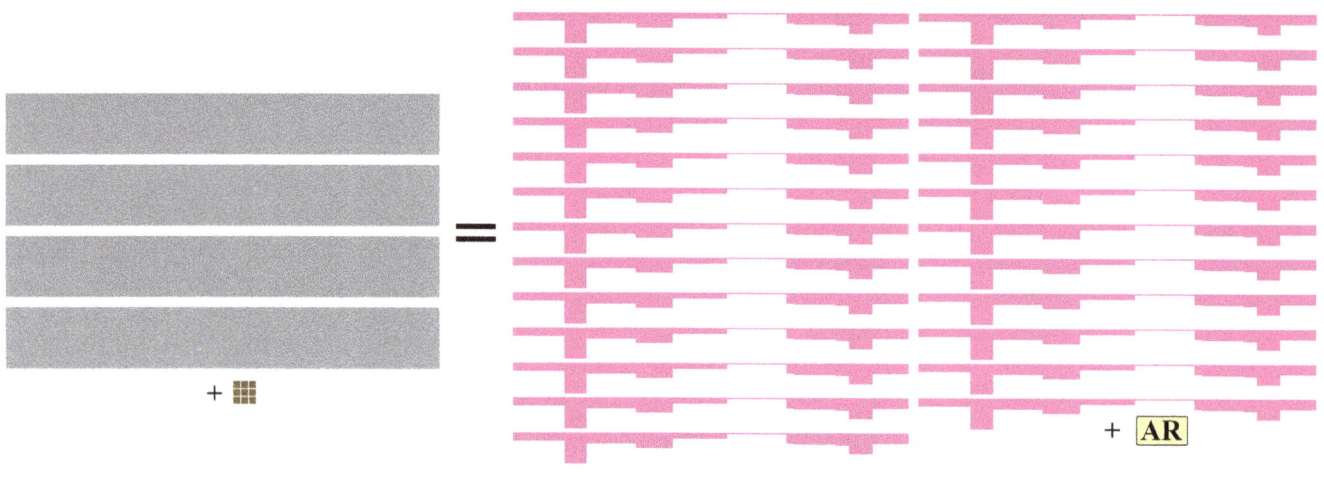

$$S + R + AR = 2A + N$$
or
$$25{,}498 + 2{,}195 + 17 = 27{,}708 + 2$$

Chart 92: Single Letters Plus Remainder Letters Plus Average Remainder Equals Two Averages Plus the 'Nun's'.

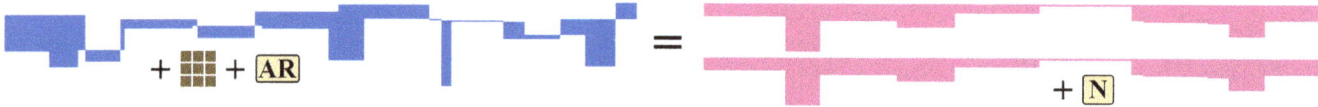

As far as the 'Keys', there seem to be three prominent ones besides **71**: the first is **103** and its multiple **309**, likely because $A + 3R - B = 309$. The second is **440** and $\frac{1}{8}$ and $\frac{1}{5}$ of it, **55** & **88**, likely because $D \div 181 = 440$. The third is **439**, which is $\frac{1}{5}$ of the Remainder Numbers, **2195**.

$$5(B + 103) + 12R + N = 5S + AR$$
or
$$100{,}650 + 515 + 26{,}340 + 2 = 127{,}490 + 17$$

Chart 93: Five Backgrounds Plus Five 103's Plus Twelve Remainder Letters Plus the 'Nun's' Equals Five Single Letters Plus the Average Remainder.

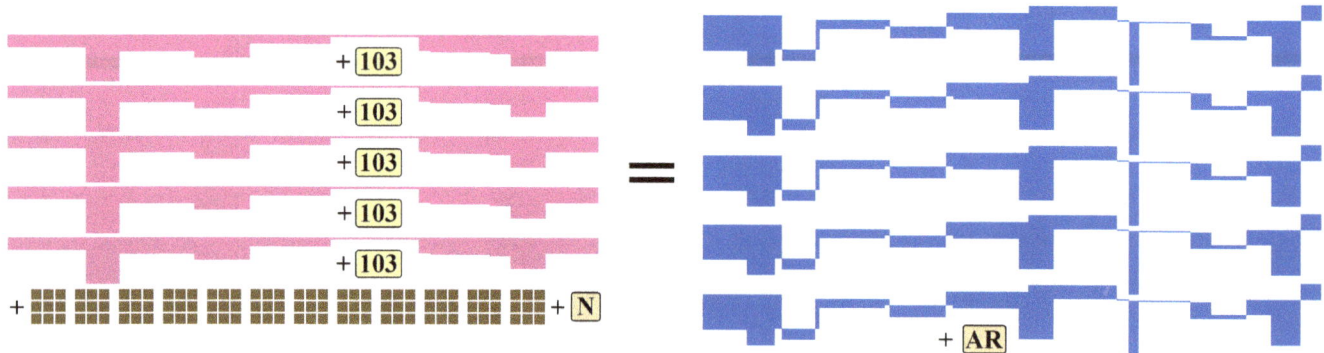

But the strangest thing found with this set is their propensity to make large 'series' numbers. We saw this initially with **B − A = 66,666** as well as **7F = 876,876**. The fact that in base 3, **2B** is **20010 20010** and **2S** is **21202 21202** is weird. And many of them are equally odd in base 11; **4B** is **55550** and **4(B − R)** is **49999**. So since this chapter is for exploration, let's look at a few of these.

$$B + R = 103 + 22{,}222$$

$$20S - 4F = 8{,}888$$

$$2S = 8R + 103 + 33{,}333$$

$$4F + 9R + 111 = 3S + 444{,}444$$

$$6B + 6(440 + 6) = 123{,}456$$

$$7T + 7D + 7R = 3B + A + 1{,}234{,}567$$

$$300S + 3(439) + 212AR = 7{,}654{,}321$$

$$1{,}500S + 31B + 30(440 + 3N) + 2R + 5AR = 5(7{,}777{,}777)$$
(If we add to this figure, $(440 + 3AR)(4S - 3(3AR + N))$, we come to **88,888,888**)

$$7F + 4AR = 2T + N + 666{,}666$$

$$S^2 + (AR^2)(240^2 - 440 - N) = 666{,}666{,}666$$

$$4000S + 29^2 S + B + 29^2 = 123{,}456{,}789$$

$$(D - (D \div 440)(100))(A + R) + 12A + 103 = 5S + 40{,}000 + 987{,}654{,}321$$

$$(71)(440 + 3AR)(S) + 55^2 + 5AR = 888{,}888{,}888$$

Now here's a bit of an odd experiment which i was debating whether to include or not (i still may not, in which case you won't be reading this). Consider the following relationship:

$$2S + R + 13(71) = 2B + A$$

Chart 94: Two Single Letters Plus Thirteen 71's Plus Remainder Letters Equals Two Backgrounds Plus the Average.

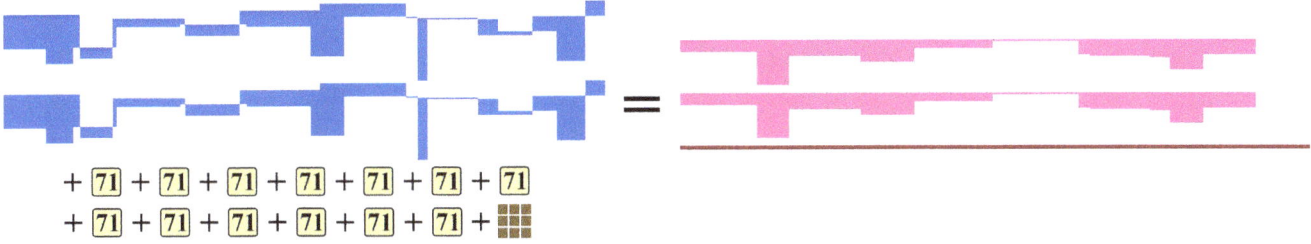

Now if we take everything after the **2S** in the first half and subtract it instead, we get **2S – R – (13·71)** = **2B – 2R – 2(13·71) + A** in which case each side equals **47,878**. Obviously, the first thing you want to do with a number like that is add it to **239F** (29,939,052), which puts us at **29,986,930**. Why **239**F? Obviously, because **13·71** equals **3(239) + 2(103)**. Now *who* this is obvious to is an entirely different question.

Three of the most important numbers in mathematics are π, e, and φ. They are the ratio of a circle's diameter to its circumference, the natural logarithm, and the golden proportion. The decimals go forever without repeating, so rounding to eight decimal points and multiplying by 100 million, we get 314,159,265 and 271,828,183 and 161,803,399 respectively. Added together, we have **747,790,847**. And of course you're immediately going to want to add this to **239F + 2S – R – (13·71)**. Here we go:

$$29{,}986{,}930 + 747{,}790{,}847 = 777{,}777{,}777$$

That was a bit convoluted, so let's just finish up with a much more balanced one:

$$A^2 + AR + 1 = A + AR^2 + 191{,}919{,}191$$

While we were concentrating on exploration, we demonstrated a lot of internal consistancy. But more importantly, we have been given several very important clues as to the nature of these very strange set-ups.

We found in Chapter V that a the 'Key' can take the form of a specific number or pair of numbers in addition to the Key taking the form of a *shape* as in Chapters III and IV. We can see that the Key is a vital clue as to the character of the subject under consideration. This leads me to think that if we narrowed our subject matter down, say to a specific book, that any Key we find would help us to understand the character of that book. This would be its character from a *numeric* perspective; to find its character from a *linguistic* point of view we would engage in the strange practice of reading it.

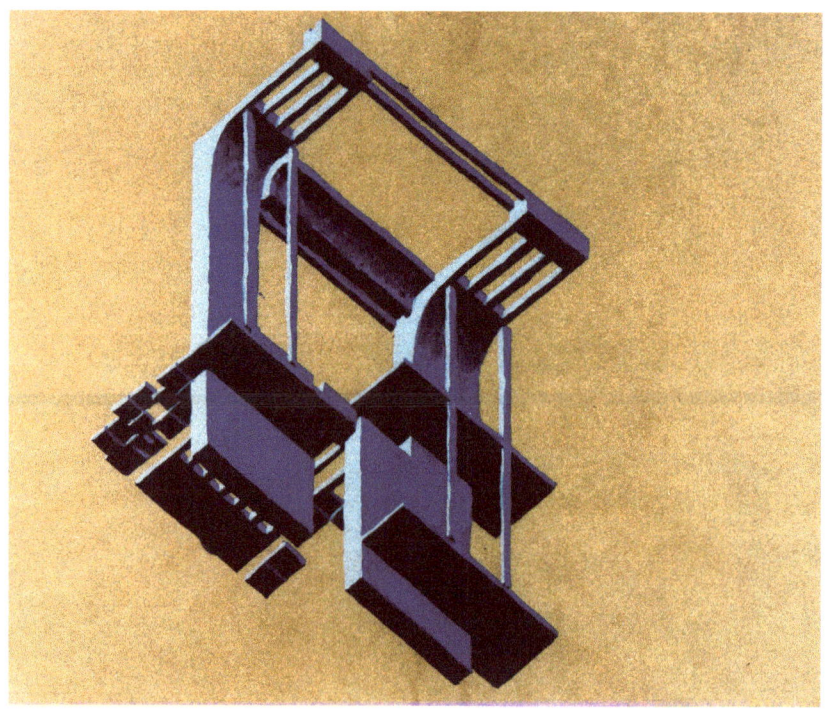

Chapter X

Almost to the Starting Line

That was a long journey. There is something about exhaustion and exhilaration combined that can keep us forging ahead.

So what have we discovered? That the Bible is letter perfect? Perhaps. That there are patterns woven throughout the ancient texts? Certainly. That the language of numbers has messages as significant as the language of letters? Indisputably. But here's the rub: *we know virtually nothing about this language of numbers*. If we found '**17**' and '**71**' in every relationship, it would be like reading a book which only had the letters '**M**' and '**N**'. It would make for very **mo**no**to**nous reading, and not be very informative.

Knowing that a language is there and learning that language are two rather different journeys.

So having set out to "apprehend" that the Bible is "letter-perfect, numerically perfect, and of a logical order that is beyond the power of investigation", how far have we come? I would venture to say *almost to the starting line*.

There are in actuality fewer than half a dozen methods employed in the previous chapters. These were not planned out but stumbled upon. It is intuitively apparent that there are thousands of methods which can be used to unlock the mathematical messages, <u>provided that they are thorough</u>, and <u>reach closure</u>. The fact that this journey handled so few attests to the enormity of the potential ahead.

"Closure" means that using only the elements found in the text, it self-validates by balancing and aligning the three dimensions (or parameters) in which it operates. In order to perform in this arena, we must be able to cleanly conceptualize. Labels will not do it, nor will formulas; they are static.

And 'methods' will not do it either. Two things we can observe from this journey are (1) the same exact method is never used twice in the same way, and (2) every time there is closure, there is also a little door, exception, or unknown quality that leads us further. In architecture (my major way back when) it is the difference between designing *in* a style (static) and designing *with* style (creative).

What i will do with the rest of this book is provide Appendixes (or appendices) that round out the subject in various ways. For the most part these are fruits plucked from journeys other than the one we just came through. While everything is related, we are rarely childlike enough in our approach to see *how* everything is related. Formulas are easy to apply and easy to memorize. But life is alive.

So thank you, dear reader, for taking this journey with me (even if you simply turned to this page first). I do not pretend that the preceding chapters *prove* anything whatsoever; one reason being that proof is unavailable to finite beings. Those of you who are infinite feel free to take exception to that remark. We have, however, *demonstrated* that hidden value can extracted by applying effort, understanding, and patience. This tends to happen measure for measure; the results do not reflect the value of the phenomena (*that* exists whether we find it or not) but the perseverance of the discoverer. As such, i do apologize for the weakness of many of the demonstrations. But hey. It was fun.

This last chapter appears to want to be brief, so let's comply. The Appendices are there to round out the picture: what the picture actually *is* will hopefully show itself as we slowly and painstakingly approach the starting line.

Appendix I

37 and 73

We have noted that each letter of both Hebrew and Greek also represents a number, as listed in Appendix III. Thus the very first verse in the Bible has the value of **2,701**, or **37** x **73**, two prime numbers. For example, "Christ" is numerically represented as follows:

$$\begin{array}{ccccccc} Χ & ρ & ι & σ & τ & o & ς \\ 600 + & 100 + & 10 + & 200 + & 300 + & 70 + & 200 \end{array}$$

The total of "Christ" in Greek is 1,480 which is 40 x **37**.

How strange to find this particular prime number in "Christ". Where else might we find it if we search?
- The total value of all the letters of the Greek alphabet is 4,995 which is **37** x 5 x 3^3.
- The value of "Jesus" in Greek is 888 which is 24 (the number of letters in the Greek alphabet) x **37**.
- The value of "Cross" in Greek is 777 which is 21 x **37**.
- The number of the beast, 666 is 18 x **37**.

Note that in the last three examples there, 18 is 6 + 6 + 6, 21 is 7 + 7 + 7, and 24 is 8 + 8 + 8. Where else do we find 37 lurking?
- II Corinthians 4:4 says "...*Christ, who is God's Image...*" The words *God's Image* have a value of 1,369 which is **37** x **37**, or **37²**.
- "*The holy of holies*" has a value of 2,368 which is **37** x 8^2.
- 2,368 is also the the value of "*Jesus Christ*".
- "*Godhead*" (from KJV Romans 1:20, other translations say "*divinity*") has a value of 592, which is **37** x 2^4. Notably, when 592 is added to the value of "*Jesus*" (888), it equals 1,480 which is the exact value of "*Christ*".
- "*The Son of Man*" from Matthew 13:37 has the value of **37** x 80. This value of 2,960 is the total of the three figures in the previous example: *Godhead* 592 + *Jesus* 888 + *Christ* 1,480.
- "*The Lord Christ*" from Colossians 3:24 has the value of **37** x 120.
- "*The Son of God*" from Galatians 2:20 has the value of **37** x 66.
- "*Of the Seed of David*" from John 7:42 has the value of **37** x 70.
- "*Christ is the son of David*" from Luke 20:41 has the value of **37** x 75.

It is apparent that the number 37 is woven into both the old and new testaments in a very specific manner. The question is *What is that manner?*

We see in example **4** above that 666 is **37** x 18. So the multiplier (18) would be the key to how to treat **37** in that case, just as the multiplier in *Jesus* (example **2**) is 24. The number **37** is established in both examples as the **core**, and the multiplier is in each case the **descriptor**.

So looking at the two descriptors here, 18 and 24, what do we find? One way (there are many) of considering them is that 18 is **3** x 6, while 24 is **4** x 6. So there is something about taking three sixes that lands us on **666**, and something about four sixes that lands us on **888**.

Looking at Appendix II, we see that three is *mechanics*, four is *universality*, and six is *freedom*. It would be possible to conclude then that to merely be interested in the *mechanics* (**3**) of freedom (**6**) leads to **666**, while being interested in the *universality* (**4**) of freedom (**6**) leads to **888**. In other words, the *mechanics* of freedom leads to self-interest, while the *universality* of freedom leads to freedom for everyone. This would be the message of the numbers here, why one descriptor (**18**) is the number of the beast, while the other descriptor (**24**) is the number of Jesus . . .when multiplying both by thirty-seven.

The above paragraph is a suggestion only. We have to be careful not to make rules in an arena in which we barely know the language.

But what about when the descriptor and the core are the same? In example above, *God's Image* equals **37** x **37**. Most remarkable. Where else might we find **37** x **37**?

And the Spirit of God moved over the face of the waters.

ת פ ח ר מ   ם י ה ל א   ח ו ר ו
400 80 8 200 40   40 10 5 30 1   8 6 200 6

ם י מ ה   י נ פ ל ע
40 10 40 5   10 50 80 30 70

And there it is in the very second verse of the Bible. Adding those letters up equals 1,369, which is **37** x **37** again.

Now if we recall, the first verse of Genesis adds up to **2,701**, or **37** x **73**. When we get to the third verse, it begins to branch out into the other significant numbers in scripture, such as the 153 fishes of John 21:11. "*And God said Let there be light, and there was light*" adds up to **813** (as does the phrase "*And God divided between the light and the darkness*" as well as the words *resurrection* and *trust* in Greek). This peculiar number is 3 x (**37** + **37** + **73** + **73** + (3 x 17)). I have underlined 3 x 17 because it equals the strange 51, which is one-third of the 153 fishes of John. But more simply, **813** = (20 x **37**) + **73**. Look at the next verse, verse 4: its value is 1776, which is 48 x **37**. It is also 2 x **888** (Jesus). It isn't until we get to the fifth verse before we find a value (2141) that isn't divisible by 37 or anything else; it's prime. However, if we subtract the previous verse's value (**2141–1776**) we get the number of days in a year (**365**) as well as the age of Enoch when he was translated. . . which oddly enough is 5 x **73**. And we get the same thing with the 6th verse whose value is **1660**; subtract from that **2141**, and we get **481** which is 13 x **37**. And the 7th verse? It's **4541**, so subtracting verses 6 (**1660**) and 4 (**2141**) from it you get **740**; 20 x **37** again. And if you like 20 x **37**, go to the next verse, the 8th, **2255**, which is **37**^{2} + (20 x **37**) + **73** + **73**. And so on throughout all the scriptures as far as we wish to explore.

Now it is somewhat valuable to know what we are doing besides playing with numbers. The section of verse two that is **37**^{2} is only half of it; the part that says the Spirit was hovering over the face of the waters. The other half adds up to the seemingly useless **2177**. But if we look at the *content* of the verses, things begin to make sense. **2177** is the section that says the earth was waste and empty and darkness was on the face of the deep.

Thus the first three verses of chapter 2 where God rests has a value of **10,502**, which gets us nowhere. But if we *subtract* the **2177** of "waste and void", we get **8325**, which is **15**^{2} x **37**. The idea is that in order for God to rest, the original problem of waste and void has to be taken away. 15 means "possession", and **15**^{2} is a very emphatic way of showing that God is taking possession of the earth again. This theme of fifteen being used for "possession" crops up a lot.

In verse 31, God looks over everything and sees that it is "very good". This verse has a value of **3065** which once again gets us nowhere with 37 or 73. But if we again subtract the "waste and void" (**2177**) we get **888** which is both the numerical value of "**Jesus**" and 24 x **37,** an indication that the "waste and void" has to be addressed before things become "very good".

Again, verses 26 through 30 deal with the creation of Man. The value of these verses is **23,942**, which once again gets us nowhere. If we add God's rest (**10,502**) from the first three verses of chapter two, we still get nowhere *until we subtract the* **2,177** *waste and void*, at which point we arrive at **35,332** which is **22²** x **73**.

Looking at Man's relationship with creation, the entirety of the sixth day adds up to **34,150**. Adding in again the creation of the land animals (**7,143**) and the whole 5th day of fish and birds (**13,689**), we arrive at **54,982** which is **37** x **2** x **743**. Seven hundred forty-three is a prime number meaning *"Finishing the full application of universal wisdom"*

But all is not rosy with the creatures over which Man has been placed. If we read carefully in Genesis, we will notice that the fish were not named by Adam; just the birds and beasts. And in Revelation when describing the new earth, it says "the sea exists no more" (21:1). So if we take verses 26-30 that talk of Man's creation (**23,942**), *add* the creation of the beasts in verses 24 & 25 (**7143**), *add* the entire verse having the Spirit hovering over the waters in verse two (**3546**), and then *subtract* verses 20 through 23 that deal with the fish (**13,689**), we end up with **20,942** which turns out to be **37** x **566**.

Take verses 3 through 5 regarding the whole First Day ("Let there be light"); the value is **4730**. Subtracting the entire **3546** of the "waste and void" verse gives us **1184**, which is **2⁵** x **37**.

Take verses 6 through 8, the second day (**8456**) and subtract the **2177** section of the "waste and void" verse, we end up with **2553**, which is **69** x **37**. Sixty-nine means judgment being meted out willy-nilly any way the judge wants; it's probably no coincidence that the second day is the only one that was not declared good.

Take verses 9 through 13 regarding the dry land and the plants; we find that it *already* has a value divisible by **37** like the first verse; they add up to **15,984** which is **3²** x **2⁴** x **37**. This and the fifth days are the only ones that needs no adjustment. Perhaps God considers the plants and birds to be just fine the way they are. The fifth day (20 through 22) except for the last verse (23) adds up to **12,629** which is **73** x **173**.

The fourth day regarding the "light bearers" from verse 14 to 19 is somewhat strange. The value of that section is **16,843**, and the first and second days (**4730** and **8456** respectively) must be *subtracted*, as well as the entire verse regarding "waste and empty" (**3546**). We are left with **111**, which is **3** x **37**.

Note that for many of our discoveries here, we are constantly subtracting the section that says "*And the earth was waste and empty, and darkness was on the face of the deep*" which has a value of **2177**. In Psalm 139:22 we have a verse with the same value of **2177**: "*I hate them with perfect hatred: I count them mine enemies.*" There seems to be hints passed back and forth with verses of related values.

In Isaiah 5:15 (also **2177**) we get message as to what needs done: "*And the mean man will be brought down, and the mighty man will be humbled, and the eyes of the lofty will be humbled*". Yet Job 4:4, whose value is **2177**, says: "*Your words have upheld him that was falling, and you have strengthened the feeble knees.*" So there is a story woven throughout scripture that can be followed in the numerics.

We have covered the last three days already, and as you can see, this quickly becomes complex, so let us touch on a few more facts and return to our subject.

- "*My wrath*" from Hebrews 3:11 has a value of **999**, which is 3^3 x **37**.
- **3** x **888** (*Jesus*) = **2,664**. Adding **37** to this gives us once again the value of Genesis 1:1, which is **2701**.
- Flipping this, **3** x **2701** = **8103**, which when we add **888** (*Jesus*) equals **8991**, which is 3^5 x **37**. It is also **9** x **999**, "my wrath".
- It is said that the end of Deuteronomy relates to the beginning of Genesis. The last two verses in the Pentateuch (first five books of Moses) add up to **7373** which is **101** x **73**.

Is there a place we can find 37 geometrically? As we've mentioned before, any number which relates to a cube is highly significant. The numbers 8, 27, 64, 125, and 216 all make perfect cubes. Where does **37** come in?

Let us take a perfect cube of 64 blocks. That is 4 x 4 x 4, or 4^3. It looks like this:

This cube is a good visual for the "*Truth*", whose value is also **64**, or 4^3, as there are **64** blocks in the cube. Of these **64**, there are **37** blocks that can be seen at any one time, and **27** (3^3) that are hidden from sight at any one time. That is one way of visualizing this strange number.

The phenomena we have seen in Genesis 1:1 of a reversed number (**37** x **73**) is found throughout scripture. For example, if we take the well known John 1:1, "*In the beginning was the Word, and the Word was with God, and the Word was God*", we find that it's value is 3,627 or 3^2 x **13** x **31**, or **39** x **93**. After a three verse introduction, Ezekiel 1:4 begins the narrative with a verse whose value is **49** x **94**. Isaiah 55:6 is often quoted; "Seek you Jehovah while he may be found; call on him while he is near" and has the value of **19** x **91**. When Jesus stumped his opponents with the question, "David therefore calls him Lord, how is he then his son?" he did so with **59** x **95**.

Note how the content matches the numerics. Compare Job 13:3 "Nevertheless I would speak to the Almighty, and desire to reason with God", and Isaiah 14:14 "I will ascend on the heights of the clouds, I will be like the Most High." Both are **61** x **16**.

Yet there is far more than we even imagine involved in the sacred text and its numbers. Let us take a brief look at 'Triangle Numbers'. These are what we get when we stack pennies. Here are the first three Triangle Numbers, **1**, **3**, and **6**:

What we are looking for here here are are the numbers **73** and **37** that make up Genesis 1:1 when multiplied together. . . and how they unfold from **Creation** into the rest of the Scriptures.

It so happens that the **73rd** Triangle Number is **2,701**, the very value of the first verse. Before we explore that let us start with the **7th** Triangle Number, **28**, as Genesis 1:1 has **28** letters. Here it is:

Now there are not only <u>Triangle Numbers</u>, but <u>Hexagon Numbers</u> and <u>Star Numbers</u>, as follows:

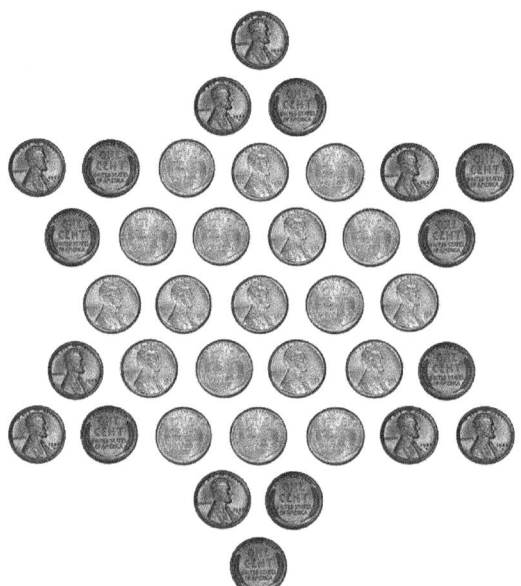

Here we have a <u>star</u> of **37** pennies nesting a <u>hexagon</u> of **19** pennies by putting an inverted **28** triangle upon itself. The Hebrew word for the *heart* is "הלב". The ordinal value of these letters (they are the 5th, 12th, and 2nd letters respectively) equals **19**. Their cardinal value (5, 30, and 2) equals **37.** And our star above has **19** pennies in the center hexagon, and **37** pennies altogether. Does this relate to Genesis 1:1? The phrase "*and the earth*" has a value of **703**, which is **19** x **37**. And **703** is also the **37th** triangle number.

Now counting from **1** to **1,000,000,000,000,000** (one quadrillion) there are only **12** numbers that can make both a star and a hexagon, and there is only **one** under **1,000**. If you guessed **37** you were right. Here is the **37**-hexagon embedded in a star:

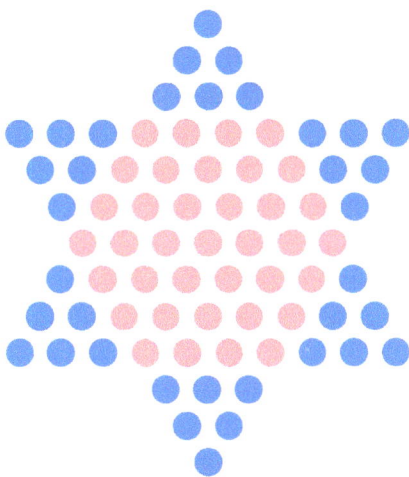

And how many pennies do we have altogether? **73**. This shape gives us a **visual map of Genesis 1:1**.

And we use a map to *find* something, so what are we to find with this? Let us consider for a moment who *else* was there with God in this beginning.

"*Jehovah possessed me in the beginning of his way, before his works of old. I was set up from eternity, from the beginning, before the earth was*" (Wisdom speaking in Proverbs 8).

Let us look at Wisdom here. Specifically, let us look at ח כ מ ה, which is "Wisdom" in Hebrew. Ordinally the four letters are the **8th**, **11th**, **13th**, and **5th**. *Cardinally* (their value) the letters are **8**, **20**, **40**, and **5**. The first adds up to **37**, the second to **73**. Thus we see that one of the great secrets hidden in the first verse of the Bible, whose value is **37** x **73**, is pointing us directly at Wisdom.

And because **37** is one of the very few numbers that can be both a star and a hexagon, what happens when we make a **37** star, and surround it with a larger star?

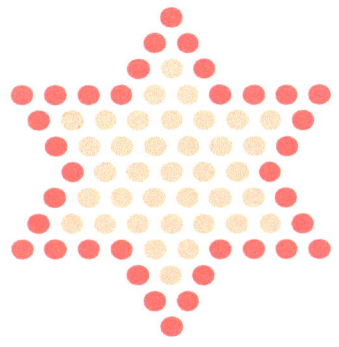

Again, our **37** star is embedded in a star of **73**. This all seems so simple and natural except for the fact that *these are the only numbers that this works for.* And they're the numbers we find in Genesis 1:1.

Now before we started looking at the triangles, we noted that John 1:1, "*In the beginning was the Word, and the Word was with God, and the Word was God*" has a value of **3,627** or 3^2 x **13** x **31**. Let us rewrite that by spreading the **3**'s over the **13** and **31** by multiplying (**3** x **13**) x (**3** x **31**) = **39** x **93** = **3,627**. Once again we have two reversed numbers, **39** and **93** (just like Genesis' **37** & **73**), describing a seminal verse.

And if we combine **Genesis 1:1 (2701)** and **John 1:1 (3627)**? We get **6,328** which turns out to be the **112th** Triangle Number. And what is **112**? It happens to be the value of

יהוה אלהים

...which we know as "Jehovah Elohim". While we are on **112**, we might note that in the letters of the book of Mark, there are **6,862** Alphas and **1,314** Omegas. We are familiar with the verse, "I am the Alpha and the Omega". These add up to **8,176**, which is **112 x 73**. And since we've spent time on **37** and **19** we might also note that all *four* gospels' Alphas and Omegas add up to 3^3 x 3719.

And while we are in John 1:1, let us look at "Logos" *(the Word)*, whose value is **373**. . .

Λ   o   γ   o   ς
30   70   3   70   200

373 is (**7 x 37**) + (**6 x 19**). Here we have **7** stars of **37** pennies each, and **6** hexagons of **19** pennies each, to equal **373**: **Logos**, made up of the very elements that were hidden in **Genesis 1:1**.

So we find that the more we explore, the *tighter* the patterns become, rather than looser as we might expect from mere happenstance. And while we're looking at geometrical aspects of Genesis 1:1 and Wisdom, consider this famous passage: "*Here is the <u>Wisdom</u>. Who has <u>the understanding</u>, let him count the number of the beast; for it is the number of man: and his number is Six hundred sixty six.*"

What does "*the understanding*" from this passage in Revelation 13:18 look like? Its value is **990**, which happens to be the **44th** triangle number. It looks like this:

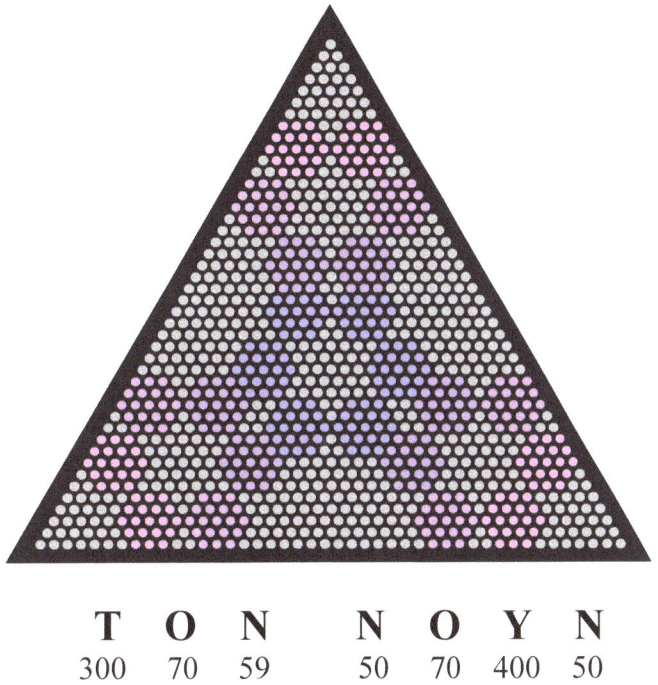

T	**O**	**N**		**N**	**O**	**Y**	**N**
300	70	59		50	70	400	50

Now understand that i have to actually make all these illustrations by hand. So where did i get this marvelous triangle of 990 circles? It ought to look familiar because i took the illustration for "Logos" above, trimmed the pokey parts from the stars on the outside, and doubled it up. Well, quadrupled really, because three of the original triangle fits under it, the middle one upside-down. Yes, "Logos" was **22** layers high, and "the understanding" is **44** layers; precisely twice as high.

Oh, and if we add "Wisdom" from Revelation 13:18 to "the Understanding" in the same verse, we get **1,771**, which is the **21st** triangular pyramid. Here's looking straight down on it:

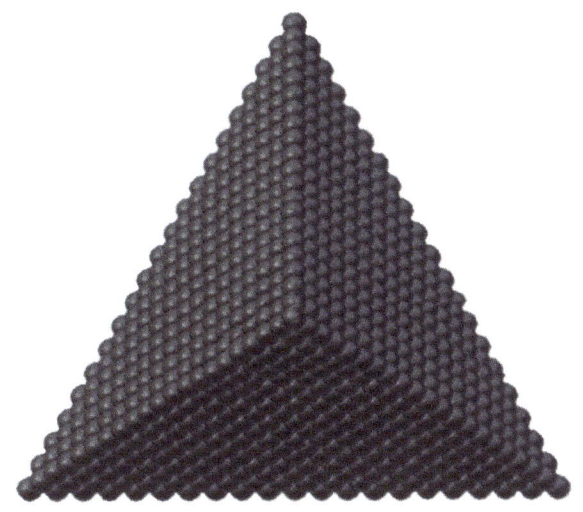

And while we're enjoying triangles, if we take the **22**-layer Logos triangle, and add **51** layers (¹/₃ of the **153** fishes at the end of John) we have our **73rd** (73 layers) triangle number, which as we have mentioned, has **2,701** (the value of Genesis 1:1) units, as follows:

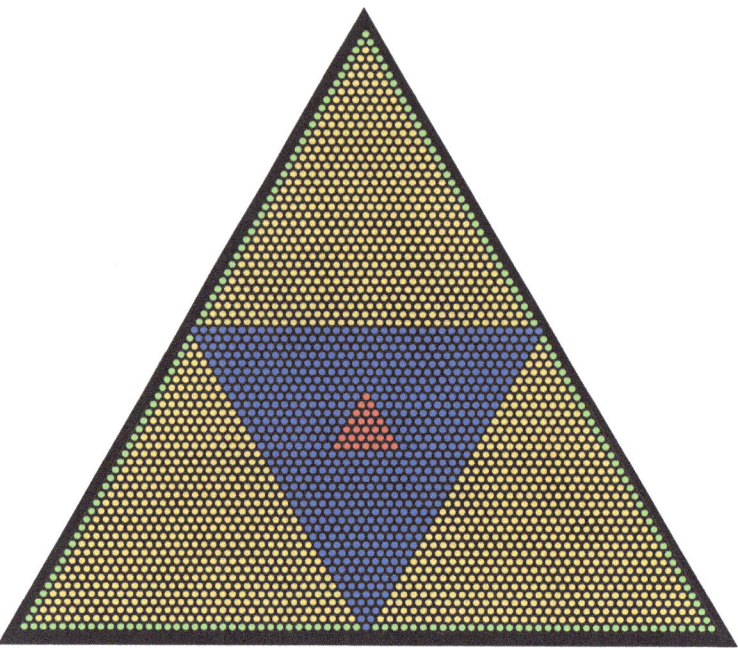

The outer edge (done in green) has **216** units which is **6x6x6**, a rather rare phenomena (one of only two from 1 to one million) in which the edges of a triangle number make a cube. Here it is:

216 is also the value of the 'wonderful numberer' (פלמוני, phalimuni) angel from Daniel 8:13 who is asked by yet a different angel about the 2,300 days of the sanctuary being trodden underfoot. The middle blue triangle is the **37th** triangle number and holds **703** letters, which is **37 x 19**. If we were to put a similar triangle fitted into the blue one, it would be the **19th** triangle number, which is quite reminiscent of our earlier 37-star with a **19**-hexagon in its center. **703** also happens to be the value of "...*and the earth*", the last three words of Genesis 1:1, as well as the Remainder Letters of Chart 39.

Furthermore, since we found Wisdom and Understanding making such a nice triangle earlier in the verse about calculating the number of the beast, we might note that the three orange triangles around the blue **703** triangle have **666** units each.

Furthermore, that middle red triangle of **28** units (the **28** letters in Genesis 1:1 which are **27** wrapped around the center) has edges of **6 + 6 + 6**. We said earlier that there are only two cubed numbers from 1 to 1,000,000 that also equal the edges of a triangle number; these are **216** from above and **27**.

Another example of a rare phenomena is to take a triangle number, double it, and end up with a new triangle number. This works for only four numbers from 1 to 1,000,000: **3** (to 6), **105** (to 210), **3,510** (to 7,020), and **121,278** (to 242,556). Why mention this? Because **105** is the perimeter of each of the three orange **666** triangles above. To see just what **105** can do for us, here are some more pretty pictures:

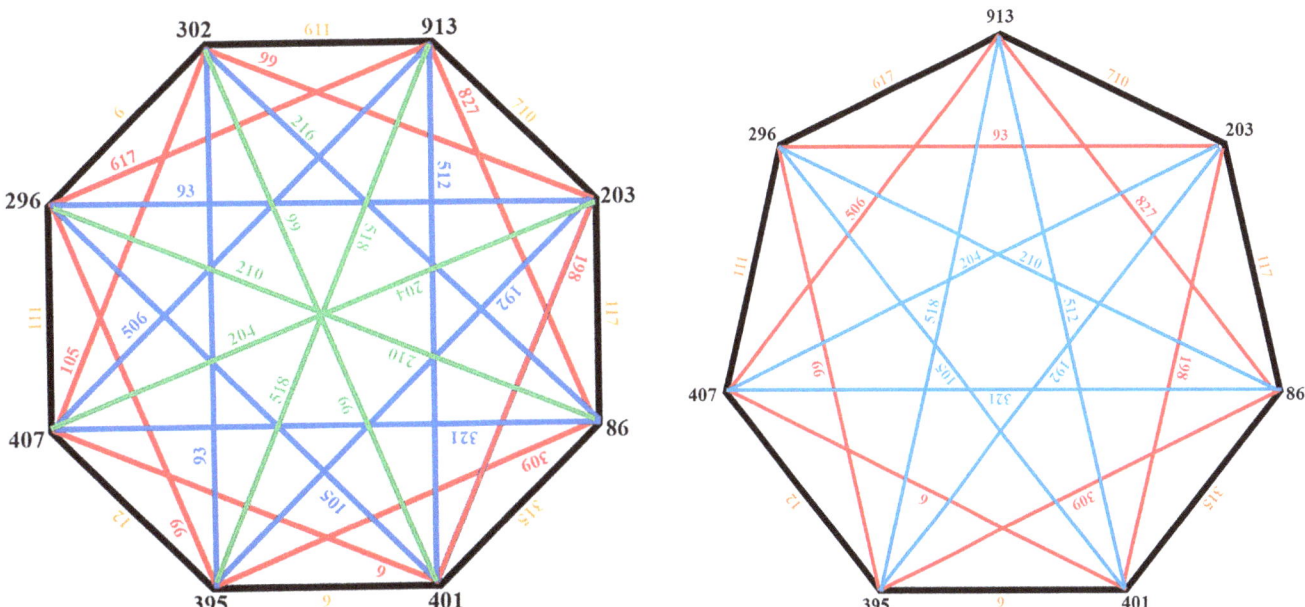

The first shows the values of the seven words of Genesis 1:1 plus the first word of Genesis 1:2 (to make an even octahedron), all in black around the edge. The second shows just the first seven words. *Both* show the difference between the value of each word to each other word; that's what all the colored lines and numbers are: subtracting each from each other.

Now let's take all these *differences* (the colored lines and the shape outline), list them, and express them in terms of **105** and **6**, our new magic numbers.

Chart 72: Differences of All Words in Genesis 1:1 Expressed by 105 and 6 in Ascending Order						
Differences of Gen. 1:1 plus first word of 1:2				**Differences of the Seven Words in Genesis 1:1**		
# of 105's	Each Difference Expressed as Multiples of 105 and 6	Value Diff.'s	# of Times	# of 105's	Each Difference Expressed as Multiples of 105 and 6	Value Diff.'s	# of Times
0	+ 6	**6**	3	0	+ 6	**6**	2
0	+ 6 + 6	**12**	1	0	+ 6 + 6	**12**	1
1 x	105 − 6 − 6	**93**	2	1 x	105 − 6 − 6	**93**	1
1 x	105 − 6	**99**	3	1 x	105 − 6	**99**	1
1 x	105	**105**	2	1 x	105	**105**	1

1 x	105 + 6		**111**	1	1 x	105 + 6		**111**	1
1 x	105 + 6 + 6		**117**	1	1 x	105 + 6 + 6		**117**	1
2 x	105 − 6 − 6 − 6		**192**	1	2 x	105 − 6 − 6 − 6		**192**	1
2 x	105 − 6 − 6		**198**	1	2 x	105 − 6 − 6		**198**	1
2 x	105 − 6		**204**	1	2 x	105 − 6		**204**	1
2 x	105		**210**	1	2 x	105		**210**	1
2 x	105 + 6		**216**	1	3 x	105 − 6		**309**	1
3 x	105 − 6		**309**	1	3 x	105		**315**	1
3 x	105		**315**	1	3 x	105 + 6		**321**	1
3 x	105 + 6		**321**	1	0	+ 6	− 500	**506**	1
0	+ 6	− 500	**506**	1	0	+ 6 + 6	− 500	**512**	1
0	+ 6 + 6	− 500	**512**	1	0	+ 6 + 6 + 6	− 500	**518**	1
0	+ 6 + 6 + 6	− 500	**518**	1	1 x	105 + 6 + 6	− 500	**617**	1
1 x	105 + 6	− 500	**611**	1	2 x	105	− 500	**710**	1
1 x	105 + 6 + 6	− 500	**617**	1	3 x	105 + 6 + 6	− 500	**827**	1
2 x	105	− 500	**710**	1					
3 x	105 + 6 + 6	− 500	**827**	1					

You mean to say that every difference in Genesis 1:1 can be expressed with **105** and **6**, *whether we include an extra word from the next verse or not*? Yup. But we have that nagging "**− 500**" in the last bunch of both lists. It has been introduced through necessity, since none of those numbers work with **105** and **6**. But it is arbitrary; there is no 'magic triangle' that produces 500 like the rest of the numbers. Hm. . .

To solve this one, i will have to make a wee bit of an aside here. While scripture says what it says, it also says quite a bit more than we suspect. If we take up the fact that sometimes ancient Hebrew was written with no spaces between the words, it means that our English bibles are our best guess as to what the text actually is saying, mostly based on the work of the Masoretes. However, it can be translated—perfectly accurately—to say more than one thing. Often, *far more*.

The first word of Genesis, "בראשית , *In the beginning*" can be divided into "ברא" and "שית". The first half is familiar; it is the same as the second word of the passage which we translate "created". The second half can either mean "he appointed (set, put, applied)" or "thorns" or "cloak". So we have a less-favored but perfectly acceptable reading of the first verse: "He created, appointed, created—God—the heavens and the earth" or even "Creating thorns, God created the heavens and the earth."

Now how appropriate those translations are or how to work out the exact meanings might be is a subject for some other discussion. What we are doing here is seeing how that particular approach affects our charts above. Now we have eight words again, and this time we are not borrowing from the second verse. Is the '**105 + 6**' phenomena strengthened or destroyed?

Let's see:

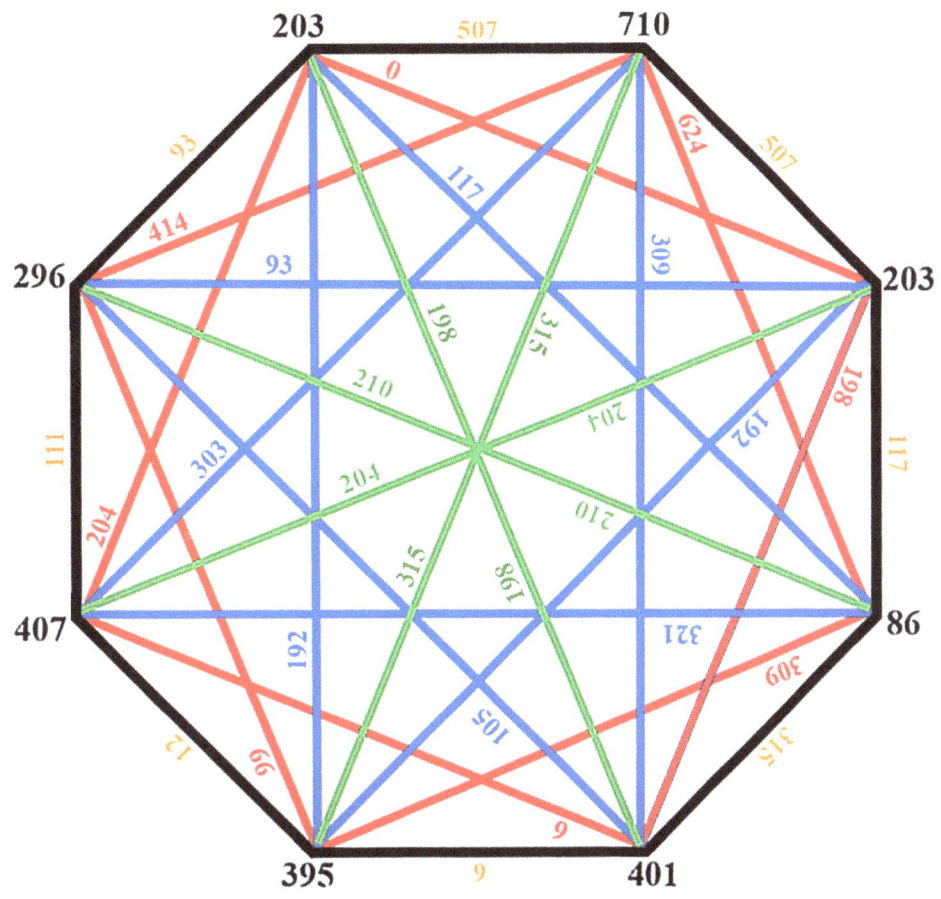

Chart 73: Differences of the Eight Words in Genesis 1:1 Expressed by **105** and **6** in Ascending Order							
# of 105's	Each Difference Expressed as Multiples of 105 and 6	Value Diff.'s	# of Times	# of 105's	Each Difference Expressed as Multiples of 105 and 6	Value Diff.'s	# of Times
0		**0**	1	2 x	105 − 6	**204**	2
0	+ 6	**6**	2	2 x	105	**210**	1
0	+ 6 + 6	**12**	1	3 x	105 − 6 − 6	**303**	1
1 x	105 − 6 − 6	**93**	2	3 x	105 − 6	**309**	2
1 x	105 − 6	**99**	1	3 x	105	**315**	2
1 x	105	**105**	1	3 x	105 + 6	**321**	1
1 x	105 + 6	**111**	1	4 x	105 − 6	**414**	1
1 x	105 + 6 + 6	**117**	2	5 x	105 − 6 − 6 − 6	**507**	2
2 x	105 − 6 − 6 − 6	**192**	2	6 x	105 − 6	**624**	1
2 x	105 − 6 − 6	**198**	2	Total: **6,081** Total each number only once: **4,050**			

And lo and behold it not only still works, but we have eliminated the "− 500" problem. Does this mean we should consider more seriously splitting the first word into two words? I haven't the faintest idea. This is an exploration, not an exegesis. It is a most remarkable phenomena though, and if you would like to have a go at John 1:1, it looks like it uses **3**, **13**, **31**, and **39**. The fact that when we add all those Genesis differences above (**6,081**) we also get the numbers for the **31ˢᵗ** 18-agonal number and the **39ᵗʰ** 16-agonal shapes points in that direction. *Lots* of room for exploration here.

Here's our visual for Genesis 1:1 that goes with the chart above. Each color is one of the words with the exception of "ברא, He Created", which is the same for the first and third words:

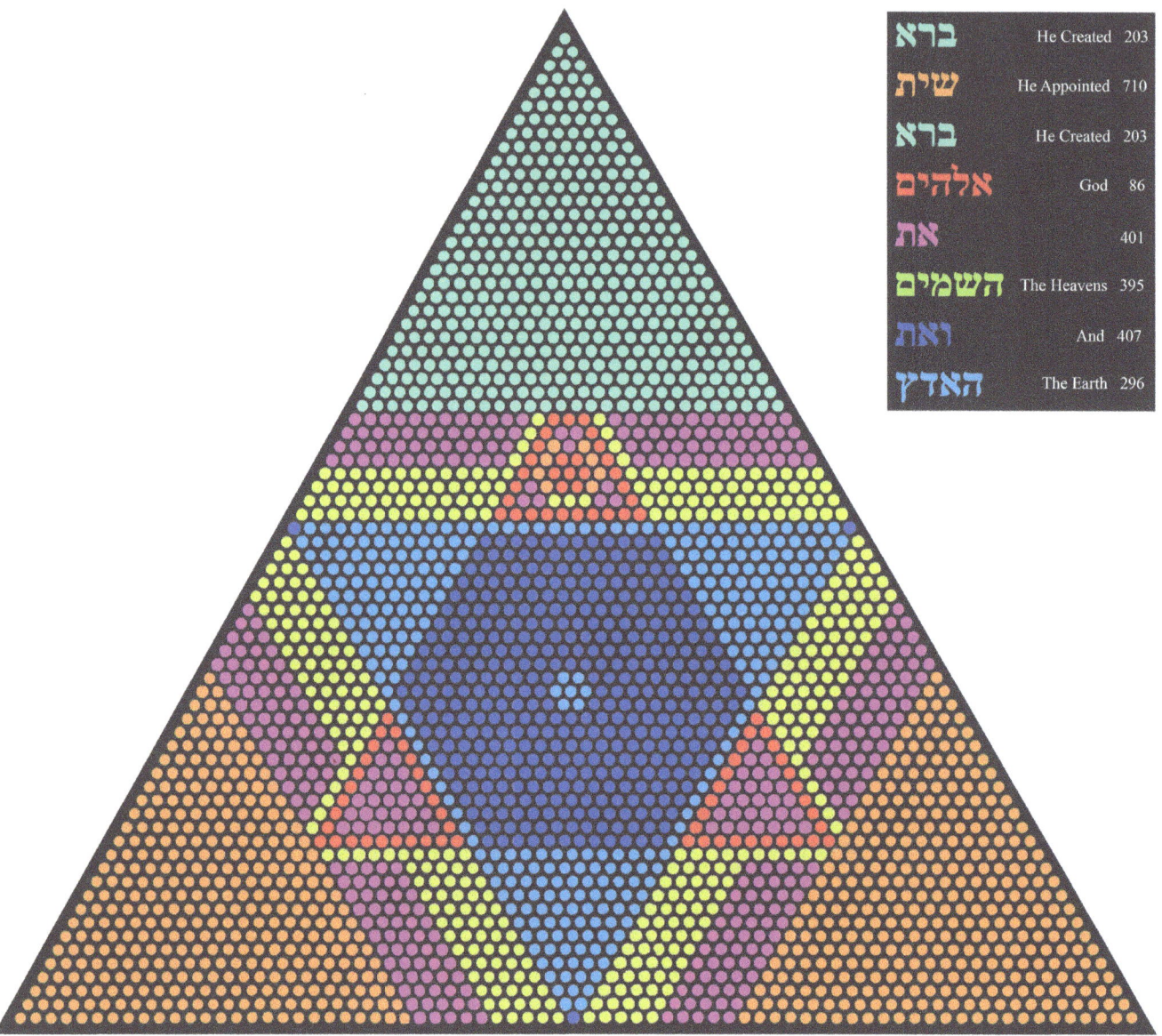

Each multicolored triangle around the central two-toned blue one has **666** units. If the central triangle were flipped on itself to make a star, it would be the **13ᵗʰ** star number, with **1,764** remaining spaces, which is the **42ⁿᵈ** square number. The star would fit perfectly within the three outer triangles of **300** each.

An upside-down triangle fitted within any of the **666** triangles (everything outside the central blue triangle, and we would trim the points to center it) has **210** units, from where we get our **105** from the previous chart. Around this **210** triangle would be three triangles of **153** units (the **17ᵗʰ** triangle number), about which number an entire book could be written.

At this point it is obvious that we could continue on this particular branch of the journey for as long as we like. Let us summarize and close this appendix.

Logos, Wisdom, Jehovah Elohim, and the Alpha and Omega are primary in Genesis 1:1, as well as the keys to unlocking mystery after mystery in the rest of the scriptures, as well as things we haven't yet begun to imagine. We are given in the first verse of Genesis elements that are woven throughout the rest of scripture and creation, and that in but a few simple words.

Appendix II
The Meanings of the First 50 Numbers

The following chart gives the meanings of each number from one to fifty. This is distilled from a much larger study which shows the relationships between the meanings and how they are derived. This is best approached visually rather than verbally to see the *geometric* relationships. The chart from which these are derived is quite large; a section of it is reproduced at the end of this appendix.

	Chart 74: The Meanings of the First 50 Numbers				
1	Unity / Being	18	Rest / Interrelationship	35	Perfected Ability: Accomplishment
2	Substance / Nature	19	Ability to Accomplish: Executabilty	36	Peace
3	Mechanics / Workings	20	Recognition / Honor	37	Artistic Capability
4	Action / Universality	21	Fulfillment	38	Solving
5	Ability / Fruit	22	Answering	39	Harvest
6	Allowance / Freedom	23	Full Action in Every Capacity	40	Proving / Testing
7	Perfection / Completion	24	Ripening	41	Enjoying
8	That which is Completed	25	Satisfaction	42	Pleasure / Awareness
9	Interaction / Full Mechanics / Judgment	26	Multiplying / Affecting	43	Stewardship Returned
10	Responsibility	27	Self-Knowledge / Knowing	44	Answered / Done
11	Response	28	Blessing	45	Indoctrination / Belief
12	Full System / Organization	29	Holding (In Understanding)	46	Accomplishing Everywhere
13	Accountability	30	Communication / Giving	47	Settlement
14	Results	31	Self-Building	48	(Perfect) Potential
15	Possession	32	Effecting	49	Fulfillment of Blessing
16	Working	33	A Running System	50	Return
17	Creation	34	Unfurling	51	Discernment

A Casual Stroll through the Meanings of the Numbers

As we start this journey, let us bear in mind that *meaning* is not *amount*. As we get higher and higher in numbers, they can seem more complicated and more powerful due to mass alone, but that is a reflection of their amounts only. As ideas, they are getting more *fragmented* and *smaller* in significance. **The lower a number is, the more powerful and far-reaching its meaning** until we get down to **ONE**, which is the ultimate number of power and of God.

Let us also note a few elements regarding their characters. Prime Numbers always produce a new idea. Scripture uses them as markers, and they are incredibly useful in seeing the 'root character' of a word. 'Israel', the name given to the lone man who stayed behind and fought with the angel, totals **541**, and is prime. In contradistinction, Mr Universal, Abraham the "father of a multitude", as both 'Abram' and 'Abraham' total **803** and **808** respectively. The first is **11** x **73** and the second is 2^3 x **101**. [That is using the 27-system which includes the 'final forms'. In the 22-system the numbers are **243** (3^5) and **248** (23 x **31**) respectively]. This is one example of how and when prime numbers are used or not used. The Loner's name comes out prime, and the Universal man's name comes out composite.

Next of importance to note is that numbers are not moral. There are no 'good' and 'bad' numbers, not even 666 or 13. These numbers can seem bad or unlucky to us *because of the way we apply them*. For example, **13** means 'accountability'. For one who has been diligent in his work, it would be an utter delight to have a day of accountability, a day of review. The trouble is, most of us are less than diligent in our work, thus we are apprehensive of the day of reckoning, thus **13** becomes 'unlucky' to us. But this does not make **13** good or bad; it simply reflects how we apply the meaning behind it.

Let us take a brief look at mathematical operations. What does it mean to add two numbers or multiply them? What does it do to their respective meanings?

Here are the guidelines to adding, subtracting, multiplying, dividing, exponentials, and roots. Bear in mind that these utilize the **concepts** behind the numbers. Merely applying 'labels' of meaning is too limited an approach to obtain results.

- When **adding** numbers, do it two at a time (if you have a long string), and use the word '**of**', '**from**' or a similar word. Thus **10** (responsibility) **plus 18** (rest and interrelationship) **equals 28** (blessing). So we would phrase it, "*The rest from responsibility is blessing*." This works for all addition operations on numbers and their meanings. Another example: **2 + 5 = 7**. Two is the 'nature' or 'substantiation' of something, five is 'ability', and seven is 'perfection'. So if one has *ability* (5), he will *substantiate* it (2) by *perfecting* (7) things.

- When **multiplying** numbers, make one **possessive**. Thus **4** (action) **times 11** (response) **equals 44** (answered, done). So we would phrase it, "*Action's response is to answer and be done*." This works for all multiplying operations on numbers and their meanings. Another example: **2 x 5 = 10**. Two is 'nature', five is 'ability', and ten is 'responsibility'. So *ability's nature* is to *respond with that ability* (response-ability), that is, if one has an ability to do something in a certain arena, when encountering that arena, he will automatically respond, and to respond with an ability is the concept behind the word 'responsibility'.

- When **subtracting** numbers, make the larger one possessive, and use the phrase, "*is derived* *from*". Thus **7** (perfection) **minus 2** (substance) **equals 5** (fruit). So we would phrase it, "*Perfection's substance is derived from its fruit*," i.e., one can tell if something is perfect by looking at the fruit it produces, as Jesus mentions in Matthew 7. This works for all subtracting operations on numbers and their meanings.

- When **dividing** numbers, ask *how it relates*, or *how we can see it*. Thus **12** (organization) **divided by 3** (mechanics) **equals 4** (action). So we would phrase it, "***How do we see** the mechanics of an organization? By its actions*." This works for all division operations on numbers and their meanings.

- To **power** numbers using an exponential (x^2), make the power a verb, and say "is defined as", or "is known as". Thus $2^5=32$; **2** (nature) **to the power of 5** (accomplishment) **equals 32** (effecting). So we would phrase it, "*Nature **accomplishing** is known as **effecting**.*" This works for all exponential operations on numbers and their meanings.

- To take **Square Root** of a number, say "*The foundation of. . .*" or "*The basic requirement for. . .*" Thus the **square root of 25** (satisfaction) is **5** (fruit). So we would phrase it, "***The basic requirement for** satisfaction is fruit*." In other words, we are not going to achieve satisfaction unless have accomplished something, or produced some fruit. This works for all roots with numbers and their meanings.

Those will help us sort through the many claims that are made regarding numbers. Numbers are designed to make sense, and their language, like every language, has very specific protocols.

Now we come to the exploration of the numbers themselves. As stated, this description is far better done visually, but an adequate chart demonstrating the geometrical relationship between numbers and their meanings would not fit on these pages. So let us start this description with the three necessary elements that contribute to each meaning.

1. **Cyclic.** All meaning found in nature, numbers, and scripture occurs in regular cycles. Sometimes these cycles are **regular**, such as every **third** number having something in common, and that having to do with the meaning of **three**. Sometimes these cycles are **progressive**, such as the Fibonacci series, which would follow the steps of 1, 2, 3, 5, 8, 13, 21, 34, 55, 81, etc., each number being a combination of the previous two. *The cyclic nature of numbers is one of the most valuable and least known tools of investigation into both numerics and mathematics.* The most common cyclic element in our lives is probably the clock.

2. **Ordinal.** In Genesis 1, days 2 through 7 are called the second, third, fourth, fifth, sixth, and seventh days respectively. Not so day one. It is not called the *first* day, but day *one*. Hebrew has a word for *first*, but it does not use it there. This is an example of **ordinal** being used for days 2 through 7 and **cardinal** being used for day 1. Ordinal simply means in what place the number is found with its companion numbers. For example, the 20th of December is the *sixth* day of the *third* week, as well as the *twentieth* day of the *twelfth* month, as well as the *three hundred fifty forth* day of the year . So we see that every number has a multitude of ordinal identities. It is necessary to know which one is significant in the context in which it is being used.

3. **Cardinal.** This is what most people think about when they think of what a number is. Cardinal is quite simply the *amount* that the number represents. The number **12** in **cyclic** would mean that it is either noon or midnight on a clock. **12** in **ordinal** would mean you got picked **12**th for

the team, which would mean you got picked last if there were 24 players available, and each team got twelve. **12** in **cardinal** means that there are a dozen apples, team members, or doughnuts. Cardinal is what we think of when we think of a number line or measuring tape. It simply means *how many*.

These three aspect of numbers are most valuable when all three are working together. It is useful to have the distinctions between them clearly in mind, for in Numerics, the fact that something is **6th** (ordinal) does not mean that there are **six** (cardinal) of that item. We see this in Appendix III on the chart of the Greek alphabet, where the value of the 24 letters are missing **6, 90**, and **900**. Thus 'Theta' (**Θ**) has a **cardinal value** of **9**, but an **ordinal value** of **8**. And its **cyclic value** depends entirely on the scale of the cycle; if we are going in a three-cycle (1, 2, 3... 1, 2, 3... 1, 2, 3...) it would land on **2**. If we are going in a four-cycle (1. 2. 3. 4... 1. 2. 3. 4...) it would land on **4**. In mathematics this is called "Mod".

In discovering and establishing the actual meanings of numbers, all three of these aspects must be used together. This is the main stumbling-block encountered by those who have attempted to assign meanings to numbers: when one fails to account for all three dimensions of numbers, the results come out 'flat' and they neither produce a workable pattern nor do they match the manner in which the numbers and their meanings are used.

Now this part can be quite complicated unless one visually draws it to see the geometry. However, these are the steps to be taken to discover the meanings of numbers.

- Choose a preferred cycle (repeating pattern) and understand its parts. Smaller ones are easier. For example, the **two** cycle has the parts *male, female; male, female;* (or *inward, outward*). The **three** cycle has the parts *issue established, issue solved, issue gone beyond (or negated)*. This repeats in a cyclic manner. Thus it is necessary to understand the **parts** of each cycle, which are different for each cycle. This is like a roadmap of how to get through the cycle. If you are going to the laundromat four blocks away, you might take a different route than when you go to the grocery store five blocks away, not just add a block to the laundromat route.

- Ordinally number your cycles. Thus there is the *first* 'male, female', a *second* 'male, female', a *third* 'male, female', and so on. We will call these ordinal groupings.

- Establish an *estimate* of the cardinal meanings of the numbers. You may not know what five means, but you're fairly sure that seven means perfection. So now you know that the seventh ordinal grouping will have something to do with perfection. But perfection of what?

- The answer to the previous question is the key: *perfection of whatever the meaning of the number of parts of the preferred cycle is.* Thus the 'male, female' cycle is a two-cycle, and the seventh ordinal grouping will be about the **nature (2)** of **perfection (7)**. It will have two parts: the *male* aspect of the nature of perfection, and the *female* aspect of the nature of perfection. In this particular example, the **seventh grouping** of the **two cycle** contains the numbers **13** and **14**. Thus the *male* aspect of the *nature of perfection* is accountability and the *female* aspect of the *nature of perfection* is results.

- Let us take that previous example into the three cycle. Its parts, as we have said, are *issue established, issue resolved, issue gone beyond (or negated)*. Thus **13** and **14** are found as the first two parts of the **fifth grouping** of the **three cycle**. Three is *workings* and five is *ability*. The *workings (3) of (+) ability (5)* is what that ability will accomplish, or *(=) that which is accomplished (8)*. Thus this grouping describes the three parts of that which is accomplished. And what do we find? Part one, issue established: *accountability (13)*; part two issue solved: *results (14)*. We arrive at the same exact meanings in the three cycle as we did with the entirely different two cycle.

- We note then, that every cycle, in its ordinal context, leads to the same cardinal meaning of the number. While this pattern is consistent and straightforward, actually analyzing each pattern and establishing the meanings properly can take many hundreds of hours. It certainly did for me.

Now. Let us embark on our journey through the first 50 numbers.

1

One is the most powerful and thus the most difficult number to understand. We are accustomed to thinking of all numbers containing it, yet in Numerics it contains all numbers. One is unity through perfect balance. When we balance something, say a bicycle wheel, we make sure every spoke weighs the same. One is the perfect balance of *diverse* parts, that is, all other numbers—each different from the rest—balance within the structure of One. It is as if we took the bicycle wheel and made every spoke a different weight, yet still balanced it. **One** is unity, power, existence, wholeness. It is also *loneliness, unapproachable light, singularity,* and *lack of need* respectively. God is One. The human was split into male and female, and thus was designed to find Oneness in relationship rather than 'being'—this being fortunate since the nature of his 'being' was somewhat damaged by what happened in the Garden. The things in scripture that are described as being One are rare and fascinating. . . and because God is One, anything that partakes of Oneness must necessarily deal with him. This is why relationships are so emphasized by Scripture; the subject of a man and a woman becoming *one* is a major aspect of Mankind's approach to God.

2

Two sets up the great Entity/Relationship pattern. *Even* numbers tend to be Entities (identifiable things) and *odd* numbers tend to be Relationships. We are generally more comfortable with Entities, because they can be labeled and described, unlike Relationships which depend entirely on what that they are relating. Two responds (to 1), fills out, effects, substantiates, and characterizes. Two is the *nature* of something, its *substance*, its *acceptance*. If One is light, Two is love.

When thinking of the **duality** involved with two, it is important to remember that numbers are not **moral**. That is to say, a true duality is not good versus bad, but inside versus outside, or ideal versus practical. Light and darkness are not a true duality; darkness is merely the absence of light, whereas light is certainly not the absence of darkness. Light and *love*, however, are a true duality, as are grace/truth or even particle/wave. . . and male/female.

Just as One is pure order, Two is pure *demonstration* of order. Two is the feminine foundation for all relationships.

3

One is **that** God is, Two is **what** God is, and Three is **who** God is. Three is the workings, the plannings, the structure of anything, thus it is used for Wisdom, Counsels, and Intelligence. Everything has three dimensions, and each dimension is completely different from its two companions with no overlap. It is not the Father's job to manifest God, it is the Son's. It is not the Son's job to teach us about himself (he teaches us about the Father) it is the Spirit's. The pattern of the roles of the Trinity are stamped on everything in creation.

Three is *capacity*, *dimensions*, and the ability to use them. One introduces God, Two introduces Creation, and Three introduces the *process* of Creating, and what that process in turn will mean to God. Three is all-inclusive and contains the secrets to the mechanics by which anything works.

4

Four is universality and action. There are four winds, four directions, four corners of the earth. The simplest, and thus first, shape in three dimensions is the tetrahedron; it has four corners and four faces. Thus four is the beginning of the formation, or **substantiating** (remember *substance* is two) of things. This formation occurs in all directions at once, and thus includes all requisite actions.

Three, being dimensions, has no reference to a center-point; Four always emanates from a center; all action has a source-point. The geometry of Four shares the same geometry of a Carbon atom; the four directions are always ≈109.5° apart... just as Job addresses his four friends (the three and Elihu) and said, "*Mark me, and be astonished, and lay the hand upon the mouth*"; this phrase has a value of 1095.

The four actions of a human soul are *being*, *believing*, *perceiving*, and *loving*. Physically, these are *breathing*, *eating*, *sensing*, and *giving* (or *doing*) respectively.

5

Five is simply an amazing number. It is the second proper Prime after **One** (2 and 3 only qualify as primes under a cardinal definition when one ignores ordinal and cyclic) and along with **9** is one of the two keys to our base-10 counting system. Five is **ability** and **fruit**. The hand with its five fingers is the ultimate symbol of ability. Ability does not stand alone, it *accomplishes*; and the result of *accomplishment* is called **fruit**. If we slice an apple sideways, we will see that the seeds are enclosed in a five-pointed star.

Five also points toward death, because true fruit always contains the Seed, and as Jesus said, unless the seed falls into the ground and dies, it abides alone. The man of ability in scripture is David, and his story is replete with fives, 8 times in Kings and twice in Chronicles for a total of **10** (2 x **5**); from the five stones he chose from the brook to the five giants killed by him and his men.

Since Five is accomplishment, it is the end of the process of **1.** Conceiving, **2.** Assessing, **3.** Planning, **4.** Doing, and **5.** Accomplishing. After this, what has been fully formed must be let go, which leads us directly into **6**.

6

Six is *releasing, allowance, freedom*. Once *accomplishing* (**5**) a project, say building a car, Six is letting your friend taking it for a spin, not knowing whether he will wreck it or not. Six is the extent to which you will let something go; thus with God, the number 666 is the extent to which he will allow evil without stepping in and stopping it.

In the **3-cycle** mentioned in the number **3**'s description, four is *that* God does (action), five is *what* God does (what he accomplishes; fruit) and six is *what God doesn't do* (what God allows). Because when God allows us to do things without stopping us, we do all sorts of ridiculous things, six is variously seen by people as failure, sin, weakness, and 'man's number'. Yet remember that numbers are not *moral*; Six is just as easily a wonderful thing as a gateway to failure; it depends on how well we are able to handle our freedom. Solomon received 666 talents of gold per year; right up to the limit of what God would allow.

7

Seven is Perfection, as our friend Ivan Panin likes to point out to us. It is 'finished-ness'; there are seven parts to every endeavor, every progression, every monument of activity. Each of the seven stages is distinct and unique. The rainbow separates itself into seven clearly defined bands; our pianos have seven clearly defined notes.

Seven is the third Prime, and as '**third**', the ordinal form of **3**, it gives the *mechanics of perfection* to any system. This is why Panin finds so many texts can be demonstrated to be part of scripture (or not part of scripture), because the **7**'s are always there to indicate the structure of a perfect system.

Seven is not all crystal and roses; to accomplish perfection in this world, suffering is necessary. Jesus said *"Go say to that fox, Lo, I cast out demons and accomplish healings today and tomorrow, and the third day I am perfected. Nevertheless, I must go on today and tomorrow and the day following: for it cannot be that a prophet perish out of Jerusalem."* The numeric value for "**the cross**" is **777**, as well as to *kill*, a *rod*, to *give*, and to *prove*. Lamentations 3:52 says *"My enemies chased me sore, like a bird, without cause"* ...which has the value of **777**.

8

Eight is that which is perfected. Eight's perfection is distinct from **7**'s perfection in that it does not have *parts* like **7**; it is in and of itself a whole new part. It is *that which is new, that which is not part of the system, yet has used the entire system*. It is often used (correctly) as the number for new creation. **888** is the numeric value of '**Jesus**'. Philippians 2:16 speaks of the hope of New Creation thus: *"Holding forth the word of life; that I may have of what to glory in Christ's day, that I did not run in vain neither toil in vain."* This passage has the value of **8888**. There are **88** words in scripture with the value of **88**; the last one is in First John 5:4 *"...because whatever is begotten of God overcomes the world; and this is the **victory** that has overcome the world: our faith."* And the first word in scripture with the value of **88** is **Noah**, who took eight souls to a **new** start for humanity.

Eight is two cubed (2^3), and according to the directions above, we would phrase it *"Nature (2) is planning (3) for new creation (8)."* The natural world, as God set it up, actually is working toward and longing for **new creation** (Romans 8:19-23).

9

Nine is a somewhat intimidating number. It is the <u>interaction of a full system</u>, whether that system be numbers or teaching man to number his days (Psalm **90**, "*So teach us to number our days, that we may apply our hearts unto wisdom.*" This verse's value is **693**, or **9** x **107**). Thus nine is used for **judgment**. Revelation 2:16 says "*Repent therefore; else I come to you quickly, and I will war against them with the sword of my mouth*"; this verse has a value of **9999**.

The physical universe is composed of Space, Time, and Energy (or matter if you will). Space has height, width, and breadth, Time has past, present, and future, and Energy has modulation, volume, and intensity (or for Matter, proton, neutron, and electron). These add up to Nine, the full system of the universe. Likewise there are nine planets and a woman's pregnancy lasts nine months, each required for a full system.

Nine is 3^3 and from the **3-cycle** that we have been looking at, **7** is *that* God perfects, **8** is *what* God perfects, and **9** is *what* God *doesn't* perfect, that is, what enters into judgment and gets burned up, as it says in Second Peter 3:10 (verse value: **11119**, prime). *Verily, Snare, evil,* and the *branch* not bearing fruit in John 15:22 all equal **99** in Greek, but so does *great, fountain,* and *draw*. The number **9** likes to be taken seriously.

10

Ten is <u>responsibility</u>; not so much what one *has* to do, but what we *have the ability to do*. Ten is **2** x **5**; five is *ability*, and five more is the *response to ability*, or responsibility. Five toes balance the foot; ten toes balance the walk itself.

The ten commandments have clued in many as to its meaning. Ten is a 'triangle number' (think of the setup of 10 bowling pins) such as 3, 6, 15, 21, 28, etc. In the *action* cycle (**4**) it is <u>capability</u>, in the *accomplishment* cycle (**5**) it is <u>response</u>, in the *freedom* cycle (**6**) it is <u>communicating</u> <u>perfection</u> <u>outward</u>, and in the *perfection* cycle (**7**) it is <u>structuring using responsive ability</u>.

As in Appendix 1 we looked at **666**, **777**, and **888** (all having **37** as a factor) for their different characters, let us list here some of the Greek words with similar values relating to **ten**. Each list has a different character.
610: *sow, laborer, work, build, continue, judge, crooked.*
710: *warm, answer, help, confirm, counsel, good, faithful, watch, find, wash, baptize, mercy, power*
810: *brother, Lord, friend, comforter, endure, purifying.*

These show some of the *facets* of what is associated with <u>responsibility</u> when put into differing numerical contexts.

11

Eleven is the secret weapon of prime numbers. He pops up in the strangest places, and often permeates a passage even more than his well-known brother **7**. **Eleven** means response. **11** answers, responds, and uses its full capacity to fulfil expectations. A good response is rare; Proverbs 9:9 says *"Give instruction to a wise man, and he will be yet wiser: teach a just man, and he will increase in learning."* This is how God likes us to respond, and the value of that verse is **1331**, or **11³** (11 x 11 x 11). The previous verse has a similar theme; *"Reprove not a scorner, lest he hate you: rebuke a wise man, and he will love you"* and has the value of **4257** (3³ x **11** x 43).

Music presents her own version of response in that the number of vibrations per second for each musical note is in multiples of eleven. And the sunspots occur in eleven-year cycles, indicating that it is possible the sun is responding to the earth as much as vice-versa.

One of the wisest responses in the Old Testament was when Solomon was faced with the two harlots arguing over a child; *"And the king said, Bring me a sword. And they brought a sword before the king."* This has the value of **1221**, or **11** x 111, as does Job's challenge for anyone to be able to respond to his words in 24:25; *"And if it be not so now, who will make me a liar, and make my speech nothing worth?"*

12

Twelve is an organization, a full system. It is contrasted from **9** (*interaction of a full system*) by the fact that it tends to be organized by a higher power, often God. For this reason it is sometimes called *administrative organization*. It is the first number whose factors include both the **dimensions** (3) and the **directions** (4); as such, it has both the **capacity** and **activity** (respectively) to provide a full structure. In music, there are **12** notes when we include the halftones.

As there were **12** disciples, the word *preach* has the value of **1728**, which is **12³** (12 x 12 x 12). And the list of twelves is almost inexhaustible; 12 tribes, twelve signs of the zodiac, 12 springs of water in Elim in the wilderness, and the list goes on and on.

In the **3-cycle** that we have been looking at, **10** is *that* God expects, **11** is *what* God expects, and **12** is *what* God *doesn't* expect, that is, he himself sets it up rather than relegating that organizing to man. In the *freedom* cycle (**6**) it is *usable perfection; response released*, and in the *perfection* cycle (**7**) it is *a made organization*.

More in-depth, learning to understand the *twelve parts* of **12** provides a comprehensive grasp on whatever subject is at hand, though it involves taking the time for to thoroughly familiarize one's self with the subject. The **twelve** elements of **mathematics** are: *measure (cycle), scale, span, orientate, standardize, reflect, define, apply, identify, extrapolate, sanctify,* and *specify*. In **art** they are *idealizing, choreographing, substantiation ordering, responding, solving (intuitive), naming, dignifying, forming, adjusting (environmental), realizing, planning (projecting),* and *embodying*. And again, these two lists are duplicate sets (though not in the same order here) applied in two differing contexts, math and art.

13

Thirteen is accountability, and as mentioned in the intro this gives it somewhat of a bad rap. In scripture, however, it is a very powerful force as well as a vital aid in navigating the infinite numerics. In Hebrew it is both the value of the word *One* and *Love*. The force of being accountable does come through loud and clear in the verses characterized by it; 13^3 (13 x 13 x 13) = **2197**, which is the value of **Exodus 34:14** *"For you shall worship no other God: for Jehovah—Jealous is his name—is a jealous God."* Likewise with **Proverbs 28:24** *"Whoever robs his father or his mother, and says, It is no transgression; the same is the companion of a destroyer."* That verse has the **22-system** value of **2197** (13^3) and the **27-system** value of **2847** (3 x **13** x **73**). Fortunately, **Psalm 86:5** gives us a little glimpse of how nice it is to have mercy in the day of accountability: *"For you, Lord, are good, and ready to forgive; and plenteous in mercy to all them that call on you."* ...with a value of **1313**.

14

Fourteen means results. If **5** represents *ability* using the *hand* with its five fingers as a model, **14** represents the *results* attainable using that ability with **14** phalanges, or finger bones (as well as **14** in each foot). There are also **14** facial bones in the human skull. It might also be of interest that an owl, who can turn his head all the way around, has **14** vertebra in his neck.

The result of Jacob working for Laban for **14** years was two wives; the result of Job's patience and double blessing was **14,000** sheep. The passover was held on the **fourteenth** day of the month, and there are three sets of **14** progenitors in Jesus' genealogy in Matthew. Paul waited **14** years before he went to Jerusalem to present his Gospel to the Apostles.

Fourteen begins the full system of three-dimensional shapes; the simplest being the tetrahedron with **6** edges, + **4** sides + **4** faces = **14**. Four (action toward formation) **plus 10** (responsibility) = form, the results of formation.

It is the nature (**2**) of perfection (**7**) to produce results (**14**).

15

Fifteen means possession. When God took repossession of the earth in the days of Noah, nearly every measurement of the ark as well as every length of time mentioned was a multiple of **15**; as Psalm 124:4 says, *"Then the waters had overwhelmed us, the stream had gone over our soul"*— this verse has the value of **1515**. And **225** (15^2) is the Greek value of the words *his, child, holy, sincere,* and *divine*.

In Leviticus 7:25 the fat of the sacrifices was owned by God; *"For whoever eats the fat of the beast, of which men offer an offering made by fire to Jehovah, even the soul that eats it will be cut off from his people."* and when David obtained possession of the promise from God that his Seed would abide, he said to God in Second Samuel 7:28 *"And now, O Lord Jehovah, you are that God, and your words are true, and you have promised this goodness to your servant..."* Both these verses have the value of **3375**, or 15^3 (15 x 15 x 15).

The earth rotates **15°** every hour, and in the **24-clock** of Greek letters (Illustration Page 118), each letter is **15°** apart. The time between the new moon and the full moon is **15 days**. In the **3-cycle** that we have been looking at, **13** is *that* God gets, **14** is *what* God gets, and **15** is *what* God doesn't get, that is, what he already possesses.

16

Sixteen means <u>working</u> with the added sense of <u>substantiating</u>. It can also be applied to the exhaustion that comes of working. **16** is both 2^4 and 4^2; it is the only reciprocal exponent. Add to this fact that **4** is both **2 + 2** and **2 x 2**, and we see that **sixteen** is a very active number. Of note among the cycles is the *freedom* cycle (**6**) in which **16** means <u>*assets in action*</u>. Greek words that equal **256** (**16²**) include *fishers, shepherd, care, arm,* and *deed*... all 'working' ideas.

16³ (**16** x **16** x **16**) equals **4096**, (and is **2¹²**), which is the value of the following verses:
Zephaniah 3:5 *"The righteous Jehovah is in the midst of her; he does no wrong: every morning does he bring his judgment to light, he fails not; but the unrighteous knows no shame."*
Daniel 8:27 *"And I Daniel fainted, and was sick, days; then I rose up, and did the king's business; and I was astonished at the vision, but none understood."*
Jonah 2:7 *"When my soul fainted within me I remembered Jehovah: and my prayer came in unto you, into your holy temple."*

17

Seventeen is the number of <u>creation</u>. **289** (**17** x **17**) is the Greek value of the words *receive, new, shape,* and *distribute*. The thought is not so much that of God creating the earth, but the manner in which one either overcomes by creating a new way of going forward in life in the face of great difficulty, or succumbs. Three examples from scripture, all of which have the value of **4913** (**17³**, or **17** x **17** x **17**):
Ruth 2:10 *"And he said, Blessed are you of Jehovah, my daughter: for you have shown more kindness in the latter end than at the beginning, inasmuch as you followed not young men, whether poor or rich."*
Judges 16:21 *"But the Philistines took him, and put out his eyes, and brought him down to Gaza, and bound him with fetters of brass; and he did grind in the prison house."*
James 4:17 *"To him therefore that knows to do good, and does it not, to him it is sin."*

18

Eighteen is <u>rest</u>, specifically the rest of interrelationship. It takes the *full interaction* of **9** and tempers it with *nature* (**2**), as **2 x 9 = 18**. In the **3-cycle** that we have been looking at, **16** is <u>*that*</u> God works (**work**), **17** is <u>*what*</u> God works (**creation**), and **18** is <u>*what*</u> God <u>*doesn't*</u> work, that is, **rest**. **Eighteen** is *freedom's counsels* (**6 x 3**), and the *counsels* bring in the idea of interrelating.

18³ (**18** x **18** x **18**) = **5832**, and Second Chronicles 30:1 has both the idea of a interrelationship and a day of rest combined nicely: *"And Hezekiah sent to all Israel and Judah, and wrote letters also to Ephraim and Manasseh, that they should come to the house of Jehovah at Jerusalem, to keep the passover to Jehovah God of Israel."* And there is the classic verse in First Timothy 2:12 (also **5832**) that addresses it: *"But I permit not a wife to teach, nor to have dominion over a husband, but to be in quietness."*

Eighteen is a reflective number, a doubling up of thought and experience. It is the only number that is twice the sum of its digits, and **18 x 20** (*recognition/honor*) gives us the **360°** of a full circle.

19

Nineteen is *executability*; the ability to *accomplish*. It is the **7th** prime, and as such plays a pivotal role in getting our bearings in Scripture. When Joshua stopped the sun in the sky, five of the kings he defeated hid in a cave. Joshua ordered them brought out in 10:23 ". . .*and they did so, and brought forth those five kings unto him out of the cave, the king of Jerusalem, the king of Hebron, the king of Jarmuth, the king of Lachish, and the king of Eglon.*" This verse has the value of **6859** which is 19^3, or **19 x 19 x 19**. When God finished all of his creation, it says in Genesis 2:1 "*Thus the heavens and the earth were finished, and all the host of them.*" This verse (in the **27**-system) has a value of **2888**, which is $19^2 \times 2^3$.

We saw in Appendix I how important the **19**-penny hexagon was to both Genesis 1:1 and John 1:1. The fact is that if one is to make a 'magic hexagon' starting with one and numbering all the spaces so that each row in each direction equals the same (in this case 38), **19** is the *only* *size* of a 'magic hexagon' to which this can be done:

Nineteen, then, has a unique role among numbers, and is a vital clue to many of the relationships that are waiting to be searched out. When we go to the verses in First John which tell us what the Word did, we find **19** throughout: "*And the Word became flesh, and tabernacled among us, and we beheld his glory, glory as of an only begotten with a Father, full of grace and truth.*"

In this verse, "*flesh*" is the key word, and is 19^2 (**19 x 19**). The phrase "And the Word became flesh" is **1273** (**19** x **67**), "Tabernacled among us" is **1501** (**19** x **79**), "*we beheld his glory, glory as of an only begotten with a Father, full of grace and truth*" is **7068** (**19** x **372**), and "*as of an only begotten with a Father, full of grace*" is **4598** (**242** x **19**).

While Vacationing in England, Moses builds a Quick Study Model for the Letter Proportions.

20

Twenty is recognition/honor; the idea is both a *display* of honor and recognition for having fulfilled responsibilities, especially in relationships. Job in 13:18 says *"Behold now, I have ordered my cause; I know that I will be justified."* ...and this verse has the value of **2020**. The number **20** also has the opposite aspect in which one does not get honor; as such, 20^2 (**400**) is the value in Greek of *deceitfulness, transgression, defile*, and *lie* ...as well as *holy*. Leviticus 21:4 has both senses when it says *"But he shall not defile himself, being a chief man among his people, to profane himself,"* also **400**. And Second Chronicles 7:20 continues the theme of dishonor: *"Then will I pluck them up by the roots out of my land which I have given them; and this house, which I have sanctified for my name, will I cast out of my sight, and will make it to be a proverb and a byword among all nations."* That verse equals **8000**, which is 20^3 (**20 x 20 x 20**).

Twenty is a triangle pyramid number as shown:

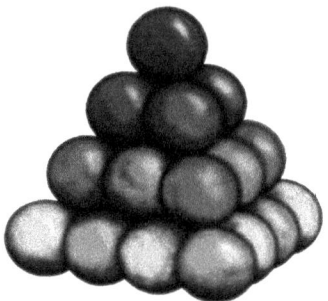

This means it relates directly to a 3-**dimensional** construct where the most intricate numerics are hidden.

21

Twenty-One is **3 x 7** and means fulfillment and fullness. In the **3-cycle** that we have been following, **19** is *that* God can finish (executability), **20** is *what* God can finish (honor), and **21** is *what* God *doesn't* finish, that is, it is already finished for him, as the honor that Christ gets for doing the work he was sent to do. Consequently, **21** is closely related to the finished work of Christ; his struggles being seen in a picture when Jacob wrestled with the Angel: *"And when he saw that he prevailed not against him, he touched the hollow of his thigh; and the hollow of Jacob's thigh was out of joint, as he wrestled with him."* ...which verse's value is **2121**.

A difficult yet important lesson that **twenty-one** teaches us is that we are to enter into God's rest as Hebrews 4 explains. Thus Matthew 5:37 says *"But let your word be, Yea, yea; Nay, nay: and whatever is more than these is of the evil one."* ...which has the value of **9261**, 21^3 (**21 x 21 x 21**). For **21 x 73 = 777**, which is *the cross*, and Christ has already done that; we enter into his God's rest in the work. There are times when the glory of God is so taken up with his appreciation for his Son that we cannot approach, as Exodus 40:35 says *"And Moses was not able to enter into the tent of the congregation, because the cloud abode on it, and the glory of Jehovah filled the tabernacle."* This verse is **2310** which is **(21 x 37) + (21 x 73)**.

22

Twenty-Two is answering. It has the sense of *distributing service, returning thankfulness,* and *responding by initiating a creation*. It is like **11**, *response*, but takes it much farther; it is *how* one responds, and *to whom*. In the negative, it is Proverbs 15:12 "A scorner loves not one that reproves him: neither will he go unto the wise" (**22²**) and the force of the positive is shown in Isaiah 40:30 "*Who has directed the Spirit of Jehovah, or being his counselor has taught him?*" ...which has the value of **2200**.

23

Twenty-Three is another powerful prime; it means full action in every capacity. It has the sense of *awaking and acting* as well as *hyperactively accomplishing* and *using everything that you are*. On the intense side it it *the accountability of responsibility* (**13 + 10**) and on the energetic side it is the *fruit of rest* (**18 + 5**), as when one wakes in the morning and attacks a project.

There is a certain abandon to **23**, as Ecclesiastes 11:1 says "*Cast your bread upon the waters: for you will find it after many days*" (**1679**; **23 x 73**). The beauty of this energy can be seen in Song of Solomon 1:19 "*I have compared you, O my love, to a company of horses in Pharaoh's chariots*" (which verse value is **2323**) and the negative of this energy can be seen in Job 12:25 "*They grope in the dark without light, and he makes them to stagger like a drunken man.*" ...whose value is **2300**.

24

Twenty-Four is the perfection of fruit; **ripening**. It has the sense of just beginning to enter into rest, and of making room for maturing to occur. The end of the fourth day in Genesis 1:19 and the seeing that the beasts that the earth brought forth were good in 25, both contain **24** as a factor. **24²** (**576**) is the value of *Spirit, honor, overshadow, kindle,* and *finish* in Greek. A good example is found in Daniel 1:19 "*And the king communed with them; and among them all was found none like Daniel, Hananiah, Mishael, and Azariah: therefore stood they before the king*" which has a value of **2424**.

And **24 x 37** is **888** (*Jesus*), while **24 x 73** is **1752**, which is Proverbs 8:23 "*I was set up from everlasting, from the beginning, or ever the earth was*" ...Wisdom speaking.

25

Twenty-Five is Satisfaction, particularly the satisfaction that comes of one's own accomplishments. Song of Solomon 8:2 has "*I would lead you, and bring you into my mother's house, who would instruct me: I would cause you to drink of spiced wine of the juice of my pomegranate*" which has the value of **2525**.

25 is both the **5th** square and **5 x 5**. It is also the sum of two squares; $3^2 + 4^2 = 9 + 16 = 25$, thus it is often used as an example of the Pythagorean Theorem ($A^2 + B^2 = C^2$) which allows us to easily calculate the third leg of a triangle.

One can see Jacob's great satisfaction in his son Judah when he blesses him: "*Judah, you are he whom your brothers will praise: your hand will be in the neck of your enemies; your father's children will bow down before you*" which has a value of **1825**, or **25 x 73**.

26

Twenty-Six is <u>multiplying</u> and <u>affecting</u>. It is the number of *influence, what others can count on,* and one's *ability to have a full effect*. As **2** x **13**, it is the *nature* (**2**) of *accountability* (**13**) meaning that when one has successfully given an account, one can then move on and use that dignity to influence what happens next. **26²** (**676**) is the value of the Greek words *doer* (from James) and *new*. When the idea is negated, one has no ability to affect, thus **676** is the value of the first verse in First Kings "*Now king David was old and stricken in years; and they covered him with clothes, but he got no heat.*" The flip side for David is First Samuel 29:5 "*Is not this David, of whom they sang one to another in dances, saying, Saul slew his thousands, and David his ten thousands?*" which has the value of **2626**, as does Ezekiel 37:2, "*And caused me to pass by them round about: and, behold, there were very many in the open valley; and, lo, they were very dry*" to which God then did some rather remarkable <u>multiplying</u> and <u>affecting</u>.

27

Twenty-Seven is <u>self</u> <u>knowing</u>. It has the sense of *self searching, self examination*, and *reexamination*. The Old Testament uses the expression "*And Adam <u>knew</u> his wife*", meaning that they made love. This is very much a part of **27**, for a man's wife is part of himself, and the marriage process is that of getting to one's <u>self</u>, that is, one's <u>wife</u>. Thus **27** is part of the mystery of Oneness.

Twenty-Seven is 3^3, and as such is central to inner counsels and workings. Both verses in Genesis 1 (26 & 27) which speak of God creating male and female and telling them to multiply and have dominion have **27** as a factor; **27** x **208** and **27** x **431** respectively. **Twenty-Seven** also has an application to knowing God, as Daniel 11:32 shows; "*And such as do wickedly against the covenant shall he corrupt by flatteries: but the people that <u>do</u> <u>know</u> their God shall be strong, and do.*" This verse has the value of **2727**.

And there is a warning against knowing one's self (or one's wife) so well that we do damage; both Exodus 20:13 and Deuteronomy 5:17 say "*Thou shalt not kill*" which in both instances has the value of **729**, or **27²**.

Twenty Seven is the number of Hebrew letters including the final forms. It is a most vital number to understanding how to put the letters into <u>three</u> <u>dimensions</u>. In two dimensions, as we saw in Appendix I, the numbers **37** and **73** are in prominence. But in three dimensions, **27** is primary. So is there a relationship between **27** and **37** & **73**? Let's shade in the **27 cube of Hebrew letters** as it sits within the **64 cube,** 'Truth':

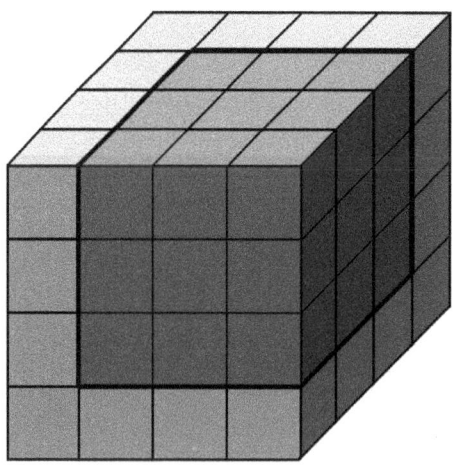

If we *remove* the **27 Hebrew letter cube**, we end up with this:

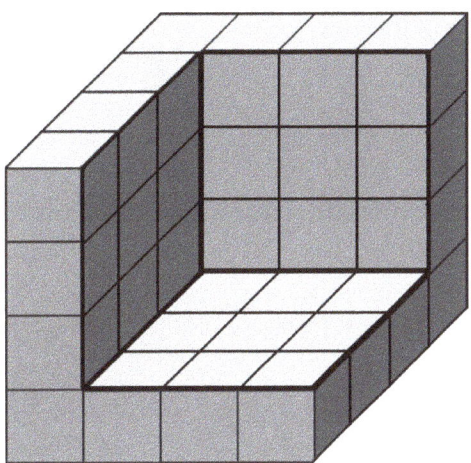

And how many cube are left? **Thirty-Seven**. But in using **64** and **27**, we used the **3rd** and **4th** cubes, skipping the first (**1³**) and second (**2³**). So let's slip all the cubes back in.

Much better; now all the cubed numbers up to **64** are accounted for. And total number cubes here? **73**.

This is one way to show that while different numbers are prominent in differing scenarios, they are always intricately related.

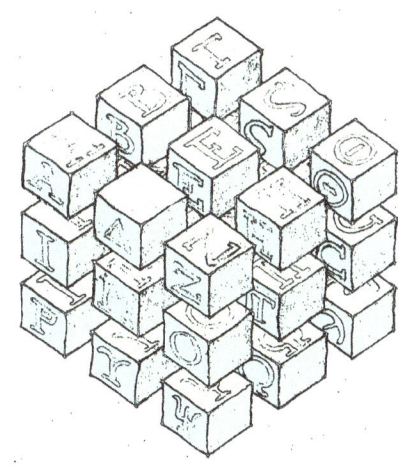

28

Twenty-Eight is the **7th** Triangle Number (a triangle of pennies with each side 7 pennies long) and means blessing. It has the sense of '*Amen!*' It is the accountability of possessions and overseeing, especially your own business or family. In the negative it can mean destroying your possessions instead of blessing them, as Zephaniah 1:2 "*I will utterly consume all things from off the land, says Jehovah*" which has the value of **784**, or **28²** (**28** x **28**). But even this has God's mercy involved, for Job 33:28 says "*He will deliver his soul from going into the pit, and his life shall see the light.*" And the woman is well blessed in Song of Solomon 6:5 "*Turn away your eyes from me, for they have overcome me: your hair is as a flock of goats that appear from Gilead.*" These two verses have the values of **2800** and **2828** respectively.

Each time in Genesis 1 that it says "*and God blessed them*", the value is **765**, or (**28** x **24**) + **7**. The value of Genesis 2:3 "*And God blessed the seventh day, and sanctified it: because that in it he had rested from all his work which God created and made*" is **4928**, or **28** x **176**. And interestingly, the only Greek word with the value of **28** is heal.

29

Twenty-Nine is holding/understanding. It is what one holds within one's self so as to understand what to do. It means having possession of the results of your experience. As the **9th** prime, it has a powerful application to inner strength. Ecclesiastes 7:10 has some advice about considering one's experience: "*Say not, How is it that the former days were better than these? for you do not inquire wisely concerning this.*" This verse has a value of **2929**. When Nebuchadnezzar wrote his letter to the whole world after his restoration, in his new understanding he says "*I thought it good to show the signs and wonders that the High God has wrought toward me*" and this verse is **2030**, which is **29** x **70**.

30

Thirty means communication/giving. It is *understanding available to be used*. In the negative we see the lack of communication or giving in Job 19:14 "*My kinsfolk have failed, and my familiar friends have forgotten me*" which has a value of **30²**, or **900**. Psalms 36:8 gives the positive "*They will be abundantly satisfied with the fatness of your house; and you wilt make them drink of the river of your pleasures.*" That verse has the value of **30** x **73**.

30 is the **4th** Square Pyramid Number after **1**, **5**, and **14**, meaning that if you stack ping-pong balls in a square pyramid, it will take **30** of them to make four levels high. The next level would take **55** balls, which is also the number of pennies in one of the two overlapping triangles on the **73/37** star of *Logos*.

When God gave the lights in the expanse of the heavens (Genesis 1:16) to communicate signs, seasons, days, and years, the verse has a value of **5820** which is **30** x **193**.

31

Thirty-One is the **10th** prime, and means <u>self-building</u>. It is also the number for **<u>naming</u>**; the sense is *actively working on one's self or one's possessions* as in Deuteronomy 3:7 *"But all the cattle, and the spoil of the cities, we took for a prey to ourselves"* which has the value of **961**, or **31²**. When Adam named the animals, the word *name* equals **301**.

The negative side of not being able to build one's self up can be quite harsh, as we see in Esau in Genesis 27:34 *"And when Esau heard the words of his father, he cried with a great and exceeding bitter cry, and said unto his father, Bless me, even me also, O my father."* That verse has the value of **3100**. But the inclusion of God in the process is nice, as we see in Psalm 139:24 *"And see if there be any wicked way in me, and lead me in the way everlasting."*, which has the value of **31 x 73**.

32

Thirty-Two is **2⁶** and means <u>working</u> <u>out</u>; **<u>effecting</u>**. Genesis 2:3 says *"And God blessed the seventh day, and sanctified it: because that in it he had rested from all his work which God created to make"*, and has the value of **4928** (**32 x 11 x 7**). Judges 20:1 shows the effectiveness of working together; *"Then all the children of Israel went out, and the congregation was gathered together as one man, from Dan even to Beer-sheba, with the land of Gilead, unto Jehovah in Mizpeh."* This verse has the value of **3200**. Likewise with Exodus 7:17 *"Thus says Jehovah, In this you will know that I am Jehovah: behold, I will smite with the rod that is in my hand upon the waters which are in the river, and they will be turned to blood"*, which has the value of **3232**.

33

Thirty-Three is a <u>running</u> <u>system</u>, a *full operation*. Ironically, the only Greek word that equals **33** is *hades*. This harkens to Luke 12:5 *"But I will forewarn you whom you shall fear: Fear him, which after he has killed has power to cast into hell; yea, I say unto you, Fear him!"* which has the value of **11,979**, which is **33³ ÷ 3**.

There are **33** vertebrae in the human spine. David reigned for **33** years over all of Israel and had **33** mighty men. Jesus lived to **33**. An example of a full operation is in Numbers 41:38 *"And the officers which were over thousands of the host, the captains of thousands, and captains of hundreds, came near unto Moses"* which has the value of **3333**.

34

Thirty-Four means <u>unfurling</u>. In the *accomplishment cycle* it has the sense of <u>unfolding</u>; in the *perfecting cycle* it has the sense of <u>unleashing</u>. The unfolding of the seas and the dry land (Genesis 1:10) has the value of **2074** which is **34 x 61**. Isaiah 43:6 says *"I will say to the north, Give up; and to the south, Keep not back: bring my sons from far, and my daughters from the ends of the earth"* which verse has the value of **3434**. Eber was **34** when he had Peleg, in whose days the earth was divided; we are not told what forces were unleashed, only that they were.

It also has the sense of <u>unfurling</u> a <u>flag</u> for battle, as in Psalm 45:3 *"Gird your sword upon your thigh, O most mighty, with your glory and your majesty"* . . .this verse has the value of **1258**, which is **34 x 37**.

35

Thirty-Five is perfected ability or accomplishment. It is the *honor* of *possessions* and *creation's rest*. It is the value of the Greek words *glass* and *amethyst*, as well as *child* and *translate*. Psalm 98 greatly praises the accomplishments of God, and verse 7 says *"Let the sea roar, and the fullness of it; the world, and they that dwell in it"* and has the value of **1225** which is **35**^{2}.

In Genesis 11:4, mankind had perfected his ability and wanted to make the ultimate accomplishment; *"And they said, Give help! Let us build us a city and a tower, and its top in the heavens; and we make for us a Name, lest we are scattering over the face of the whole earth."* This verse has the value of **3535**. Joel 3:10 says *"Beat your plowshares into swords, and your pruning hooks into spears: let the weak say, I am strong"* which has the value of **3500**.

35 is the sum of the first five Triangular Numbers, making it a Triangular Pyramid Number as follows:

This construct has **35** spheres. The last time we saw this was with number **20**, this time with an additional level. The next will be **56**.

36

Thirty-Six is <u>peace</u>. It has the sense of *outspreading* and *leading toward awareness*. It is 6^2, the 6th square number and also the product of two squares: $2^2 \times 3^2$. It is also the 8th Triangle Number and the only triangular number whose square root (**6**) is also a triangular number. The sum of the numbers from **1** to **36** is **666**. Here is what we mean by both a square number and a triangular number (both have 36 pennies):

There was a sense of outspreading peace from the moon and the sun when "*God set them in the expanse of the heavens, to give light on the earth*" in Genesis 1:17, and the value of this verse is **36** x **67**.

One of the most beautiful passages about peace is the first half of John 14:27: "*I leave you peace; my peace I give to you: not as the world gives, give I to you.*" The value of this verse is **36** x **244**, and even **244** is $2^2 \times 61$ . . .**sixty-one** being a most mysterious number that is the primary numeric key to **Psalm 119**. The first half of this phrase "*I leave you peace; my peace I give to you*" has the value of **3360**, which is **36** x **33.33333**. . .

John 18:9 says "*That the word be fulfilled, which he said, Of those whom you have given me, I lost not one*", which has the value of **7776**, which is $36^3 / 6$.

37

Thirty-Seven has had more said about it in this book than perhaps any other number. Here we mention a few things that have not been said.

37 means <u>artistic</u> <u>capability</u> and *solving*. It is closely connected with *creating* and the process of *translating* from one realm to another, including from this life to the next. Jeremiah 52:31 states that "*in the <u>thirty-seventh</u> year of the captivity of Jehoiachin king of Judah, in the twelfth month, on the twenty-fifth of the month, that Evil-Merodach king of Babylon, in the year that he began to reign, lifted up the head of <u>Jehoiachin</u> king of Judah, and brought him forth out of prison.*" Jehoiachin has the value of **111** which is **3** x **37**. Ishmael, Levi, and Amram lived to **137** (Sarah lived to **127** and Jacob to **147**).

Isaiah 52:15 has the value of **3737** and says "*...so will he astonish many nations; kings will shut their mouths at him; for what had not been told them will they see, and what they had not heard will they consider.*" Habakkuk 1:12 also has the value of **3737** and says "*Are you not from everlasting, Jehovah my God, my Holy One? We will not die. Jehovah, you have ordained Him for judgment; and you, O Rock, have appointed him for correction.*"

38

Thirty-Eight means solving, primarily through *planning* and *organizing*. In Deuteronomy 2:14 it states that it took **38** years for the generation of the men of war to be consumed from the midst of the camp. In John 5:5 a man had been infirm for **38** years by the pool called Bethzatha whom Jesus healed and told to sin no more lest something worse befall him—promptly went and tattled on Jesus to the Pharisees. Yet Jesus was using that very situation to organize the first of many discussions with the religious leaders that continue through the rest of the book; he was laying down the gauntlet, so to speak, having planned out and organized his approach to the severe attitudes against God of the day.

One form of the word *heal* (ιαθηι) in Greek has the value of **38**. There is then the question of who has the ability to size up a situation and solve it, as it says in Jeremiah 9:12 *"Who is the wise man, that may understand this? and who is he to whom the mouth of Jehovah has spoken, that he may declare it, for what the land perishes and is burned up like a wilderness, that none passes through"* . . .with the value of **3838**. And God is not interested in false solutions, as he says in Amos 5:22 *"Though you offer me burnt offerings and your meat offerings, I will not accept them: neither will I regard the peace offerings of your fat beasts"* which has a value of **2774**, which is **38** x **73**.

Psalm 111:2 says *"The works of Jehovah are great, sought out of all them that have pleasure in them"* which has the value of **1406** which is **38** x **37**. . . as does Proverbs 17:3 *"The fining pot for silver, and the furnace for gold: but Jehovah tries the hearts."*

39

Thirty-Nine is harvest; *fulfillment of rest*. Jeremiah 50:34 talks of this *"Their Redeemer is strong; Jehovah of hosts is his name: he will thoroughly plead their cause, that he may give rest to the land, and disquiet the inhabitants of Babylon."* The value of this verse is **3939**. And after everything that the woman goes through in Song of Solomon, her final way of phrasing what she says in so many forms is *"I am my beloved's, and his desire is toward me"* with a value of **1443** (**39** x **37**). Sharing that value, Psalm 128:6 says *"Yea, you wilt see your children's children, and peace upon Israel."*

Contrasted with a negative harvest, such as Zephaniah 1:15 *"That day is a day of wrath, a day of trouble and distress, a day of ruin and desolation, a day of darkness and gloominess, a day of clouds and thick darkness"* . . .is the positive of Jeremiah 33:12 *"Thus says Jehovah of hosts; Again in this place, which is desolate without man and without beast, and in all the cities thereof, shall be a habitation of shepherds causing their flocks to lie down"* and Deuteronomy 16:13 *"You shall observe the feast of tabernacles seven days, after that you have gathered in your corn and your wine"*. All three of these verses have the value of **2847**, which is **39** x **73**.

40

Forty is well-known as proving and testing. Scripture is replete with **40**'s; **40** days and **40** nights of rain in the flood, **40** days between when the ark rested and Noah opened the windows, the age of Isaac when he took Rebecca as wife, the age of his son Esau when he took two Canaanite wives, **40** days of embalming Jacob, **40** years of the Israelites eating manna, twice Moses on the mountain for **40** days and **40** nights, **40** silver bases under the boards on both the north and south sides of the tabernacle, **40** days of the spies searching out the land, **40** years of wandering in the wilderness (that do not exactly correspond to the **40** years of eating manna; they are offset by two years), maximum amount of stripes allowed when punishing someone under law, Moses' life of **120** was divided into **3** sets of **40**: Egypt, Jethro, and Israel; **40** years the land rest after Othniel, then Deborah, then Gideon; **40** sons of Gideon, **40** years under the rule of the Philistines until God raised up Sampson, **40** years Eli judged Israel, **40** days that Goliath defied Israel, the age of Ishbosheth Saul's son when he became king, the number of years David reigned, the age of Absalom when he tried to usurp the kingdom, . . .and we are not even halfway through the occurrences.

One of the lesson we can see in this pattern of **40**'s is that they all—without exception—require God's involvement. The following two verse give this idea clearly, both of which have the value of **1600**, or **40²**; Psalm 107:28 says *"Then they cry unto Jehovah in their trouble, and he brings them out of their distresses"* and Psalm 65:2 says *"O you that hear prayer, unto you will all flesh come."*

In Judges 6:4 we have Gideon testing Jehovah *"And God did so that night: for it was dry upon the fleece only, and there was dew on all the ground"* and in Job 36:9 Elihu explains how God proves people: *"Then he shows them their work, and their transgressions because they have increased."* Both these verses have the value of **1480**, or **40 x 37**. . . the same numerical value as **Christ**.

And we'll finish with this example of the ultimate test of life or death: *"Then the king held out the golden scepter toward Esther. So Esther arose, and stood before the king"*, Esther 8:4. This verse has the value of **4040**.

41

Forty-One means enjoying, using, and appreciating. The only Greek word with the value of **41** is *salt*, which allows us to appreciate food. Certain kings enjoyed the fruits of labor provided by those who came before them; Rehoboam was **41** when he began to reign; his grandson Asa reigned **41** years as did Jeroboam over Israel. Psalm 78:5 describes the use and appreciation of the law; *"For he established a testimony in Jacob, and appointed a law in Israel, which he commanded our fathers, that they should make them known to their children"*, this verse has the value of **4100**. On the negative side, here are some who did *not* appreciate the prophet Elisha in Second Kings 2:23: *"And he went up from there unto Bethel: and as he was going up by the way, there came forth little children out of the city, and mocked him, and said unto him, Go up, you bald head; go up, you bald head"* . . .which verse also has the value of **4100**. Note that the two she-bears that came out of the wood tore **42** of them; leading to the next number with a corresponding meaning to enjoying/using.

But Psalm 69:34 brings us back to enjoying; *"Let the heaven and earth praise him, the seas, and every thing that moves in it"* with a value of **1517** (**41 x 37**).

42

Forty-Two is <u>pleasure</u> and <u>awareness</u>, connected with *fulfillment substantiated*. It is different from the enjoying of **41** in that it is an outward sharing of pleasure rather than an inward <u>using</u> for one's self. **41** and **42** are a good example of a **meaning pair** in which two numbers occur beside each other which have the <u>male</u> and <u>female</u> meaning of the same idea.

The negation of **42** can be seen in the **42** months that the nations tread under foot the outer court of the temple, the **42** months that the Beast pursues his career, and the **42** royal persons from Judah that Jehu killed when establishing his kingdom—and breaking the truce between Israel and Judah. For the positive we have the **42** cities that were set aside for the Levites which would double as Cities of Refuge.

And the positive side is meant to be *outward*; to others or to God as Numbers 29:6 "*Beside the burnt offering of the month, and his meat offering, and the daily burnt offering, and his meat offering, and their drink offerings, according unto their manner, for a <u>sweet savor</u>, a sacrifice made by fire unto Jehovah*", this verse has the value of **1746**, which is **42²**.

43

Forty-Three is <u>stewardship</u> <u>returned</u>. It is the *recognition* (**20**) that one has *acted fully in every capacity* + (**23**). It is the one good thing that Jehu did in Second Kings 10:19 when he was given stewardship of the kingdom by Elisha's servant: he extricated Baal from Israel by slaying all his prophets: "*Now therefore call unto me all the prophets of Baal, all his servants, and all his priests; let none be wanting: for I have a great sacrifice to do to Baal; whoever will be wanting, he will not live. But Jehu did it in subtlety, to the intent that he might destroy the worshipers of Baal.*" This verse has the value of **4343**. *Judge* (κρινομαι) and *deed* (πραξιν) in Greek both have the value of **301**, which is **43** x **7**.

And the comment regarding the woman in Song of Solomon 3:6 when she returns to her beloved with the stewardship of his love: "*Who is this that comes out of the wilderness like pillars of smoke, perfumed with myrrh and frankincense, with all powders of the merchant?*" This verse also has the value of **4343**. The Greek work *espouse* (μεμνηστευμενηι) has the value of **1161**, which is **43** x **37**.

Of course, God can *demand* an accounting of stewardship as he did to Job in 38:3, "*Gird up now your loins like a man; for I will demand of you, and answer you me*" and in Jeremiah 13:20, "*Lift up your eyes, and behold them that come from the north: where is the flock that was given you, your beautiful flock?*" These two verses are **1161** (**43** x **37**) and **3139** (**43** x **73**) respectively.

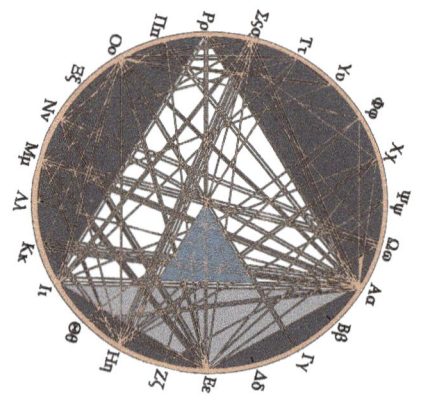

44

Forty-Four is answered/done, making another **meaning pair** with **43**. It is the 4th Octahedral Number (see page 124). It also has the sense of being in *readiness for what is next*. In John 4:49 "The nobleman says unto him, Sir, come down before my little child die. (50) Jesus says to him, Go, your son lives." Verse 49 there in which the request was already answered and done, has the value of **4444**.

In First Samuel 1:27, Hannah presents Samuel to Eli and says *"For this child I prayed; and Jehovah has given me my petition which I asked of him."* This verse has the value of **4400**. Eli had told her when he saw her last that Jehovah would grant her petition; answered and done. And in Genesis 24:65 *"And she is saying to the servant, What man is this that walks in the field to meet us? And the servant is saying, It is my master: and she is taking a veil, and she is covering herself."* This verse also has the value of **4400**, and has double the meaning; she was already considered married (*done* and *in readiness for what is next*) and now that Isaac was married, the servant's new master was Isaac, not Abraham as previously.

Because God knows our requests before we even make them, and because prophecy from God is as sure as if the event had already happened, both pray (προσευχομενη) and prophecy (προφητευομεν) in Greek have the value of **1628**, which is **44** x **37**. These are the only two Greek words with this value.

45

Forty-Five means indoctrination and belief. The idea is to saturate a problem with the solution; to be wholly occupied with something, as Paul says to Timothy in 4:15, "Meditate upon these things; give yourself wholly to them; that your profiting may appear to all", which has the value of **5200** (**45** x **115**) + **5²**.

Levi (through Phinehas) completely immersed himself in Jehovah's word in Deuteronomy 33:9, *"Who said unto his father and to his mother, I have not seen him; neither did he acknowledge his brethren, nor knew his own children: for they have observed your word, and kept your covenant."* Likewise in Numbers 24:1, Balaam finally realized that it was *Jehovah's* word, not some other entity *"And when Balaam saw that it pleased the LORD to bless Israel, he went not, as at other times, to seek for enchantments, but he set his face toward the wilderness."* Both these verses have the value of **4545**.

Habakkuk 1:13 gives a good example: *"You art of purer eyes than to behold evil, and cannot look on iniquity: for which reason look you upon them that deal treacherously, and keep silent when the wicked swallows up a man more righteous than he."* And Second Timothy 2:12 gives us the difference between truly believing and not: *"If we endure, we will also reign together: if we will deny him, he also will deny us."* Both these verses have the value of **4500**.

And as to the character of doctrine, it is something we need to *get*, and get from a place where it is held. The four Greek words with the value of **1665** (**45** x **37**) are *have* (κυριευουσιν), *have* (εχωσιν), *obtain* (τετευχεν), and *synagogue* (συναγωγης).

45 is also a triangular number, as well as the sum of the digits 1, 2, 3, 4, 5, 6, 7, 8, and 9.

46

Forty-Six is <u>accomplishing</u> <u>everywhere</u>. It is as if one is in overdrive. It is also the number of human chromosomes. Accomplishing everywhere at once can be seen in Habakkuk 2:14, *"For the earth shall be filled with the knowledge of the glory of Jehovah, as the waters cover the sea."* And the excitement is almost palpable in Genesis 29:12 *"And Jacob told Rachel that he was her father's brother, and that he was Rebekah's son: and she ran and told her father."* Both of these verses have the value of **2116**, which is **46²**.

And we have the romantic side in Ruth 4:13: *"So Boaz took Ruth, and she was his wife: and when he went in unto her, Jehovah gave her conception, and she bare a son"* which has the value of **3358**, which is **46** x **73**.

Then we have the beginning of the last paragraph of the Old Testament; Malachi 4:4, which says *"Remember you the law of Moses my servant, which I commanded unto him in Horeb for all Israel, with the statutes and judgments.,"* with the value of **4646**.

47

Forty-Seven is <u>settlement</u>, as the fulfillment of multiplying. Note that the planet Mars settles back into the same place every **47** years. The only Greek word with its value is *herd* (αγελη).

In Second Chronicles 7:2 the glory settled on the house of God *"And the priests could not enter into the house of Jehovah, because the glory of Jehovah had filled Jehovah's house."* This verse has the value of **1739**, or **47** x **37**. Its negation—the opposite of being settled—is in Job 18:18; *"He is driven from light into darkness, and chased out of the world."* This has the value of **1269**, or **47** x **27**.

And we have the romance of settlement in Proverbs 5:19, *"Let her be as the loving hind and pleasant roe; let her breasts satisfy you at all times; and be you ravished always with her love."* Then with God we have the settlement of events past, present and future in Isaiah 44:7: *"And who, as I, will call, and will declare it, and set it in order for me, since I appointed the ancient people? and the things that are coming, and shall come, let them declare unto them."* As well as the immovability of the settled heavens in Job 38:31; *"Can you bind the sweet influences of Pleiades, or loose the bands of Orion?"* These three verses have the value of **3431**, or **47** x **73**.

48

Forty-Eight is <u>perfection</u> <u>of</u> <u>potential</u>. It is what is achieved when the maturing process is healthy. **48** cities were given to the Levites in the land. **48** is most often seen in setting up a peaceful and stable scenario that has take an enduring consistent effort to produce. We see this in Genesis 47:12, *"And Joseph nourished his father, and his brethren, and all his father's household with bread, according to their families"* and First Chronicles 16:2 *"And when David had made an end of offering the burnt offerings and the peace offerings, he blessed the people in the name of Jehovah."* Both of these verses have the value of **2304** (**48²**), as well as the negation, one of which is found in Proverbs 25:28, *"He that has no rule over his own spirit is like a city that is broken down, and without walls."* **48** is also the 3rd Icosahedral Number (see page 125).

In Isaiah 50:4 we have *"The Lord Jehovah has given me the tongue of the learned, that I should know how to help by a word him that is instructed: he wakens morning by morning, he wakens my ear to hear as the instructed."* This verse has the value of **4800**.

49

Forty-Nine is **7²** and both its digits, **4** and **9** are squares. **49** means <u>fulfillment</u> <u>of</u> <u>blessing</u>, as it is mentioned in Leviticus 25:8 "*And you shall count seven sabbaths of years, seven times seven years; so that the days of the seven sabbaths of years be unto you <u>forty-nine</u> years.*" And this verse even has the value of **7524**, or **(49 x 153) + 3³**. And in First Samuel 16:3 God finally gets the king he wants "*And call Jesse to the sacrifice, and I will show you what you will do: and you will anoint unto me him whom I name unto you.*" This verse has the value of **4949**.

In Joshua 21:43 we have "*And Jehovah gave unto Israel all the land which he swore to give unto their fathers; and they possessed it, and dwelt therein*" with a value of **4900**. And the negation is seen in Acts 13:40 when Paul is preaching, "*Beware therefore, lest that come upon you, which is spoken of in the prophets. . .*" also with a value of **4900**.

50

Fifty is <u>return</u> with the sense of *glory*; each **50** years in Israel was the <u>Jubilee</u>, in which all possessions returned to their original owners, from slaves to property, and all debts were erased. **50** is **1² + 7²** as well as **5² + 5²** as well as **3² + 4² + 5²**. as well as **5³ - 4³ - 3³ + 2³ + 2³**. The two Greek words with the value of **50** are *righteous* (δικαιε) and *I* (εμε).

First Corinthians 10:31 says "*Whether therefore you eat, or drink, or whatever you do, do all to the glory of God.*" Likewise in Genesis 17:1 "*And when Abram was ninety years old and nine, Jehovah appeared to Abram, and said to him, I am the Almighty God; walk before me, and be you perfect.*" Both these verses have the value of **5050**. And in Exodus 34:35 Moses returned with so much glory that they couldn't look at him: "*And the children of Israel saw the face of Moses, that the skin of Moses' face shone: and Moses put the veil upon his face again, until he went in to speak with him.*" That verse has the value of **5000**.

And if something cannot return glory to God? Matthew 7:19: "*Every tree that brings not forth good fruit is hewn down, and cast into the fire.*" This verse has the value of **3650**, or **50 x 73**.

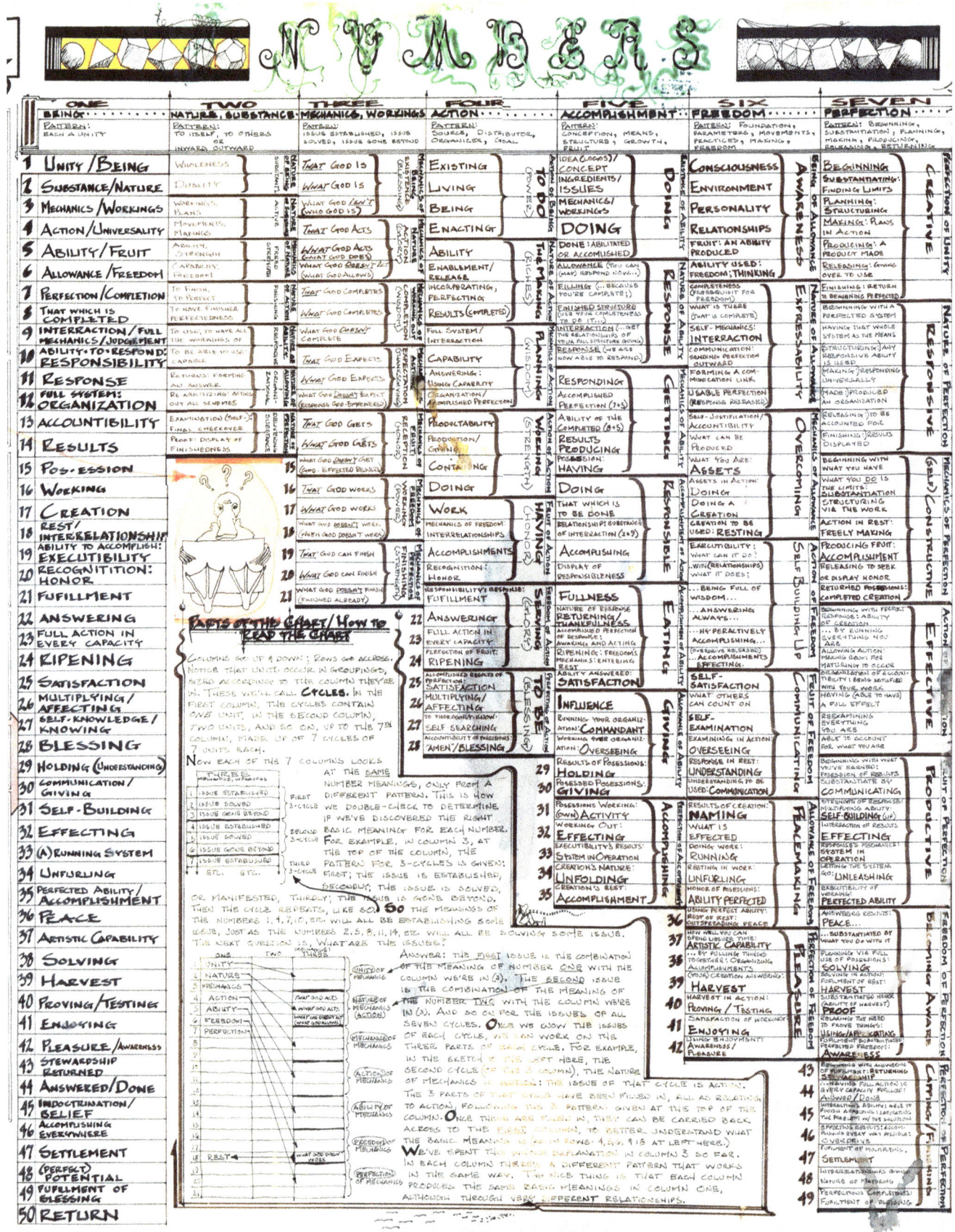

Section of the Original Number Chart

Appendix III

Gematria Systems for Hebrew and Greek Letters

\<td colspan=6\>					
<td colspan="6" align="center">**Chart 75:** Hebrew Letter Gematria Values</td>					
Letter	Name	Final Form?	Numeric Value	Place Value	English Sound
א	Aleph		**1**	1	a as in 'as'
ב	Beth		**2**	2	b, bh
ג	Ghimel		**3**	3	g, gh
ד	Daleth		**4**	4	d, dh
ה	Hé		**5**	5	h, hé as in 'hospitalize'
ו	Vav		**6**	6	o, u, v, w, f as in 'vow'
ז	Zayin		**7**	7	z
ח	Chet		**8**	8	h, hé, ch see note
ט	Tet		**9**	9	t
י	Yod		**10**	10	i, ai, soft j, y
כ	Kaf	ך	**20**	11	c, ch, k see note
ל	Lamed		**30**	12	l
מ	Mem	ם	**40**	13	m
נ	Nun	ן	**50**	14	n
ס	Samekh		**60**	15	s, x
ע	Ayin		**70**	16	h, wh
פ	Pe	ף	**80**	17	p
צ	Zadi	ץ	**90**	18	tz as in 'klutz'
ק	Qof		**100**	19	k, qu see note
ר	Resh		**200**	20	r
ש	Shin		**300**	21	sh
ת	Tav		**400**	22	th, t

The previous page shows the **Hebrew** letters with both their Numeric Value in Hebrew counting and their Place Value, that is, order in the alphabet. There are five 'final forms', meaning that if one of these five letters is the last letter in a word, the final form is used instead. The total of this the Hebrew chart above is 1495; below we add the final forms.

Note: Pronunciations often have a progression of soft to hard like Hé, Het, Chet, and Qof (ה, ח, כ, ק) that ranges from a soft 'h' to a hard 'k'. And there is some overlap of sounds in examples like these.

The 'final forms', when used in the numbering system, have the following values:

Chart 76: Gematria Values for the Hebrew Five Final Forms			
Letter	Name	Numeric Value	Place Value
ך	Kaf	**500**	23
ם	Mem	**600**	24
ן	Nun	**700**	25
ף	Pe	**800**	26
ץ	Zadi	**900**	27

This rounds the chart out nicely to include all requisite numbers from 1 to 900. It also makes the letters into a perfect cube, as 27 is 3^3, they can be arranged into a construct like a Rubik's Cube. This is important, because numbers that can be represented in three-dimensional form turn out to be very useful. The total of this chart comes out to 4995, which turns out to be a significant number in Bible Numerics. Here are two examples of verses whose values add up to 4995:

Even to them will I give in my house; and within my walls a place and a name better than of sons and of daughters: I will give them an everlasting name, that will not be cut off. **Isaiah 56:5**

Wherefore comfort one another with these words. **First Thessalonians 4:18**

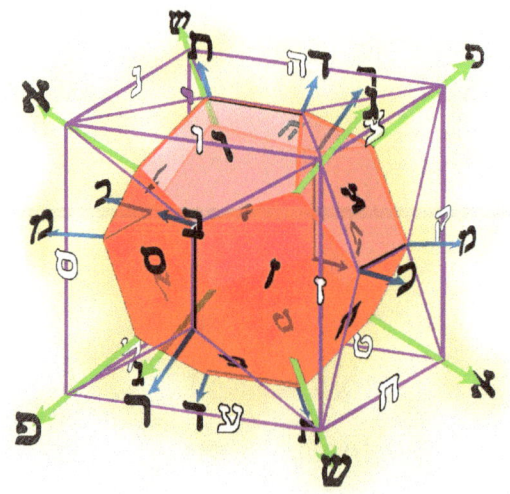

<u>The next page shows the values for the 24 letters of **Greek**.</u>

Note that Stigma (ς), Koppa (C), and Sampsi (ϡ) with the respective values of 6, 90, and 900 had fallen out of usage as letters of the alphabet by the time the New Testament was written, but were retained for the numbering system. Thus they are not included in 'place values' but have a numerical equivalent. The only difference that their inclusion makes is that it give the whole numbering system a total value of 4995, just as the addition of the five "final forms" do for the Hebrew. None of these three 'extra' letters occur in the New Testament.

So to give an example of gematria, 'Logos' (Λογος) means 'Word' and is where we get our English word 'logic' from. Looking at the chart, **Λ = 30, o = 70** (twice), **γ = 3**, and **ς = 200**. Adding those up gives us a value of **373** (which is a prime number) for the **numeric value** of word Logos.

Looking in the column that has its **place value**, we see that **Λ = 11, o = 15** (twice), **γ = 3**, and **ς = 18**. Adding those up gives us a value of **62**. We could add the article ('the') which in this case is Omicron (**o = 70**) again. This brings the **numeric value** up to 443 (also prime) and the **place value** to **77**, or **7 x 11**. Added together they equal **520**, or **13 x 40**.

So we can see the immense range in totals with Greek words. In Mark 14:36 we have **Αββα** (dad), which has a total numeric value of **6**. In 14:46 we have **αυτω** (him), which has a total numeric value of **1501**. Each word has only four letters, yet the range between **6** and **1501** is immense.

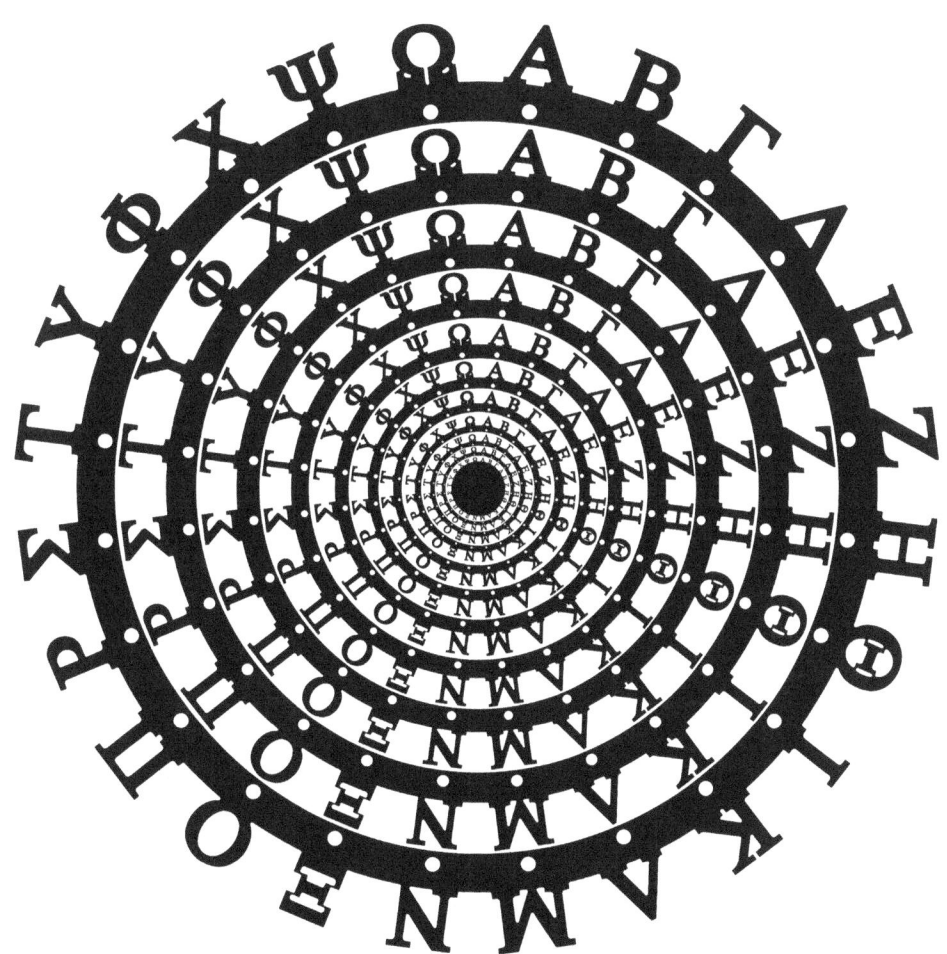

Chart 77: Greek Letter Gematria Values					
Letter		Name	Final Form?	Numeric Value	Place Value	English Sound
A	α	Alpha		1	1	a as in 'father'
B	β	Beta		2	2	b
Γ	γ	Gamma		3	3	g
Δ	δ	Delta		4	4	d
E	ε	Epsilon		5	5	e as in 'endure'
Ϛ	ϛ	Stigma		6		archaic unused letter
Z	ζ	Zeta		7	6	z
H	η	Eta		8	7	ê as in 'hey'
Θ	θ	Theta		9	8	th as in 'thrust'
I	ι	Iota		10	9	i as in 'iterate'
K	κ	Kappa		20	10	k
Λ	λ	Lambda		30	11	l
M	μ	Mu		40	12	m
N	ν	Nu		50	13	n
Ξ	ξ	Xi		60	14	ks as in 'appendix'
O	o	Omicron		70	15	o as in 'often'
Π	π	Pi		80	16	p
Ϙ		Koppa		90		archaic unused letter
P	ρ	Rho		100	17	p
Σ	σ	Sigma	ς	200	18	s
T	τ	Tau		300	19	t
Y	υ	Upsilon		400	20	u as in 'put'
Φ	φ	Phi		500	21	f
X	χ	Chi		600	22	ch as in 'bellyache'
Ψ	ψ	Psi		700	23	ps
Ω	ω	Omega		800	24	ô as in 'escrow'
ϡ	ϡ	Sampsi		900		archaic unused letter

Appendix IV

153

I have decided that *not* having an explanation of this most peculiar number would be remiss. While it appears throughout the text, this chapter will introduce it primarily as a *mathematical* phenomena. As to *natural* phenomena, the square root of 153 (12.37) is the number of full moons in a year. Here we are exploring facts such as 1!+2!+3!+4!+5! = 153 (there are only 14 such numbers from 1 to a trillion).

If we were investigating, say, prime numbers, we would have to set parameters, because there is a practical infinity of samples. Note i say "practical"; the word 'infinity' is bandied about as if it means something in and of itself. As far as the human experience and conceptual reality are concerned, there is no such thing as 'infinity' though something may be described as 'infinite' if used properly.

However **153** is found as a part of a limited and unique set of numbers, giving us the opportunity to see the 'whole picture', provided we take the time to look at all of it. Thus this chapter will investigate phenomena that serves primarily as a repository for further investigation.

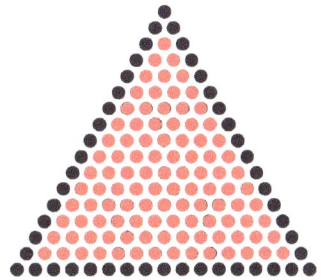

We begin by noting that it is the 17th triangle number. Inside it holds the 14th triangle of **105**, which is one of only four triangles from 1 to 1,000,000 that when doubled, also makes a triangle.

A more striking aspect is the fact that it is the sum of its cubes. This means that $1^3 + 5^3 + 3^3 = 153$, making it one of only five numbers for which this works.

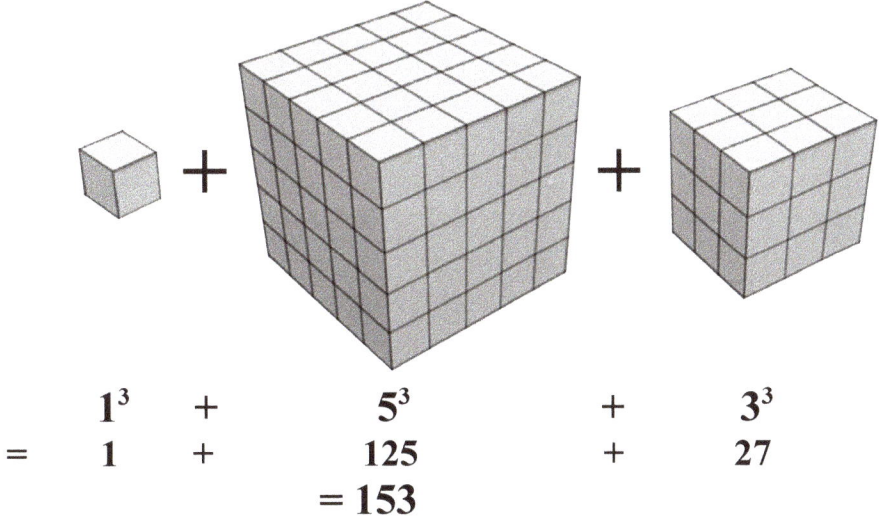

$$1^3 + 5^3 + 3^3$$
$$= 1 + 125 + 27$$
$$= 153$$

Not *only* is it the sum of its cubes, but a full one-third of all numbers culminate at 153 when we keep summing their cubes to get a new number.

Let's use 6 as an example, it's a nice long one. $6^3 = 216$. Then we do the digits of 216. $2^3 + 1^3 + 6^3 = 225$. Then we do the digits of 225. $2^3 + 2^3 + 5^3 = 141$. Then we do the digits of 141 and on and on to find the final result:

$1^3 + 4^3 + 1^3$	=	66
$6^3 + 6^3$	=	432
$4^3 + 3^3 + 2^3$	=	99
$9^3 + 9^3$	=	1,458
$1^3 + 4^3 + 5^3 + 8^3$	=	702
$7^3 + 0^3 + 2^3$	=	351
$3^3 + 5^3 + 1^3$	=	153 ...Here we arrive at 153,
$1^3 + 5^3 + 3^3$	=	**153** ...and here we stay at 153.

So the idea is to keep going until the number reaches an endpoint or endpoints. <u>Precisely one third of all numbers have 153 as their endpoint</u>, specifically every number divisible by three. Because 153 produces itself, the buck stops there.

Where else does the buck stop?

Let's do **2**. . . $2^3 = 8$

8^3	=	512
$5^3 + 1^3 + 2^3$	=	134
$1^3 + 3^3 + 4^3$	=	92
$9^3 + 2^3$	=	737
$7^3 + 3^3 + 7^3$	=	713
$7^3 + 1^3 + 3^3$	=	371 ...Here we arrive at 371,
$3^3 + 7^3 + 1^3$	=	**371** ...and here we stay at 371.

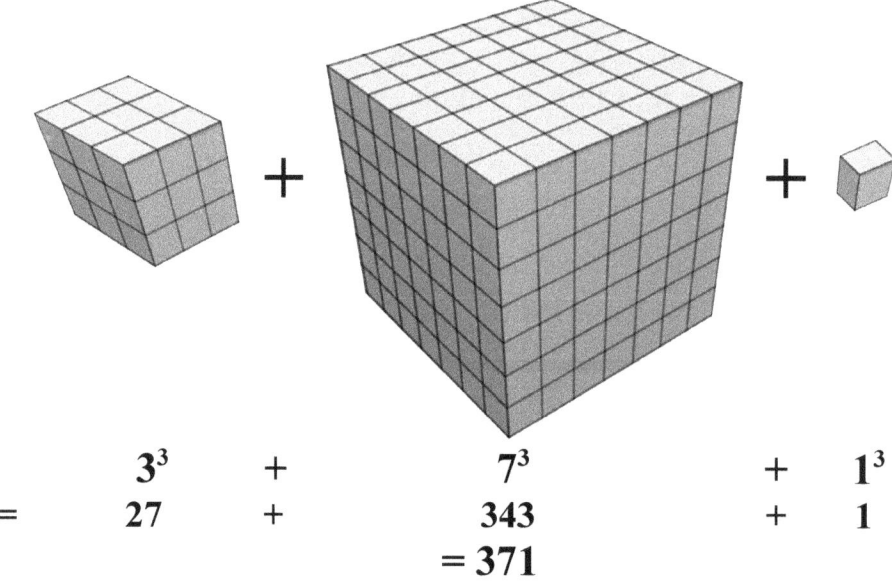

$$= \quad \mathbf{3^3} \quad + \quad \mathbf{7^3} \quad + \quad \mathbf{1^3}$$
$$= \quad 27 \quad + \quad 343 \quad + \quad 1$$
$$= 371$$

For 2, the buck stops at **371**. If we would continue, we would find that for 7, the buck stops at **370**, for 1 and 112 the buck stops at **1**, and for 47 the buck stops at **407**. Is that our magic five numbers? **1, 153,**

370, **371**, and **407**? Almost, but if we're going to look at the whole picture, we can't skip details.

So let's do **4**:

4^3	=	64
$6^3 + 4^3$	=	280
$2^3 + 8^3 + 0^3$	=	520
$5^3 + 2^3 + 0^3$	=	133
$1^3 + 3^3 + 3^3$	=	55
$5^3 + 5^3$	=	250
$2^3 + 5^3 + 0^3$	=	**133**
$1^3 + 3^3 + 3^3$	=	**55**
$5^3 + 5^3$	=	**250** These last three look familiar...
$2^3 + 5^3 + 0^3$	=	133
$1^3 + 3^3 + 3^3$	=	55
$5^3 + 5^3$	=	250 ...and yes, they keep repeating.

Four ends in a *set* of numbers: **133**, **55**, and **250**.

What kind of sense do we make of all this? Well first we need our data. And since, for example, 112, 121, and 211 all use the same digits, they make 3 *numbers* but just one *set* of numbers. Note here the use (in straight mathematics) of numbers such as **37**, **73**, and **27** which are also foundations of sacred literature:

- How many unique sets of numbers are there from 1 to 999?   **3 x 73 = 219**
- How many total number are there from 1 to 999?   **27 x 37 = 999**

We will find constant cross-overs like these as we proceed. It is good to be familiar with both worlds.

So we can organize these in three groups of 333: the numbers in the first group are all under **153**, the second group is under **371** and **470**, and the third group is under two *single* numbers, two *double sets*, and two *triple sets*:

153:   3, 6, 9... and every third number counting from 3. (**333** under 1000, **75** different sets)

371:   2, 5, 8... every third number counting from 2 *except* for the numbers following **470** just below, which also are part of this third of all numbers. (**303** under 1000, **64** different sets)

407:   47, 74, 77, 89, 98, 407, 449, 470, 494, 578, 587, 668, 686, 704, 707, 740, 758, 770, 785, 788, 809, 857, 866, 875, 878, 887, 890, 908. 944, 980... (**30** under 1000, **7** different sets)

1:   1, 10, 100, 112, 121, 211, 778, 787, 877... (**9** under 1000, **3** different sets)

370:   7, 19, 34, 37, 43, 58, 67... every third number counting from 1 *except* those found in series **1** above and the **sets** below. (**174** under 1000, **39** different sets)

Set (**55, 250, 133**):   4, 13, 25, 28, 31, 40, 46, 52, 55, 64, 82, 103, 130, 133, 205, 208, 250, 256, 265, 280, 289, 298, 301, 310, 313, 331, 349, 394, 400, 406, 439, 448, 460, 484, 493, 502, 505, 520, 526, 550, 562, 589, 598, 604, 625, 640, 652, 679, 697, 769, 796, 802, 820, 829, 844, 859, 892, 895, 928, 934, 943, 958, 967, 976, 982, 985... (**66** under 1000, **13** sets)

> Set (**160, 217, 352**): 16, 22, 61, 79, 97, 106, 115, 127, 151, 160, 172, 202, 217, 220, 229, 235, 238, 253, 271, 283, 292, 325, 328, 352, 382, 388, 445, 454, 457, 475, 511, 523, 532, 544, 547, 574, 601, 610, 709, 712, 721, 745, 754, 790, 823, 832, 838, 883, 907, 922, 970... (**51** under 1000, **11** sets)
>
> Set (**919, 1459**):   49, 94, 199, 337, 373, 379, 397, 409, 478, 487, 490, 733, 739, 748, 784, 793, 847, 874, 904, 919, 937, 940, 973, 991... (**24** under 1000, **5** sets)
>
> Set (**136, 244**):   136, 163, 244, 316, 361, 424, 442, 613, 631... (**9** under 1000, **2** sets)

I have several notebooks full of ramifications and extrapolations on this phenomena; here we wish to get a clear summary and extract some usable details. I will note in passing that all the numbers in the third group which are used as culmination points can be expressed as a multiple of 3^3 with 1^3 added except for 133, 160, 250, and 370 which have their own cube relations as follows:

1       $0(3^3) + 1^3$ =   1
55      $2(3^3) + 1^3$ =   55
133 E $5^3 + 2^3$ =   133 and $5(3^3) - 2$
136     $5(3^3) + 1^3$ =   136
160 E $5^3 + 3^3 + 2^3$ =   160
217     $8(3^3) + 1^3$ =   217 and $6^3 + 1^3$
244     $9(3^3) + 1^3$ =   244
250 E $2(5^3)$ =   250
352     $13(3^3) + 1^3$ =   352
370 E $7^3 + 3^3$ =   370 and $5^3 + 2(4^3 + 2(3^3 + 2(1^3))) + 1$
919     $33(3^3) + 1^3$ =   919 and $6 \times 153 + 1 = 919$
1459 $54(3^3) + 1^3$ =   1459 and $729 \times 2 + 1 = 1459$

   Average 55, 133, and 250 = 146 $3(3^3) + 4^3 + 1^3$
   Average 136 and 244 = 190 $7(3^3) + 1^3$
   Average 160, 217, and 352 = 243 $9(3^3)$
   Average of 919 and 1459 = 1189 $44(3^3) + 1^3 = 1189$

   Summation of 136 and 244 = 380 $14(3^3) + 2$
   Summation of 55, 133, and 250 = 438 $2(5^3) + 7(3^3) + 1^3$
   Summation of 160, 217, and 352 = 729 $27(3^3)$ and $9^3 = 729$
   Summation of 919 and 1459 = 2378 $88(3^3) + 2 = 2378$

As you can see, there is no upper limit on interesting discoveries, so let's rein this in a bit. Let me give an example of an application.

Each number or set of numbers above applies to a limited amount of cases. For example the set (**919, 1459**) only culminates **5** of the **219** possible combinations from 1 to 999. And **370** culminates a whopping **39** in comparison. So suppose we weight each number or set according to both how much it is and how useful it is. The two easiest ways of doing this is use either the *average* or *summation* of the sets with multiple numbers. This can easily turn into a rabbit-hole, so i'll simply give the results. This one uses the *summations* of the multiple-number sets:

   First group: (**153**) x number of times used (**75**) = 11,475
   Second group: (**371**) x number of times used (**64**) = 23,744

Third group:
(**407**) x number of times used (7) = 2,849
(**1**) x number of times used (3) = 3
(**370**) x number of times used (39) = 14,430
(**380**) x number of times used (2) = 760
(**438**) x number of times used (13) = 5,694
(**729**) x number of times used (11) = 8,019
(**2378**) x number of times used (5) = 11,890
Total 78,864

Because the number of letters in Genesis (Chart 1) can be expressed as

(**153**) x (.2222+2^1+2^2+2^3+2^4+2^5+2^6+2^7+2^8)

...i had been looking to compare this study on cubes to Genesis. Oddly enough, the total above of **78,864** is precisely 800 more than the total number of letters in Genesis, **78,064**. That's close enough to smell a clear relationship hiding in there somewhere. And doing this with the *averages* of the multiple-number sets lands within 133 of the number of letters in Exodus and Numbers.

Does this round out the picture? Not quite. Everything above that we have done was using the summed cubes of numbers. In picture form, we were in this realm:

What about *these* realms?

  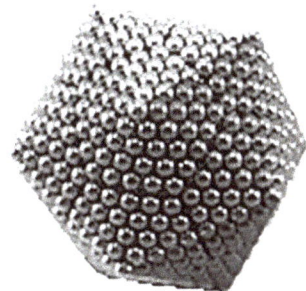 

These are the other four of the five golden solids, the only regular three-dimensional shapes available to us. They were considered sacred in every ancient culture. So if we get a specific set of useful numbers from summing cubes, do we get similar sets from summing tetrahedrons and dodecahedrons?

Yes we do. Here they are.

Tetrahedral Numbers $\dfrac{n(n+1)(n+2)}{6}$

1:   (**15** combos)
24:   (**8** combos)
289:   (**1** combo)
Set 4, 20:   (**27** combos)
Set 71, 85, 155:   (**7** combos)
Set 5, 35, 45, 55, 70, 84, 140, 21: (**161** combos)
   3 Singles, **1** Double, **1** Triple, **1** Octuple

Summations of Summations: **76,576**
Summations of Averages: **11,302.5**

Octahedral Numbers $\dfrac{n(2n^2+1)}{3}$

1: (**1** set)
593: (**11** different sets)
739: (**1** set)
Set [237, 256]: (**8** different sets)
Set [148, 389, 852, 435]: (**198** different sets)
   3 Singles, **1** Double, **1** Quadruple

Summations of Summations: **372,359**
Summations of Averages: **99,523**

Icosahedral Numbers $\dfrac{n(5n^2-5n+2)}{2}$

1: (1 set)
3 Set **[553, 558, 1633]:** (3 different sets)
20 Set **[1236, 517, 998, 4386, 1756, 1454, 504, 379, 2419, 1766, 1655, 967, 2827, 1894, 2882, 2280, 1152, 269, 2097, 2383]:** (102 different sets)
25 Set **[126, 469, 2209, 1653, 760, 1198, 2759, 2638, 1644, 705, 997, 4000, 124, 137, 791, 2372, 814, 1253, 316, 505, 510, 256, 723, 802, 1140]:** (113 different sets)

1 Single, **1** Triple, **1** Vigintuple, **1** Quinvigintuple

Summations of Summations: **6,723,788**
Summations of Averages: 305,862.62

Dodecahedral Numbers $\quad \dfrac{n(3n-1)(3n-2)}{2}$

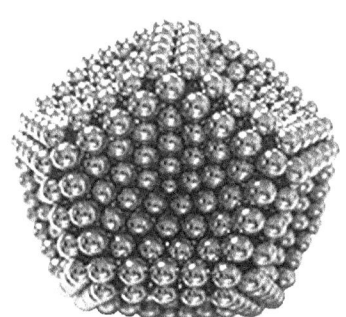

1:	(1 set)
2:	(2 sets)
21:	(1 set)
240:	(1 set)
241:	(3 sets)
304:	(2 sets)
324:	(13 sets)
440:	(1 set)
441:	(1 set)
1356:	(12 sets)
2167:	(7 sets)
2484:	(1 set)
2583:	(1 set)
2860:	(2 sets)
3009:	(5 sets)
3029:	(1 set)
3093:	(1 set)
3249:	(2 sets)

Summations of Summations: **1,846,161**
Summations of Averages: 460,921.279

Set **[40, 220]:** (4 sets)
Set **[41, 221]:** (5 sets)
Set **[170, 1333]:** (1 set)
Set **[475, 2005]:** (5 sets)
Set **[480, 2244]:** (3 sets)
Set **[895, 5404]:** (3 sets)
Set **[1078, 3355]:** (4 sets)
Set **[2783, 3458]:** (10 sets)
Set **[3049, 3229]:** (1 set)
3 Set **[560, 1271, 1352]:** (2 sets)

3 Set [920, 2945, 3620]:   (**10** sets)
3 Set [995, 6305, 1355]:   (**13** sets)
4 Set [305, 539, 3464, 1340]:   (**3** sets)
4 Set [261, 837, 3438, 2421]:   (**7** sets)
4 Set [2386, 2944, 3385, 2647]:   (**23** sets)
5 Set [125, 476, 2366, 1736, 2231]:   (**4** sets)
5 Set [188, 4049, 3365, 1439, 3230]:   (**7** sets)
6 Set [3820, 2128, 2065, 1291, 2947, 4495]:   (**17** sets)
7 Set [87, 3354, 843, 2328, 2148, 2265, 1311]:   (**11** sets)
7 Set [707, 2260, 1652, 1292, 2966, 4577, 3335]:   (**5** sets)
7 Set [759, 4710, 1551, 912, 2946, 3981, 5034]:   (**12** sets)
7 Set [458, 2699, 6686, 4472, 1790, 4256, 1511]:   (**12** sets)

18 Singles, **9** Doubles, **3** Triples, **3** Quadruples, **2** Quintuples, **1** Sextuple, **4** Septuples
[40 Sets, 101 Points]

All 5 Shapes Summation of Summations: 9,097,748   (11^2 x 2^2 x 18,797)
All 5 Shapes Summations of Averages: 941,006.4 (11 x 2 x 42,773)
[64 Sets, 190 Points]

We have more than enough information for exploration above. Each one of the numbers is a microcosm of answers, but they want *organized*. For example, **250** is an oddball part of the set 55, 133, 250 culmination in the cube section. He is 2 x 5^3 and an exception to the $x(3^3) + 1^3$ rule. But if we add 153 to him (403) and subtract this from the gematria sum of all letters (4,995, see page 117) we get **4,592**. Not a terribly useful number until we realize that 17 x **4,592** = 78,064, the exact number of letters in Genesis.

I have pages and pages of such details, but in my opinion, unless they reach *closure*, unless they are part of an organized and unique structure, they are simply stray orphans waiting for a home. This has been as distilled a summary as i can provide of the magic of 153 and where it leads.

So have fun.

Appendix VII

The Geometric Structure of the Hebrew and Greek Alphabets

Have you ever seen something beautiful or amazing and asked, "So what?"

There are applications to the discoveries in this book that are as far-reaching as the imagination and/or research will allow. One of them we can apply to the structure and meaning of the alphabet itself.

If we draw the alphabet as a path on a cube, the 'blocks' can be represented by the eight corners, twelve edges, six faces, and the center. This will give us our 27 places for letters. Or if you like, simply take each block of a Rubik's Cube including the center.

The idea is to draw a continuous path that positions each of the letters in a geometrically significant arrangement. There are several very practical applications to doing this, not the least of which the fact that it would allow us to *see* words as geometrical shapes.

The two parameters we will use are (1) one unbroken line and (2) each of the six ancient letters (Aleph א, Hé ה, Vav ו, Het ח, Yod י, and Ayin ע) that doubled as vowels (before there were vowel points) must land on one of the six faces. We will be using the five final forms (Kaf ך, Mem ם, Nun ן, Pe ף, and Tsadi ץ) to make the full 27.

Using these parameters, the path unfolds as follows:

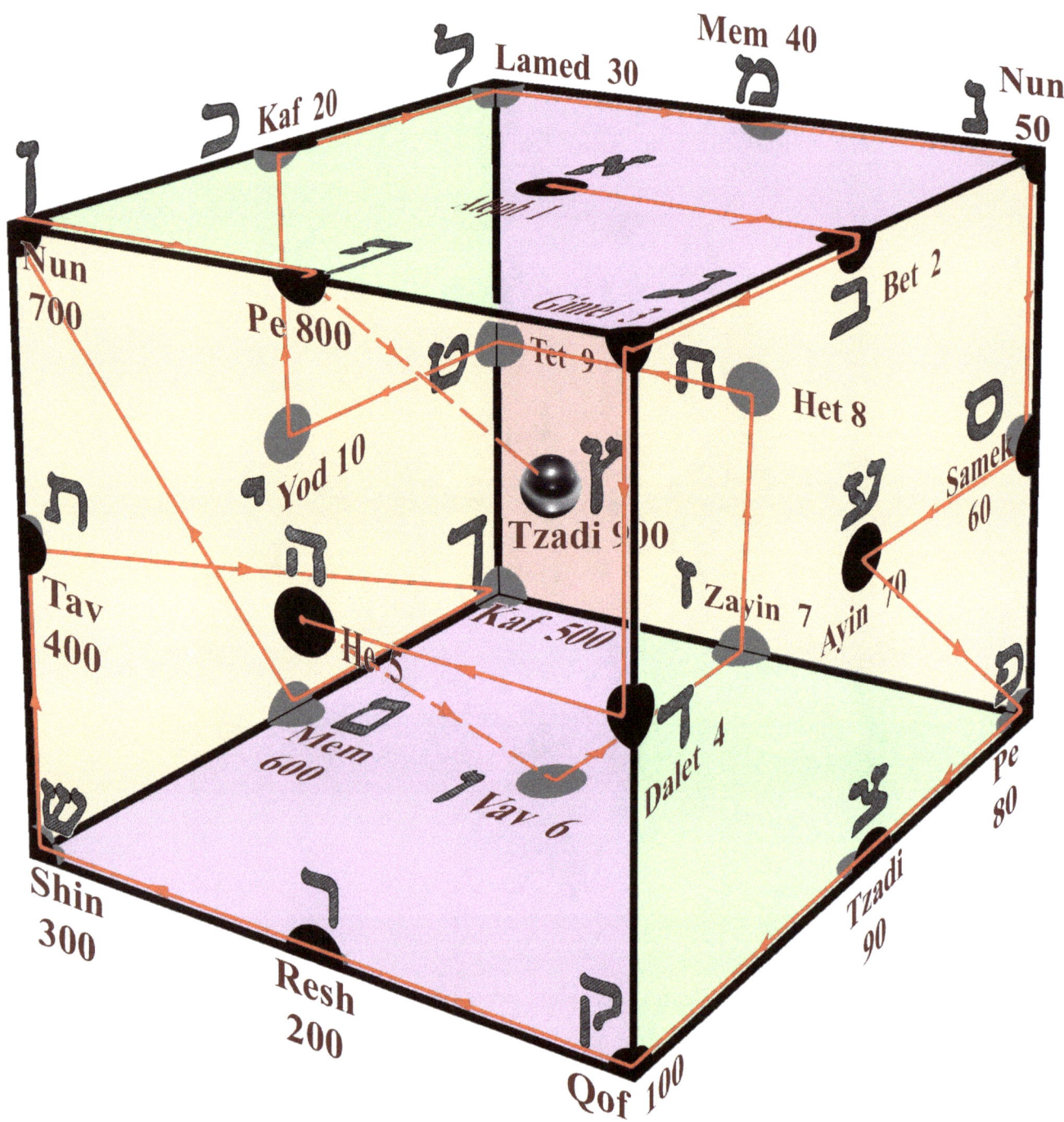

This arrangement turns out to have more than its share of interesting features. For one, the faces added together equal 100, and the faces with the center added together equal 1000. The corners with the center are 47×7^2, and the corners without the center are two primes, 43×41. The edges, being *connectors* denoting relationships are completely opposite, being divisible by *all* of the following: 1, 2, 3, 4, 6, 8, 9, 12, 18, 24, 31, 36, 62, 72, 93, 124, 186, 248, 279, 372, 558, 744, and 1116.

While the numbers tempt us into another branch of this journey, let us move on to the traditional (and some actual) meanings of each letter, and see what what this arrangement shows:

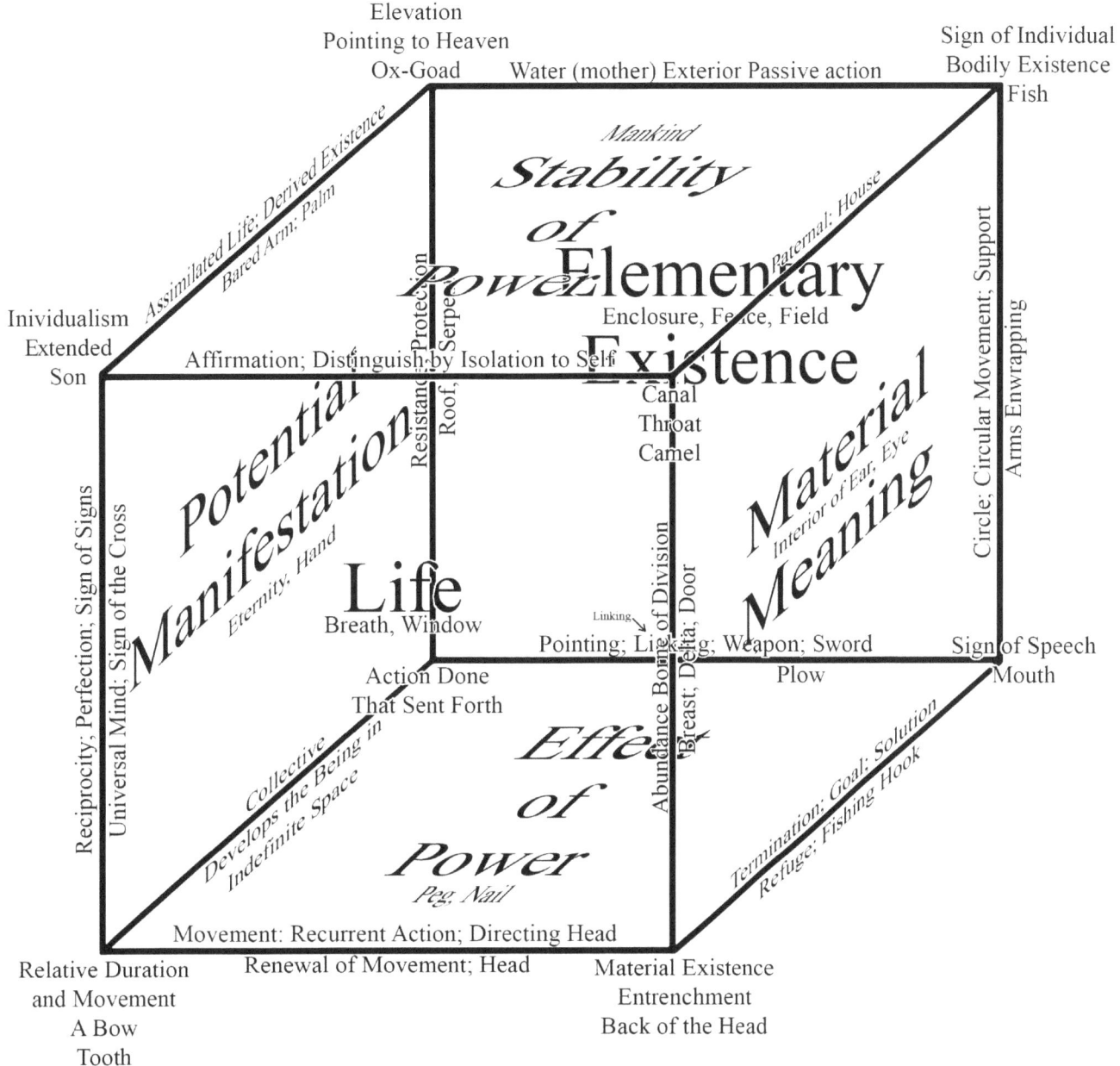

What we have done here is replace each letter with its meaning. Appropriately, the meanings line up with respect to one another. On one corner is *Material Existence, entrenchment* and on the opposite corner is *Elevation, pointing to heaven*. On the top face is *Stability of Power* and on the bottom face is *Effect of Power*. And so on. If we take the face on the right, *Material Meaning*, and look at the four edges and four corners surrounding it, they all relate to the idea of that which is material and physical. If we take the opposite face, *Potential Manifestation* and look at the corners and edges surrounding it, they all relate to that which is ethereal. This is an example of a three-dimensional arrangement that works with the (1) geometry, (2) numerics, and (3) meanings.

So we have an introduction to the subject of geometry; it is vast. We might note before moving on that most flat charts and diagrams that yield good results are actually three-dimensional constructs that have been 'unfolded', or in some cases simply 'flattened' for the sake of being able to represent them in a drawing. The real value is when we find how to expand them back out into three dimensions, for it is there that the hidden relationships spring into life.

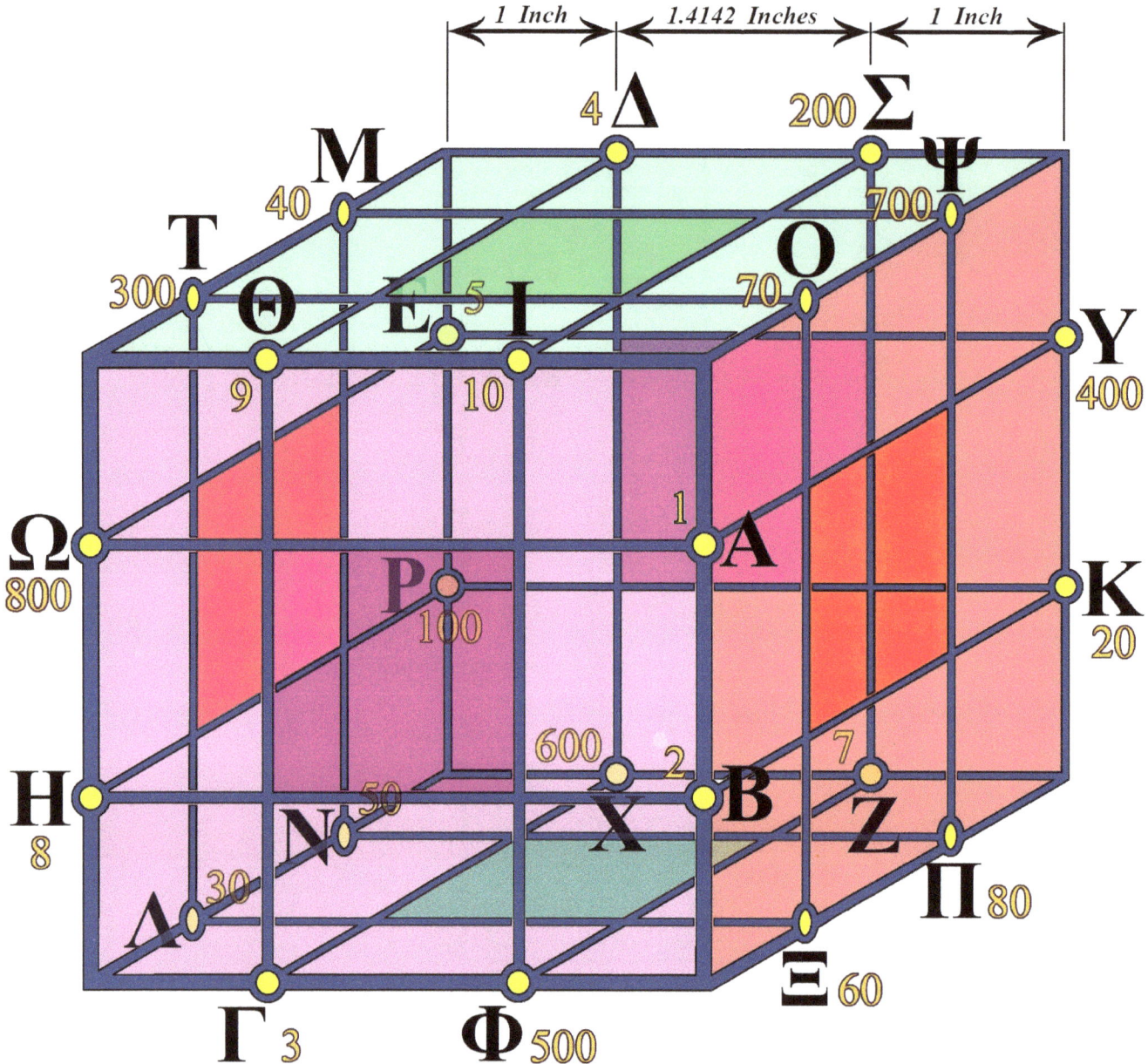

This is the Greek alphabet in its three dimensional form. In this construct, the exact spacing is vital so that the distance relationships contribute to the symmetry. For example, it is precisely the same distance from Alpha (A) to Iota (I) as it is from Alpha to Bet (B) or Alpha to Omicron (O) even though there are both perpendiculars and diagonals represented. This is especially useful when making diagonal relationships that cut through the inside of the construct; the letters maintain their peculiar distance proportions. The distance from Aleph (A) to Nu (N), Xi (X), and Rho (P) are identical, likewise the distances from Aleph to Delta (Δ), Zeta (Z), Lamed (Λ), and Mu (M). Altogether there are only **7** distinct distances that can be found between any two letters throughout the entire construct *including* diagonals that transverse the interior.

The top face, front, right, and left faces all have the value of **1,333** when the eight letters on each face are added up. However, the backside has three more, **1,336**, and the bottom three less for **1,330**, a mere **6** apart, and the edge between them is just where the **90** would be if it were included. However, neither the **6** nor the **90** have letter equivalents in the Greek used for the New Testament. This is a hint as to why the Greek was arranged as it was at the time.

Note that the Greek letters are located on the 'cracks' between where the Hebrew letters from the previous chart are found. The two languages thus fit together within a larger (unshown) structure of pure conceptual meaning. It is this larger structure which holds the keys to the understanding of everything from physics to emotion, from history to prophecy. I have not seen its like in ancient texts, but will continue to search. It's not the kind of thing that translates into a doodle or chart very easily.

An enormous amount of material hides within these geometries. . . i have several books worth of material, including the arrangement of the Hebrew letters in which each face matches each other mathematically (that would make an excellent challenge for anyone who considers themselves competent). These are not merely self-validation discoveries like this book; they open up the lost patterns of grammar, morphology, and syntax of the ancient languages. Yes, i am using these to translate the Old Testament; *Genesis Unfolded* is finished and should be available by the time this book is published. Yes i am putting together a lexicon of Hebrew roots by which the meaning of every word (and the more difficult names) in ancient Hebrew can be accurately ascertained. I am about halfway finished with that one as of of the writing of this paragraph. The work appears to be more than one lifetime long, but we shall see.

It is enough here to introduce them as tools that have been helpful both in understanding numerics and in translating text. When multiple relationships are organized into a sensible and self-referential (recursive) order, things which otherwise seem obscure jump into the foreground and introduce themselves. And they are beautiful.

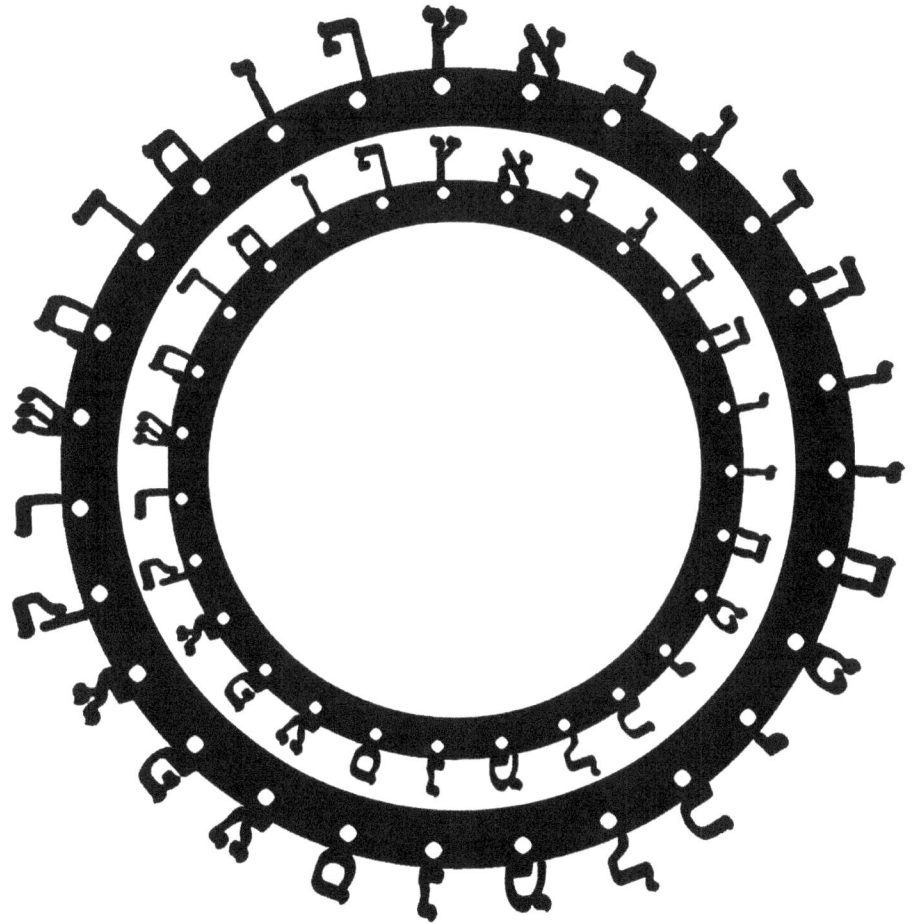

Appendix VIII

A Simple Way to Understand the Meanings of Letters

Letters offer themselves to us. They beg to be understood. Whether Hieroglyphics, Hebrew, Chinese Oracle Bone Script or English, a child (and it often takes one) can decipher the message that are bursting from these intricate shapes.

Let us note a few peculiarities of these letters—and when i say 'letter' the expression includes Egyptian hieroglyphics and Aztec petroglyphs as well. The first oddity we can note is that they universally are composed of *lines*.

Of course, there are exceptions. . .

. . .but they are rare and usually ancient. Plus they have their own protocols beyond our present scope.

Starting with the English letters of our own alphabet, we notice that there are three kinds of lines used. Perpendicular:

        | — as used in **E F H I L T**;

Diagonal:

        / \ as used in **V W X**;

and Curved:

        ⊃ C as used in **C O S**.

The rest of our letters are combinations of these three.

Each of these shapes is a universal communicator. The Perpendiculars connote dignity, individuality, seriousness, and stability. The diagonals communicate dynamics, action, movement, and reaction. The curves speak of sensitivity, community, wholeness, and centrality.

In the *relationships between* these three realms of existence lies the power to communicate virtually any thought, from imaginary dragons to stock market trades. So let us take stock of these simple shapes.

Diagonals

/// The forward diagonal (reversed if the language is read from right to left) is momentum, intention, initiation, and any kind of moving forward.

\\\ The backward diagonal is reaction, prevention, denouement, release, and counsel.

V Joined at the bottom is response, vitality, ability, and a hint of individuality.

∧ Joined at the top is mystery, private energy, finality, and possession.

X Q Crossing another line is expression, annulment, the past, cessation, and peculiarity.

...and we could go on to dozens of more forms, such as between horizontals or verticals, combined with the various kinds of curves, etc. but this is an appendix, not a textbook, so let's move on.

Perpendiculars

||| The vertical is identity, individuality, timelessness (or eternity), and dignity,.

≡ The horizontal is rest, the background, stability, extension, and holding power.

The serifs (top and bottom horizontal pieces) on the I give it stability, which is why they are often added when no other letters in the same sentence have serifs.

A certain newspaper writer who was given the job to do the financial reports wanted to be taken seriously, so he used as his pseudonym "E. F. Hilt", which is all the pure perpendicular letters in order.

Curves

C The forward curve is most useful for starting words; it is 'moving forward comfortably' with confidence.

⊃ The backward curve is 'deliberation in removing obstacles' and 'the force of history to the now'.

∩ The downward curve is provision, maternal, protection, and materialism.

U The upward curve is containment, reception, withholding, and self-centeredness.

O The complete curve is centrality, wholeness, and completeness.

Openness and Direction

Almost all the English letters are open toward what is yet to be read. The only slight exception is the letter 'N', which is possibly why the Russian alphabet reverses theirs (И). Yet the Russians allow Я, З, Э, and Л; all of which point 'backwards' to the left. Hebrew has only Qof (ק) as their exception, and Greek has no exceptions at all. The Arabic alphabet has at least six: غ ح خ ج ع though geometrically there are only two forms there. Recall that Hebrew and Arabic read so that 'backwards' for them is pointing or being open to the right.

This is somewhat instructive. Letters in words have lines that tend to point forward to the next letter. This tells us that a prefix is quite different from a suffix. Thus 'unfaithful' has quite a different meaning than 'faithless', though in each case all we are doing is adding a negation to the beginning or end of 'faith'.

This also tells us that there are 'pointer' letters ('E' has three horizontals pointing forward) and 'balanced' letters (A, H, I, M, O, T, X,). One might conclude that a 'MATH AXIOM' is very balanced. U, V, W, and Y are slightly different as they point upward. T and M have a slight downward orientation.

Now given all this, let us make a simple chart of the English letters. A proper chart, or even one limited to the abbreviated information above, would not fit on this page. This is to note how geometrically balanced—or unbalanced—the English alphabet is. . . and thus the English mindset.

	Chart 89: The English Letters Arranged by Shape					
	Source	**Distribution**	**Organization**	**Sink**	**Combo**	**Total**
Seriousness	I il	E F L	H T	t		6
Dynamics	V W vw	y	X x			3
Sensitivity		C c	O o	S s		3
Serious/Dynamic	A	K k	N Z z	M Y		6
Serious/Sensitive	B D P abdpq	G f	J j u	U	eghmnr	6
Dynamic/Sensitive	Q					1
Serious/Dynamic/Sensitive	R					1

We find some very revealing things about our culture. Seriousness (6) is twice as important to the English mind than Dynamics (3) or Sensitivity (3). Even our combinations that include seriousness have **6** members each, while the combination of Dynamics and Sensitivity has only **1**, the rarely used 'Q'. Furthermore, we have only **1** letter that combines all three shapes, the letter '**R**'. As pleased as i am with my heritage, i must say that this analysis does *not* bode well for being confident of a well-balanced culture. Let's compare our culture to Greek.

	Chart 90: The Greek Letters Arranged by Shape					
	Form 1	**Form 2**	**Form 3**	**Form 4**	**Form 5**	**Total**
Seriousness	Γ Ε	Η Ξ Π Τ τ	Ι ι			7
Dynamics	Λ ν	Χ				2
Sensitivity	Ο ο	α δ	ε ζ ξ ς	ω		1
Serious/Dynamic	Α Δ	Σ Κ κ	Μ Υ	Ν	Ζ	8
Serious/Sensitive	Β Ρ β ρ	Θ θ σ	Φ Ψ φ ψ	Ω	η μ π υ	6
Dynamic/Sensitive	γ λ	χ				0
Serious/Dynamic/Sensitive						0

. . .and we find that the Greek alphabet is even more severe than English, with *no* letters in the last two categories (we had one in each) and **8** in the Serious/Dynamic row, which may explain Alexander the Great's character. And Greek has half the number of pure Dynamic and pure Sensitivity letters as English.

In fact, if we would continue this pursuit, it would not be until we get to the Arabic, Hebrew, and Chinese before the shapes begin to balance out.

So let us give an example of shapeliness and meaning with the word LOVE. Interestingly, each of these letters is pure: **L** is pure perpendiculars, **O** is pure curves, **V** is pure dynamics, and **E** is pure perpendiculars. Furthermore, the first and last letters (the serious ones) are both pointing forward; the **L** to the rest of the word, and the **E** to whatever unknown quantity comes next. Love points forward.

But the core of love is completely balanced. **O** is wholeness and completeness, yet it shares a space with **V**, which is response, vitality, ability, and a hint of individuality. These are two very different ideas, bordered by forward movement before and behind.

L, which introduces the word, is the individual **I** extending its base of stability forward; an invitation, a reaching out. **E** extends every part of itself—that self being the wholeness of **O** and the vitality of **V**—forward toward whatever the object of the love is.

That was straightforward. Let us look at HATE. Starting at the end since we just saw it in LOVE, the **E** is extending all that precedes it to whatever the object of the hate is. The other three letters are perfectly balanced; no forward movement at all. This is especially important with the first letter, which gives its character to the rest. All three first letters simply sit there, much like a HAT that one is wearing. Now if you were to take your hat (or your shoe in many cultures) and throw it toward something, what emotion would you be communicating?

The **H** is dual individuality (**I-I**) connected by holding power. It means that the matter has been explored and a firm decision has been reached. This decision is taken up by **A**, which has the same holding power (-) in the center of **Λ**, private energy, finality, and possession; in other words, these emotions are *not* shared, but withheld from their object. The **T** acts as a signpost of dignified self absorption picked up by the **E** and projected full force into whatever object is the recipient of **H**'s decision and **A**'s privacy.

There are no elements of sensitivity in HATE, just private thoughts extended forward by the last letter. Were it HAVE, the dignity of the **T** would be replaced by the containership of the **V**; were it HARE, the universal 'relater' **R** would give a much-needed forward movement and connect the serious 'moving on' character of the **E** with the dignity of private energy of the **HA-**.

Once again, fairly straightforward. Bear in mind that this investigation is of the *shapes and sequence only*. We could do a similar study with the *sounds* or even, as this book investigates, the numerics.

And how important is the sequence? Well take the **E** in HATE and move it to after the **H** and we have HEAT. Now the only forward-pointing is projected not outward, but to the **AT**, both balanced, giving a word that has just as much vehemence, but is at rest rather than being projected.

The three concepts we are dealing with here are **Character** (the shape), **Order** (the sequence), and **Context** (all that surrounds, including the parameters of what is acceptable in that particular language.)

These three ideas relate straight across to Cardinal, Ordinal, and Cyclic discussed at the beginning of Appendix II, as well as the concepts of of Unique, Common, and Field which unearthed themselves in the process of discovering the textual patterns.

There are worlds to explore and this is but an introduction to the subject. It might be best to close here and leave the full exploration to a forum in which it can blossom more naturally. Again, have fun.

www.ingramcontent.com/pod-product-compliance
Lightning Source LLC
Chambersburg PA
CBHW051247110526
44588CB00025B/2905